The Barbados Community College Experience

The Barbados Community College Experience

Leading the Anglophone Caribbean in a Global Movement

VIVIENNE ROBERTS

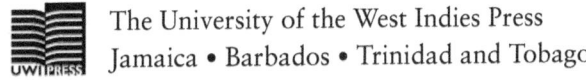

The University of the West Indies Press
Jamaica • Barbados • Trinidad and Tobago

The University of the West Indies Press
7A Gibraltar Hall Road, Mona
Kingston 7, Jamaica
www.uwipress.com

© 2020 by Vivienne Roberts

All rights reserved. Published 2020

A catalogue record of this book is available from the National Library of Jamaica.

ISBN: 978-976-640-762-9 (paper)
978-976-640-763-6 (Kindle)
978-976-640-764-3 (ePub)

Front cover illustration: Joyce Daniel, *Change*

Back cover photograph: Barry Tudor, Barbados Community College, Howell's Cross Road entrance

The University of the West Indies Press has no responsibility for the persistence or accuracy of URLs for external or third-party Internet websites referred to in this publication and does not guarantee that any content on such websites is, or will remain, accurate or appropriate.

Printed in the United States of America

For Sir Lloyd Erskine Sandiford, Barbados Community College initiator, founder, leader, recipient of a BCC honorary doctorate and teacher par excellence,

and

in tribute to Alvin Barnett, who brought calm to many a storm; Norma Holder, who gave wings to good ideas; Hinkitch Bell, who lived and breathed public health; and Peggy Inniss, who was the embodiment of service. May they rest in peace.

Contents

List of Figures / ix

List of Tables / xii

Preface / xiii

Acknowledgements / xxi

Abbreviations / xxv

1. Context, Concepts and Processes / 1
2. The Global Community College Context / 11
3. The North American Community College Experience / 22
4. The Global Movement and Community College Counterparts / 34
5. The Community College in the English-Speaking Caribbean / 48
6. The Barbados Community College: The Establishment Year, 1968 / 89
7. The Establishment Years under Clyde Best, 1969–1976 / 99
8. Filling the Gap with Arthur Sealy, 1976–1978 / 122
9. Growth and Consolidation Years under Alvin Barnett, 1978–1988 / 127
10. Expansion, Outreach and Reputation Building with Norma Holder, 1988–2004 / 155
11. A Phase of Uncertainty for Gladstone Best, 2004–2014 / 193
12. The Golden Age of Opportunities for Ian Austin and Others, 2015–2018 / 217

Conclusion / 234

Appendices

Appendix 1: List of Principals / 253

Appendix 2: List of Deputy Principals / 253

Appendix 3: List of First Staff Members / 254

Appendix 4: Board of Management Chairs / 255

Appendix 5: Registrars, Bursars and Supervisor / 255

Appendix 6: List of Senior Tutors / 256

Appendix 7: Some Department Heads / 258

Appendix 8: Staff Profile 2016 / 258

Appendix 9: Establishment Dates of Divisions / 259

Appendix 10: International Formal and Informal Articulation Arrangements / 260

Appendix 11: Articulation Arrangements with the University of the West Indies / 261

Appendix 12: Dates of Introduction of Programmes / 262

Appendix 13: Guild Presidents and Vice-Presidents / 264

Appendix 14: Scholarship Regulations / 265

Appendix 15: Annual Student Enrolment / 275

Appendix 16: Questionnaire for Past Staff / 277

References / 279

Index / 291

Figures

Figure 5.1. Alternative pathways to and through tertiary education in the anglophone Caribbean / 50
Figure 5.2. Tracking the community college movement in the anglophone Caribbean / 81
Figure 5.3. Montego Bay Community College, Jamaica / 84
Figure 5.4. Excelsior Community College, Jamaica / 84
Figure 5.5. Portmore Community College, Jamaica / 85
Figure 5.6. Moneague College, Jamaica / 85
Figure 5.7. University College of the Cayman Islands / 86
Figure 5.8. Anguilla Community College / 86
Figure 5.9. H. Lavity Stoutt Community College, British Virgin Islands / 87
Figure 5.10. Sir Arthur Lewis Community College, St Lucia / 87
Figure 5.11. Dominica State College / 88
Figure 5.12. St Vincent and the Grenadines Community College / 88
Figure 6.1. Eric Armstrong, first chair of the Barbados Community College, 1969–1971 / 96
Figure 6.2. Sir Keith Hunte, chair, 1971–1977 / 96
Figure 6.3. Dr Leonard Shorey, chair, 1977–1986 / 96
Figure 6.4. Colin Kirton, chair, 1986–1995 / 96
Figure 6.5. Professor Trevor Hassell, chair, 1995–2000 / 97
Figure 6.6. Lolita Applewaite, chair, 2000–2003 / 97
Figure 6.7. Dr Asquith Thompson, chair, 2003–2006 / 97
Figure 6.8. Desmond Critchlow, chair, 2006–2008 / 97
Figure 6.9. Bertram Carter, chair, 2008–2011 / 98
Figure 6.10. Stephen Broome, chair, 2011–2018 / 98
Figure 7.1. The Harbour site (west view): Home of Barbados Community College, 1969–1975 / 120
Figure 7.2. The Harbour site (east view) / 120
Figure 7.3. Sherbourne House: Home of Barbados Community College, 1969–1976 / 121

x | Figures

Figure 7.4. Division of Technology – first buildings at the Eyrie site, opened 1973 / **121**
Figure 8.1. Arthur Sealy, acting principal of the Barbados Community College, being received by Queen Elizabeth II / **124**
Figure 8.2. Eyrie House, home of the BCC Project Office (1968–1974) / **124**
Figure 8.3. A group of first BCC students, 1969 / **125**
Figure 8.4. Fine Arts portfolio class of 1991 / **126**
Figure 9.1. The Tercentenary School of Nursing Building, used by Division of Health Sciences 1975–1991 / **152**
Figure 9.2. Marine House, home of the Barbados Hotel School from 1973 to 1980, and the BCC Division of Hospitality Studies from 1980 to 1996 / **153**
Figure 9.3. Division of Health Sciences staff, 1986 / **154**
Figure 10.1. Hospitality Institute, opened in 1997 / **191**
Figure 10.2. The Barbados Language Centre, officially opened in 2008 / **191**
Figure 10.3. Sir Lloyd Erskine Sandiford, prime minister of Barbados, 1987–1994 / **192**
Figure 10.4. Sandiford receiving an honorary doctorate in 2004 / **192**
Figure 11.1. Clyde "Charlie" Best, principal, 1969–1975 / **210**
Figure 11.2. Alvin Barnett, principal, 1978–1988 / **210**
Figure 11.3. Norma Holder, principal, 1988–2004 / **210**
Figure 11.4. Gladstone Best, principal, 2004–2015 / **210**
Figure 11.5. Ian Austin, principal, 2016–2017 / **211**
Figure 11.6. Annette Alleyne, principal, 2019–present / **211**
Figure 11.7. Eureka Brathwaite, registrar/bursar, 1977–1979; and first bursar, 1979–2000 / **211**
Figure 11.8. Sydney Arthur, registrar, 1995–2015 / **211**
Figure 11.9. Former deputy principals, registrars and librarian / **212**
Figure 11.10. Hetty Stoute-Oni, librarian, 2004–2016 / **212**
Figure 11.11. Former senior tutors at the Barbados Community College / **213**
Figure 11.12. Arthur Sealy, senior tutor, liberal arts, 1969–1976; and principal (acting), 1976–1978 / **213**
Figure 11.13. Arthur Fingall, senior tutor, technology, 1979–1980 and 1985–1992 / **214**
Figure 11.14. Hubert Bynoe, senior tutor, commerce, 1979–1993 / **214**
Figure 11.15. Vivienne Roberts, senior tutor, science, senior tutor 1985–1991, on leave 1991–1996 / **214**

Figures | xi

Figure 11.16. Lucene Bishop, senior tutor, liberal arts, 1989– / **214**

Figure 11.17. Barbara Babb-Cadogan, senior tutor, commerce, 1993–2011; deputy principal (acting), 2011–2012 / **215**

Figure 11.18. Neville Badenock, senior tutor, liberal arts, 1994–2004 / **215**

Figure 11.19. David Hallsworth, senior tutor, science, 1997–2011 / **215**

Figure 11.20. Vincent Sisnett, senior tutor, health sciences, 1996–1998 (acting), and 1998–2008 / **215**

Figure 11.21. Allison Thompson, senior tutor, fine arts (acting), 2009–2017 / **216**

Figure 11.22. Frederick (Freddie) Inniss, the first BCC college counsellor / **216**

Figure 11.23. Esther Maynard, physical education head, 1980–2004 / **216**

Figure 12.1. The Planning and Advisory Committee at the Barbados Community College (2017) / **232**

Figure 12.2. Oraco's vision of the University College of Barbados – Eyrie Campus / **232**

Figure 12.3. The Muscavado Mural in the Hotel PomMarine, Hospitality Institute / **233**

Tables

Table 5.1. Establishment Date of Community and Other Relevant Colleges by Country / **56**

Table 5.2. Classification of Institutions into Community Colleges and Other Colleges / **58**

Table 5.3. Community Colleges Formed through Amalgamation of Pre-existing Institutions / **60**

Table 5.4. Five Models for Anglophone Caribbean Community College Development / **80**

Table 9.1. Other Exchange Visits between the Barbados Community College and St Clair College of Applied Arts and Technology / **148**

Table 11.1. Barbados Scholarships and Exhibitions, 2001–2014 / **202**

Preface

Few of us have had the good fortune to have lived a life which has followed a master plan: be born in a nuclear family, attend traditional schools at the appropriate ages, move along our educational journey at set intervals, find and work in traditional jobs of our choice, achieve the milestones we set ourselves, retire at a set time and live happily ever after. For most of us, life's journey has been complicated.

Often, we have had to take the road less travelled or, on occasion, create a path where one did not exist. Whether in politics, religion or education, living, surviving and maturing have meant making sense out of nonsense, searching for answers to questions which seemed unanswerable, living with uncertainty and ambiguity, and yet creating a reality and finding a course of action which seems at least appropriate, defensible, sensible, satisfying or just comfortable.

From childhood to adulthood, some of us have struggled with the concept of the Trinity in religion, grappling with the idea of three in one and one in three. In the end, many have come to embrace an unshakeable belief that God the Father, God the Son and God the Holy Spirit, though three persons, are joined by a unity of purpose.

As citizens of the English-speaking Caribbean, joined by a common language and a similar history but separated by the expanse of the Caribbean Sea, generations of politicians have sought to forge a federation or Caribbean community. In the meantime, ordinary citizens have managed to create a unity, tapping into the common core values of the region while enjoying the freedoms and opportunities inherent in differences.

Practitioners in education realize, only after considerable reflection, that there is as much artificiality in the established levels of education as there is in the separation of knowledge and understanding into subject disciplines of science and arts. After all, the organization into kindergarten, primary, secondary, further, tertiary and higher may very well be merely an administrative tool designed to create order and efficiency, in the same way that the scientific method transcends the borders of science and design crosses the boundary of the arts. Youngsters show us today that linear thinking blocks the gateway to creativity and matrix thinking unlocks unforeseen possibilities.

Across the region, there are similar educational institutions variously labelled as national colleges, state colleges, community colleges, colleges, university colleges and even universities. There are technical colleges, technical institutes and polytechnics. There are even schools that are called *colleges* and colleges that are called *schools*. There are grammar schools, high schools, secondary schools, specialist schools and comprehensive schools, and even secondary modern schools. Reflecting on these labels, one may ask: What is in a name? Are these labels the legacy of politics, the whimsy of leaders or the musings of semanticists? Do they constitute the general reality or someone's specific agenda, in an attempt to make sense of a given situation?

Perhaps that was the line of thinking that Thomas Henry Huxley (1888, 204) was following when he stated:

> It was badly received by the generation to which it was first addressed, and the outpouring of angry nonsense to which it gave rise is sad to think upon. But the present generation will probably behave just as badly if another Darwin should arise, and inflict upon them that which the generality of mankind most hate – the necessity of revising their convictions. Let them, then, be charitable to us ancients; and if they behave no better than the men of my day to some new benefactor, let them recollect that, after all, our wrath did not come to much, and vented itself chiefly in the bad language of sanctimonious scolds. Let them as speedily perform a strategic right-about-face, and follow the truth wherever it leads.

Some of us have had the challenge of trying to make sense of religious denominations with conflicting viewpoints on salient matters like Sabbaths and Lord's Days, salvation by grace, and rewards of faith or works. Others have had the opportunity to live in different countries and experience the disorientation of variable cultural norms. Yet others quickly shift their points of reference depending on the situation – for example, where driving on the right in one place is as correct as driving on the left in another. Many of African heritage have undergone a metamorphosis from the idea of being well groomed being signalled by cropped or straightened hair in a colonial era to one of attractive kinky, less ordered and natural Afros, locks and twists.

The challenges in setting up a new educational institution must be daunting. However, a community college in a newly independent, anglophone Caribbean country is a novelty; operationalizing it would have been quite perplexing, as the leaders figured out what should be adopted, what adapted, and what created fresh. Although no one said it publicly in those words, sceptics may even have considered the idea nonsensical, not meaning it to be foolish; but more so, a misfit, as described by Zukav (1979) as not fitting into the prearranged patterns which we have superimposed on reality.

It should not be too difficult to imagine the experience of working in a newly formed community college that was trying to establish its credibility as a tertiary institution to a sceptical public. It was an institution which was daring to assert its differences, while at the same time teaching traditional advanced-level subjects, like some secondary schools. It was a college where only a few weeks earlier, many secondary school teachers had been transformed into tertiary teachers by a small allowance, and perhaps the Midas touch.

This was a college that quickly needed to build the self-confidence of a heterogeneous student body in which young students may have been trying to fend off an inferiority complex, and mature students were striving to find a place; full-time students were making sense of freedom from uniforms and coping with a newfound responsibility for time on task, while part-time students were searching for legitimacy and carving out more hours in a working day.

Teachers were searching for their own identities as assistant tutors, tutors, instructors, or even facilitators in an environment where the practice should no longer be guided by pedagogy for pupils, but rather by andragogy for the adult learner. The founder of the college had declared that it was to be neither a transplant from the United States nor a hybrid between a university and a secondary school. As an implementer of that vision in the first community college in the region, leaders were challenged to create a homegrown institution. It could choose to spend many years on either defending what it was not or diligently asserting what it could be. Reflecting on the African proverb "A snake does not measure its shape against the rainbow", it needed to come to terms with how it would present and assess itself.

At this stage of life, reflection has become a daily practice. Since retirement, memories have become a familiar companion. History has magically reshaped past discomforts, resolved many former contradictions and transformed several ensuing disappointments into life lessons. I sometimes wonder which of these musings are facts, which are only ideas and which are figments of the imagination. My scientific training raises those questions, but my life experiences instruct me that there is intrinsic value in any recollection, both to self and others.

I did not search for my first teaching job after graduation. It found me and took me to a place that I have never forgotten. It was elitist, isolated, orderly, selective, structured, quiet, clean and traditional. Clean-cut, middle-class young women, destined for the professions or business or leisure, were busy in the sixth forms preparing for A-level studies in the sciences. A new graduate, bursting with knowledge and energized by recent success, I was excited about my lifelong dream of being a teacher, elated about imparting what I knew, ready to help students gain new skills and overflowing with excitement to take them through two gruelling years of study to achieve the goal of not just passing, but getting good grades in those prized examinations.

On reflection, up until 1974, I was unaware of community colleges, which were never a part of my educational journey or landscape. That changed when I decided to leave a familiar place behind and move to Barbados. I learned then that teaching positions might be available at the five-year-old Barbados Community College. Perhaps because my application was late (or perhaps not), it was not accepted. However, I was far more successful on that September morning when I walked into the office of the deputy chief education officer on Jemmotts Lane and enquired about a teaching job. I am not sure if I had already presented my credentials, but I recall her surprising response: "When would you like to start?"

A few days later, if not the next day, I made the journey from my home in Haggatt Hall, St Michael, to West St Joseph Secondary School (now Grantley Adams Memorial), where that too has left an indelible memory. There stood an old imposing but somewhat rundown plantation house on tree-lined grounds. Much of my time, however, was to be spent not in the house, but in smaller outer buildings which housed the science laboratories and doubled as classrooms as well.

In many ways, this was opposite to what I had left behind – large classes, noisy environs, younger pupils, less structure, less order, new principal, mixed student body in terms of gender, educational abilities and interest. For the few months I spent there, I enjoyed experiencing a different culture, meeting committed teachers and interesting students, many of whom had serious academic dreams and focus and who worked hard with me – an untrained teacher who was willing to try different pathways to success, albeit mainly in external examinations.

The Ministry of Education was just working on my appointment when I got news through my growing local network about a possible teaching post at the Barbados Community College. Those prospects seemed more appealing, so I applied, and this time I was successful. It was at the interview that I realized that I was not going to be teaching A-level science subjects, as I had anticipated. Instead, I was to apply my knowledge as an assistant tutor in the newly established Division of Health Sciences.

It was on arrival at Jemmotts Lane that I came to know that I was the only full-time member of the staff, apart from the senior tutor, Alvin Barnett. I also learned that training allied health personnel in public health inspection, medical laboratory technology, pharmacy, occupational therapy and medical records technology was the goal. These disciplines were transitioning from apprenticeship training to formal full-time education at the college, and curricula for science and general education courses needed to be urgently developed for inclusion in these programmes. I learned quickly that institutions such as the College of Arts, Science and Technology, Mona Rehabilitation Centre and West Indies School of Public Health in Jamaica had gone that route in earlier years. For Barbados Community College, this was a first; for me, it was another new experience, never to be forgotten.

I seem to have an affinity for old buildings, or they for me. Classes were conducted in the old Tercentenary School of Nursing building, which would also later house a small library. The laboratories were located next to the offices in a small, repurposed old building near a prominent tamarind tree, cherished for its shade for cars and groups as well as for its delightful fruits. The programme coordinators and part-time tutors were seasoned practitioners in their disciplines. Many of the students were older than I was, had much practical experience in their field and all were focused on quickly improving their knowledge and skills. With their family duties and other adult responsibilities, they had little time and minimal opportunity for extracurricular activities, and they had little in common with their peers in another space – young students at the Eyrie campus.

There were no computers – only typewriters, Gestetner copiers, stencils, styluses and spirit duplicators. There was no Internet to quickly access information. I knew no colleagues in Barbados with prior experience in college-level science courses for Allied Health. The senior tutor was a quiet, steady, transformative leader who guided and allowed you to be adventurous, even if you made mistakes. I had no blueprint and no teacher training.

However, I had access to the valuable experience of the practitioners in several health disciplines; the list of competencies required for various jobs; the ears of the senior tutor, who himself had a science background; a few manuals; my own books for reference; a disposition to listen; and a sound education which included learning how to learn. Pursuing a diploma in education soon after gave me some important tools in curriculum design, as well as practice in the art and science of teaching. There was a sense of purpose, a pervading pioneering spirit and an excitement about the work in the Division of Health Science, as we diligently created a path that hitherto did not exist.

It was during my studies in the United States for a master's degree in educational leadership in 1983 that I pursued a course called "The Community College". This was an eye-opener. I discovered the protean nature of the community college in the United States, and even that the concept existed in a few other countries. I appreciated its inclusiveness and symbiotic relationship with the community and the world of work. I was fascinated with an anecdotal definition that a community college is an institution that "will teach anything to anyone, anywhere and at any time, as long as the resources allowed". It was at that time that I reconstructed my concept of the community college so it was enlarged well beyond the image of a two-year or an A-level college.

It came to mean a place of learning where adults are provided with opportunities to embark on different educational journeys in preparation for further study, work, the pursuit of interests and leisure activities, periodic retooling, and even the discovery of self. It became clear that a community college is a special institution, unconstrained by the traditions of past centuries and ever evolving to meet emerging societal needs. It came to mean to me an institution of opportunities for students of all ages and at all stages, as well as leaders and staff endowed with a spirit of enterprise, nested in an incubator of unlimited possibilities in relation to curricula, projects and innovations. It stood out as a key instrument in human resource development and an important partner in nation building.

I left the Barbados Community College in 1991, but I took a part of it with me to the University of the West Indies (UWI). I carried with me its commitment to openness, access and innovation, the value it placed on articulation and partnerships, its penchant for flexibility and embracing change, the knack for breaking down the barriers imposed by labels, and the worth of lifelong learning. Those understandings served me well as I worked on the other side of the fence at UWI, first in the UWI/USAID (United States Agency for International Development) Development Training Project, the Tertiary Level Institutions Unit and later, in helping to shape the UWI Open Campus.

Working at different levels and locations in Caribbean tertiary education has provided me with an important and unique vantage point to observe and influence growth and innovation, experience success and failure, confront setbacks and, through strategic repositioning in the sector, achieve recovery. Many lessons have been learned, and there are many stories which can be told. Some may be merely interesting, but more importantly, many would be instructive to tertiary education students – including potential students and alumni, educators, administrators, planners, employers, community leaders, policymakers and civil society as they continue to reinvent a vibrant tertiary education sector.

This book is a personal attempt to make sense out of nonsense, not only for oneself but also for others of like mind. It is an articulation of the essence of a community college in the Caribbean that would become a place of learning and development for adults, an institution responsive to postsecondary educational needs and a community-oriented institution reflecting openness and flexibility, geared towards preparation for work, studies and life itself. In the end, this book seeks to celebrate opportunities seized and look ahead to future possibilities.

In the 1990s, I researched and wrote on access to tertiary education in Barbados and St Lucia and the Barbados Community College was a focal point. It is true to say that my encounter with that institution was a career-changing (indeed life-changing) one. It is that experience that has inspired me to this point, where I shall attempt to share with whoever has the time and interest to read it, my musings on the community college in general, but on the Barbados Community College in particular: its origins, intentions, relationships with other institutions, opportunities – seized or lost, successes and possibilities. Perhaps the occasion of the fiftieth anniversary of the establishment of the Barbados Community College is an appropriate time to document its journey and celebrate its achievements.

Acknowledgements

I am grateful to several persons who contributed to the production of this book. Special thanks to Joyce Daniel for permitting the use of her painting, *Change*, for the cover of the book. Photographer and designer Barry Tudor provided the photograph for the back cover and gave invaluable assistance and advice in taking and selecting relevant photographs and in designing the figures. The Sherbourne House, Marine House and Harbour Site have been demolished, and the Tercentenary School of Nursing and Eyrie House are in ruins. Therefore, I am especially grateful to the Barbados Government Information Service (BGIS) for earlier photographs of these historic structures. The donation of other photographs from community colleges across the region and the Barbados Community College Hospitality Institute, as well as from the personal collections of Hartley Alleyne, Joyce Daniel, Peter Peter, Edlyn Inniss, Laura Yard, Stephen Sealy, Annette Alleyne and Lucene Bishop is deeply appreciated.

Thanks to Annette Blackman, for lending me her thesis on the first two decades of the college. I am also grateful to the board of management, which gave permission to access college documents, and to the acting principal, Dr Cheryl Weekes, who responded to my numerous requests. Many staff members of the Barbados Community College were extremely accommodating as well, and their assistance is appreciated. I acknowledge the help of staff of the Barbados Library Service and the UWI Cave Hill West Indian Collection, especially for looking up old newspapers. The library of the Barbados Community College proved to be a reservoir of useful information and resourceful staff. Sherrol Gaskin, in the principal's office, was also extremely helpful.

I am especially grateful for the editorial assistance and comments given by Sylvia Lauretta Hackett, newly appointed BCC principal Annette Alleyne, and Jocelyn King. The documents and comments from Gladstone Best were very valuable. The comments by Professor Joel Warrican, exchanges with Jacqueline Moniquette, encouragement by Beth Hagan of the Community College Baccalaureate Association and the feedback and advice from Professor Glen Jones of the University of Toronto were much appreciated.

xxii | Acknowledgements

The book was made more relevant through interviews granted by the following persons, to whom I am deeply grateful:

Colin Kirton – first principal and former chairman of the board

Kay Thompson – former student, curriculum development officer and former senior tutor in the Division of Commece

Sylvia Lauretta Hackett – former director of the Language Centre and deputy principal (acting)

Esther Phillips – one of the first students in 1969, tutor and retired senior tutor

Joyce Daniel – first tutor and senior tutor in the Fine Arts Division

Anne Hewitt – one of the first assistant tutors in 1969

Nigel Bradshaw – one of the first assistant tutors in 1969, retired senior tutor and deputy principal

Cheryl Weekes – former senior tutor, deputy principal 2016 and principal (acting), 2017

Samuel Rouse – current senior tutor and former deputy principal (acting)

Eureka Brathwaite – the Barbados Community College's first bursar (retired)

Hartley Alleyne –senior tutor in the Fine Arts Division (retired)

Esther Maynard – the Barbados Community College's first physical education tutor (retired)

Roger Worrell – current registrar and former senior tutor

Sherrol Gaskin – principal's secretary to Norma Holder, Gladstone Best, Ian Austin and Cheryl Weekes

Zann Ward – acting senior tutor in the Fine Arts Division

Gladstone Best – former student, assistant registrar, senior tutor, deputy principal and retired principal (acting)

Patrick Rowe – former assistant registrar, University College of Barbados project manager and director, Higher Education Development Unit

Samuel Miller – current research officer

Joseph Inniss – one of the first students in 1969, former Staff Association president and current curriculum development officer

Jean Butcher-Lashley – senior tutor (acting) in the Liberal Arts Division

Denyse Menard-Greenidge – former senior tutor in the Fine Arts Division

Angelita Sandiford – former senior tutor in the General and Continuing Education Division and deputy principal (acting)

Peter Peter – senior tutor in the Technology Division

Monica Simmons – the Barbados Community College's first college librarian (retired)

Antonia Coward – the Barbados Community College's first coordinator of bachelor's degrees in technical and vocational education

June Caddle – head of physical education and senior tutor (acting) in the General and Continuing Education Division

Bernice Critchlow-Earle – former tutor, senior tutor in the Division of Hospitality Studies and director of the Barbados Hospitality Institute (retired)

Sir Lloyd Erskine Sandiford – former minister of education and prime minister; founder and assistant tutor at the Barbados Community College

Barbara Babb-Cadogan – former senior tutor in the Commerce Division and deputy principal (acting)

Trevor Marshall – head of the History Department (retired)

Abbreviations

ACTI	Association of Caribbean Tertiary Institutions
AIB	Association of the Institute of Bankers
BCC	Barbados Community College
BGIS	Barbados Government Information Service
CAPE	Caribbean Advanced Proficiency Examinations
CARICOM	Caribbean Community
CASE	College of Agriculture, Science and Education
CCID	Community Colleges for International Development
CGA	certified general accountant
CIDA	Canadian International Development Agency
CSEC	Caribbean Secondary Education Certificate
CXC	Caribbean Examinations Council
ELAP	Emerging Leaders in the Americas Programme
FISU	International University Sports Federation
GPA	grade point average
LCC	London Chamber of Commerce
MLT	Medical Laboratory Technology
NIFCA	National Independence Festival for Creative Arts
OAS	Organization of American States
OECD	Organisation for Economic Co-operation and Development
OECS	Organisation of Eastern Caribbean States
PAHO	Pan American Health Organization
PSD	private secretary's diploma
SJPP	Samuel Jackman Prescod Polytechnic
TAFE	technical and further education
TSAP	Tertiary Institutions Sports Association of Barbados
TSN	Tercentenary School of Nursing
TVET	technical vocational education and training
UCB	University College of Barbados
UNDP	United Nations Development Programme
USAID	US Agency for International Development
UWI	University of the West Indies
WHO	World Health Organization

1.

Context, Concepts and Processes

A community college was established in Barbados in July 1968, and that institution, the Barbados Community College, admitted its first students in January 1969. The desired institutional model was announced earlier as a junior college, in a context where there was an inadequate number of places to cater to the educational needs of a growing number of secondary school graduates who had successfully completed British external examinations. The country had become independent from Britain only recently (in 1966) and was urgently in need of greater numbers of middle-level managers and skilled workers – many more, and a wider variety than the local hotel school and technical institute could supply. The training and adult education capacity and scope of the extramural department of the University of the West Indies were limited. The twenty-year-old University of the West Indies was expected to continue to educate and train primarily professionals, leaders and top managers. The demand for training was urgent and growing.

The minister of education of Barbados at that time saw the need for local adaptation of the familiar British educational system. He had floated the idea of the institution he wanted but had never visited a US community college. The public had heard of junior colleges filling the gap between the secondary schools and the university. In the light of strong political and public opposition to this advanced-level college, which from this perspective would compete with the sixth-form schools, the minister defended and perhaps amended his idea. There seemed to be all-round ambivalence about what the institution would be and could do. However, its advocate was clear about what the institution should *not* be. Barbados had recently ended a colonial era, and the minister was adamant that the institution should not be a transplant from the United States. He also argued that it should not be a hybrid of the secondary school and university. He was equally clear about its major purpose – a dual function of postsecondary education for transfer to university as well as a means of addressing manpower development for the workplace.

Public perception was that the community college was a US creation. It was not generally acknowledged then that the late-nineteenth-century community college model had itself emerged from the German *Volkhochschulen*, which had inspired postsecondary, pre-university institutions not only in Europe, but also in Canada and the United States (Raby and Valeau 2012; Wiseman et al. 2012). Additionally, there were limited scholarly publications that would have pointed out that it was only a few years before, in 1960, that the California Master Plan for Higher Education had created a state tripartite system from which the prototype of the community college emerged as an integral pillar of the postsecondary system (Raby 2001).

It took a few years for Barbados to translate the community college concept into reality. Initially, the new principal of the college, Clyde Best, visited eleven community colleges in the United States to gain first-hand experience. Mentoring of the fledgling college was offered by Penn State University in the United States and the University of the West Indies. About a decade later, new dimensions emerged from a prolonged, symbiotic relationship between the St Clair College of Applied Arts and Technology in Ontario, Canada, and the Barbados Community College, sponsored mainly by the Canadian International Development Agency (CIDA) and World Bank. By then, perhaps in response to expanding information technology and the prevailing socioeconomic conditions, similar entities were emerging on other Caribbean islands and also in several other parts of the world.

As the scholarship of the community college grew, as increasing numbers of community college staff studied in the United States and Canada and the use of communication technology increased, transnational boundaries became more permeable and the Barbados Community College expanded, adopted some prevailing ideas, adapted existing policies and programming, revised its mission, assimilated best practices and took on a character of its own. In relation to the community college concept, mention had been made of the Caribbean experience in the international literature, that "in Barbados, two post-secondary institutions have recently been amalgamated to form a community college that in many respects resembles the typically American version" (Kintzer 1979).

Looking back at the foundations of this development, one may wonder how the Barbados Community College came to be. Was it imposed from above? Was it exported from abroad? Did it emerge organically from below? Was it borrowed from the United States? If so, what was borrowed, and why? What was rejected? It seems appropriate to use the framework of educational borrowing articulated by Raby and Valeau (2013) to do the following:

- Interrogate the relevant historic and contemporary global patterns in terms of north/south flows.
- Examine the types of flows which took place in terms of purposeful or spontaneous adoption.

- Explore the extent of reinvention of the institution's form, in terms of dependency and localization contributors.

In exploring reinvention, it may be interesting to analyse the Barbados Community College experience in terms of a borrowed British jingle, traditionally associated with weddings: "Something old, something new, something borrowed, something blue". On this occasion, the phrase would be reconstructed as "Something old, something borrowed, something new".

Globalization has resulted in the rapid spread of information, ideas, technology, structures and policies. Among other developments, this has facilitated the establishment and emergence of community college counterparts worldwide. Educational borrowing has been instrumental in this exchange. Often, this has been effected by way of north/south unidirectional flows, aided by the work of bilateral agreements, consortia and multinational and international development agencies. For some countries, these circumstances evoke neocolonialism, and critics condemn them as cultural penetration, while proponents laud their value.

Additionally, there is increasing evidence that globalization is providing growing opportunities for south/south and south/north flows, as well as global convergence. Paradoxically, globalization not only has resulted in mirroring of the valued US model, but also in reinforcing new local models. It also has brought greater transparency to spontaneous mirroring of global counterparts. In these circumstances, variability can be seen as the result of both globalization and the rejection of education borrowing, reflecting sensitivity and preferential response to local political, economic, social and cultural realities, but with full consciousness and respect for the global context.

These developments are consistent with the adage "Think globally, network regionally, act locally." It may be that in this global world, the idea of community has to be reconfigured as the constructs of space and time are experienced in new ways. In this study, an appropriate question is: to what extent have globalization and educational borrowing influenced the emergence and development of community college counterparts in Barbados and the anglophone Caribbean?

Purpose and Significance

Much has been written about the early history and operations of the community college in the United States (Brubacher and Rudy 1958; Cohen and Brawer 1984, 1987; Kintzer 1979, 1982; Kintzer and Wattenberger 1985; Ratcliff 1994; Baker 1994; Dougherty 1994). Additionally, several writers (Campbell 1971;

Leslie 1980; Dennison and Gallagher 1986) have published research on the early development of the Canadian Community College. More recent work on internationalization and global counterparts has been done by Raby and Tarrow (1996), Levin (2001), Raby (2000), Raby and Valeau (2009, 2013, 2018), and Wiseman et al. (2012).

In a comprehensive review of the global development of the community college movement, Elsner, Boggs and Irwin (2008, 2015) edited and presented the work of several authors, including Geremie Sawadogo on French West Africa; Glen Fisher and Marianne Scott on South Africa; Mary Gershwin on Brazil; Michael Skolnik on Canada; Mary Crabbe Gershwin, Philip Cary, Marcelo Von Chrismar, Cristobal Silva and Shelley L. Wood on Chile; Paul Elsner and Roberto Navarro Sanchez on Colombia; Don Doucette on Haiti; Cebert Adamson on Jamaica; Bertha Landrum, David Valladares Aranda, and Arturo Nava Jaimes on Mexico; George Boggs and Judith Irwin on the United States; Gerard Postiglione, Liangjuan Wang, and Don Watkins; and Gerard Postiglione and Yiwei Chen on China; Gerard Postiglione and Steven Sai Kit Kwok on Hong Kong; Allen Cissell and Harris Iskandar on Indonesia; Joyce Tsunoda and Yasuko Iida; and Joyce Tsunoda and Keiichi Yoshimoto on Japan; Paul Elsner and David Ponitz on Qatar; Paul Elsner and Sabrina Loi on Singapore; Allen Cissell and Tanom Inkhamnert on Thailand; Ahmet Aypay on Turkey; Paul Elsner and James Horton, Mark Drummond and Philip Hartley, and Tayeb Kamali on United Arab Emirates; Diane Oliver, Sandra Engel, and Analy Scorsone on Vietnam; Nabeel Alsohybe on Yemen; Stuart Rosenfeld and Cynthia Shapiro on Denmark; Hugh David and Geoff Hall on England; Frank McMahon on Ireland; Coen Free on the Netherlands; Sandra de Bresser and David Roldan Martinez on Spain; Antoine Barnaart on Australia; Jim Doyle on New Zealand; John Halder on India, the Dominican Republic and Georgia; and Edward Valeau and Rosalind Latiner Raby on India.

Research is also available on community college counterparts in Japan (Anazi and Paik 2012), Tunisia (Hagedorn and Mezghani 2013), China (Song and Postiglione 2011) and Taiwan (Wang and Seggie 2013), to name only a few.

On the other hand, little has been written about the community college in the Caribbean region. Peters (1993, 2001), Raby and Valeau (2009), Grant-Woodham and Morris (2009), Morris (2012), and Roberts (1999, 2001, 2003a, 2003b, 2003c, 2003d, 2006a, 2006b, 2006c) examined aspects of community colleges in the anglophone Caribbean, but very little has been documented and published on these colleges in general. It must be noted, though, that Adamson (2015) has written on the community colleges in Jamaica, as well as on the Council of Community Colleges of Jamaica, which coordinates their work. Alleyne (1995) has written about Trinidad and Tobago; and Howe (2003) considered community colleges in his review of tertiary education in the English-speaking Caribbean.

Published work on the Barbados Community College is sparse. Rosen (1979) conducted a study of the first nine years of the college. For Annette Blackman's library studies thesis (1990), she conducted a study on the college's first two decades (1968–1989). Sisnett (1982) looked at the Barbados Community College in relation to the US community college model. There are also unpublished studies of the Barbados Community College reported to have been done by history students under the supervision of historian Trevor Marshall at the college itself.

This work seeks to give an overview of the global community college movement – to add to the literature on the community colleges in the anglophone Caribbean region in general, and in particular, focus on the Barbados Community College. It brings to the fore the reality that in this region, there are at least twenty-four relevant institutions. There are about fifteen community colleges with that name, one of which has graduated to a university college, as well as nine community college–like institutions, one of which has also become a university. It also recognizes Barbados as the community college pioneer in the anglophone Caribbean and as a fairly early entrant in the worldwide community college movement. It seeks, therefore, to set the Barbados experience in its local, regional and global contexts.

It has taken on the challenge to record for posterity some of the important milestones in the Barbados Community College's fifty-year development, as well as some of the key players involved in its evolution. The voices of many of the founding staff members, past leaders and stalwarts have been silenced by their deaths. However, the words of many of them are quoted in this text. Oral stories told by living participants are recounted to reinforce and enrich the existing written reports and records.

This study aims to celebrate the college's contribution to higher education in Barbados and the region; to record its successes and identify some lessons learned; to examine some strategic reorientations which have been made over the years; and look ahead at future possibilities. It also looks at the changing public perception about the college over time and points to some indicators of its impact on the society in which it has operated.

It also tells the story of a man who has been associated with this institution for more than fifty years. There is no doubt that he has had tremendous impact on the community college. Whether viewed as founder, teacher, politician, leader or member of the community, his impact has been deep, wide-ranging and significant. He was the initiator of the idea of the college, overseer of its establishment legislation, teacher at different periods at the college, facilitator of policies effecting change, leader from inside and outside, and teacher par excellence. As minister of education, he has had the task of policymaking and fundraising; as prime minister, of steering its course; as private citizen, influencing strategic repositioning; and as recipient of its first and only honorary doctorate so far, speaking out to preserve the college's basic mission while breaking new ground. He has been dedicated to the cause of creating the college and helping it find its place in the higher education landscape – locally, regionally and internationally. That person is Sir Lloyd Erskine Sandiford.

The Barbados Community College experience is also a story of the contested mission surrounding its establishment; the power of partnerships with the St Clair College of Applied Arts and Technology and other institutions; the quest for quality assurance, including external validation and articulation; the value of leadership from the middle and in the trenches by senior tutors and department heads; the payoff of the persistence of pioneers; the gains in creatively moving forward with ideas, even when resources are not quite there yet; and the possibilities inherent in finding niches and opening up opportunities through adult and continuing education.

It is my expectation that as this book looks back at the past, it will catalyse the discourse on future possibilities and serve as an inspiration to present and future leaders, teachers and students, as they reflect on the journey so far and focus on the endless possibilities on the road ahead.

In sum, this book should be useful to:

- Historians with an interest in the evolution and policies of institutions of higher education
- Caribbean historians generally
- Scholars who are interested in community college counterparts in the region and globally
- Students with an interest in educational management and administration
- Members of the wider public in Barbados, the rest of the Caribbean and the diaspora who are interested in civics, cultural studies and educational affairs

Methodology

This work has three main objectives. The study itself works its way from the general to the specific – from the outer world to the Caribbean to the nation of Barbados in particular. It begins by scanning the origin and movement of the community college globally. It moves to exploring the narrower context of the community college in the anglophone Caribbean, drawing on the few published works, the information in their college handbooks and on college websites and forty years of experience emerging from direct contact with these institutions and their early leaders. The book is, however, primarily a case study of the Barbados Community College – a study based on a very limited pool of relevant scholarly and other publications, as well as on forty-five years of first-hand experience with the institution.

The literature reviewed focused on historical writings tracing the evolution of the community college model; research tracking the development of community college scholarship; discourse on the globalization of the community college concept and the associated philosophical, economic, social and political dimensions, and the rationale, processes and outcomes of educational borrowing.

In relation to the anglophone Caribbean, information was gathered mainly from books, journals, college websites and personal communications. For the Barbados Community College, information was drawn from four primary sources. The views and experiences of political leaders were found in national development plans and cabinet papers from the government, available in the public library and cabinet office. The positions and experiences of college leaders were gleaned from unpublished strategic plans and annual reports found mainly in the Barbados Community College Library. Views of the public were sought from newspaper stories from the *Barbados Advocate* (formerly *Advocate News*) and *Nation* newspapers (including *Daily Nation, Nation News, Weekend Nation* and *Sunday Sun*), many preserved in the West Indian Collection of the Sydney Martin Library on the Cave Hill campus of the University of the West Indies. The first decades of the college's establishment were targeted because this was a period of controversy, public discourse and growing legitimacy.

Using speeches and statements of purpose at the establishment of the community college and the literature, questionnaires were prepared and sent by e-mail to interviewees with a cover letter explaining the purpose and encouraging participation. (A copy of the questionnaire is included as appendix 16.) These e-mails were followed up by telephone calls. Interviewees were given the option of a subsequent face-to-face interview or a discussion over the phone. A slight majority opted for telephone interviews, all conducted by me. The intention was to conduct structured interviews with as many as possible of the nineteen teachers who were at the college from the beginning. About half of them were deceased, and others were indisposed or unwell. Five were interviewed, though, and their responses recorded.

Of the first de facto principal and the nine later principals, four were deceased. Similar interviews were conducted with the remaining five, including the first. Of the ten deputy principals, one had become principal and thus had already been interviewed, and two were deceased. The remaining seven were interviewed along similar lines. The first and longest-serving bursar and the first and longest-serving librarian were also interviewed. Because all the preceding registrars were deceased, only the current one was interviewed. All of the current senior tutors were interviewed, as well as the current curriculum development officer and the head of the physical education department.

In compiling this work, I was faced with the challenge of presenting information which would have value for and engage the attention of community college administrators and educators, while at the same time creating a document which would appeal to the layperson and the general public. I was also faced with the challenge of blending the formal exploration of the global with the less well documented experiences of the regional, and also with the stories emerging from the lived experiences with the Barbados Community College. Striking a balance was difficult.

In the end, in relation to the former, the decision was made to pursue both ends but to use short chapters and segments with captions. With this arrangement, it is envisaged that each reader will be able to navigate an informed path through the document, choosing topics related to her or his areas of interest. In relation to the latter, it was decided to address the global mainly through a review of the literature; to portray the regional mainly through available facts and to use the storytelling approach in relation to the Barbados Community College.

Analytical Framework

The opening chapters briefly establish the genesis of the Barbados Community College and the immediate and wider context within which globalization and educational borrowing are operating. Following this, the book examines the North American community college experience, which has strongly influenced that in the Caribbean. The global community college movement and its associated longstanding and emerging global counterparts are also surveyed. Subsequently, there is an attempt to provide a window into the community college experience in the anglophone Caribbean, looking mainly at the models of development and the scope of the institutions' offerings.

Having set this context, five approaches are taken to explore the development of the Barbados Community College. First, there is an ongoing account of places, people, programmes and processes. It looks at where the activities of the Barbados Community College took place, and also at the major players who were involved in these activities. In the main, it focuses on "firsts," as well as on persons who have played leadership roles. In addition, it mentions selected students who have been identified by the college or who have identified themselves by volunteering information. It references many of the various programmes of study which were developed over time and delivered to students, and the processes which evolved to guide the development, delivery and assessment of these programmes.

Second, this account is an analysis of the development of the Barbados Community College through its linear phases. These can be described as five stages: establishment, consolidation, expansion and reputation building, uncertainty and reinvention. Alternatively, the stages can be looked at metaphorically as childhood, adolescence, adulthood, midlife crisis and reincarnation.

Third, it examines the college in terms of the evolution and expansion of its traditional community college functions. It looks at its widening scope of operations, from transfer through vocational, community engagement, remediation, to baccalaureate, as well as to adult and continuing education roles.

Fourth, from a quality assurance perspective, it interrogates the extent to which the college has demonstrated the traditional community college values of accessibility, affordability, flexibility, community engagement and innovation. It also looks at the impact of the community college in terms of student success, stakeholder satisfaction and fulfilment of mission.

In sum, over the course of this book, I hope to address the following pertinent questions:

- Who were the main leaders of the Barbados Community College?
- Where is the community college in terms of its evolution?
- As an institution, is it a hybrid (a cross between a secondary school and a university), a transplant (a North American institution) or a homegrown institution?
- Has it demonstrated accessibility, affordability, flexibility, community engagement and innovation?
- To what extent has the college answered the educational, cultural, societal and economic needs of Barbados?
- Has it shown leadership locally, regionally or internationally?
- To what extent has it been affected by globalization and educational borrowing?

Fifty years is a long time in the life of a vibrant community college. The size, diversity, dynamism, scope of work, flexibility, networks and resource challenges amplify its complexity. Therefore, despite the good intentions, there will be important information and many gaps which will not be addressed. These undoubtedly will raise questions for further enquiry, research and writings.

Organization

This chapter has served as an introduction, background and guide to the overall content of the book. Chapter 2 looks at the global community college context. Chapter 3 reviews the North American community college experience. Chapter 4 surveys the global community college movement. Moving closer to home, in chapter 5, there is a survey of the community colleges in the Caribbean. Chapters 6–12 then look at the Barbados Community College over the years, breaking the story into periods under the presiding principals – Clyde Best, Arthur Sealy, Alvin Barnett, Norma Holder, Gladstone Best and Ian Austin. The conclusion highlights lessons which have been and can be learned, as well as areas for further research and action. It concludes with an analysis of the impact of the college itself on its society, as well as the influence of globalization and education borrowing on its development.

The deliberations on the Barbados Community College presented in chapters 6–12 are distilled mainly from annual reports compiled by the principals. The narrative also draws on newspaper reports and individual interviews. To improve the readability of the document, specific references will be cited for newspaper articles and individual interviews. All other information is attributed to the annual reports of the relevant dates.

2.

The Global Community College Context

To establish the context for this discussion, it is important to define some relevant terms which appear in the literature. These include short-cycle institutions, nonuniversities, community college models and community college global counterparts, which are terms used to describe institutional types. It is also necessary to clarify the concepts and processes of globalization and educational borrowing, filling in some detail about purposeful and spontaneous adoption, dependency context, north/south flows and localization contributors. Other important topics to be mentioned include relevant political, economic and cultural factors which promote reinvention of these forms.

The pool of community college global counterparts shows great diversity. Over the years, it has expanded in both size and diversity. In the past decade, forty-seven institutional types were identified (Raby and Valeau 2012). Over time, these institutions became classified as community colleges, further-education colleges or vocational colleges. Sometimes they were grouped by their length of study, as short-cycle or two-year colleges; at other times, the criterion used was the level of study, such as postsecondary or tertiary. They were even defined in terms of what they were *not* (such as nonuniversities), and at other times, by their major focus (such as lifelong learning, transfer education or vocational education).

Community colleges and similar schools were defined by scholars in the 1970s up to the 1990s as short-cycle higher education institutions (Kintzer 1979, 1993, 1998; Eskow 1974). This label formally contrasted them against universities, which normally offer programmes that last longer than three years. However, this time-based categorization was problematic because duration itself was a variable within the short-cycle group, and there were many other characteristics which needed to be factored into a workable definition. The duration of these college offerings varied, depending on the length of compulsory education in a country. For example, when compulsory education ended early, community college education tended to be four to five years. On the contrary, when built on ten or more years of compulsory education, community college education tended to be two years or less (Cohen 1991). This reality made that short-cycle definition unreliable.

The institutions were often viewed in the US setting as two-year as opposed to four-year colleges. However, beyond duration, there were many other features that they had in common. The unifying characteristics of short-cycle institutions were noted as a focus on personnel training for paraprofessionals and other workers; open access, in order to provide greater equality of opportunity; regionality and decentralized decision-making; innovation and student-centredness; and low cost (in aspiration, even if not in reality). The drivers were seen as critical shortages of midlevel personnel, high unemployment and insufficient postsecondary education institutions to meet the demand. Their certificates did not generally have the same market value, social prestige or general reception as those from traditional universities (Kintzer 1979).

This grouping was found in the United States, New Zealand and western Canada; in the form of regional colleges in Norway; higher education schools in Yugoslavia; colleges of further education in Britain; regional technical institutes in Latin America; French university institutes of technology; colleges of advanced education in Australia; community colleges in New Zealand; and even colleges in Israel (Kintzer 1979). That group also included comprehensive colleges and specialized institutions. In general, the colleges which focused on a single technology and preparation for work suffered from a "second-class" ranking. They included regional technological institutes in Mexico, Japan's junior colleges, and colleges in Taiwan, Singapore, Sri Lanka and Tanzania. Even specialized institutions with greater concentration on the university transfer function in the People's Republic of China and upper secondary schools in the Soviet Union were embraced (Kerr 1963; Kintzer 1979).

Short-cycle higher education institutions included both binary institutions, on a parallel but separate higher education track from universities; and dual institutions, which allowed university transfer as well as certification for work. Binary systems were shown to exist in Britain and Australia, having separate tracts for practical and professional schools, as opposed to academic and further-education ones, which had limited community involvement. The former sometimes also ventured into credit transfers. The dual arrangement in Yugoslavia, South America, Chile, Venezuela and Colombia, as well as in the French university institutes and upper-technician-level training schools in West Germany (mainly for adult part-time students) showed attempts at combining short- and long-cycle higher education into a single organization, driven by financial and quality assurance concerns.

Nonuniversities

In the 1990s, many observers diverted their focus from the duration and content of schools to their type, shifting the discourse to a more direct comparison with universities. Short-cycle institutions were now referred to as the nonuniversity higher education sector (Neave 1991; Kintzer 1995). By definition, these nonuniversities included all private and public higher education institutions that were not universities. In many countries, this represented the majority of higher education institutions which collectively registered the majority of students. This grouping included about four thousand institutions in about 180 countries (Raby 2001). This classification was problematic, however, in that it had an elitist bias and did not define what the group really was, but rather underscored what it was *not*. Several European scholars, for example, found this classification limiting in an environment where the Bologna process was seeking to promote convergence and create harmonization within the binary system to achieve greater compatibility and international competitiveness (Taylor et al. 2008).

Community College Models

By the latter part of the twentieth century, it was felt necessary to arrive at a more concise, all-encompassing, nondegrading, nonelitist and nonethnocentric term to describe this type of school. In an increasing multiethnic, multicultural and multilingual world, the proposal was for a community college that acknowledged, embraced and respected diversity (Raby 2001). Consistent with that thrust, scholars had been using the term "community college model" (Kintzer 1979; Raby and Valeau 2001; Burgos-Sasscer and Collins 1996; Raby and Tarrow 1996; Schugurensky and Higgins 1996; Ural 1998).

Notwithstanding the diversity within the group, five homogenizing characteristics of community college models were advanced, including their postsecondary, postcompulsory nature, as well as their locally driven budget and curriculum; their specified purpose, which advocates a singular element such as vocational training; relatively low status afforded to it by governments, universities, scholars and the public; and responsiveness to local needs and relatively low tuition, which is intended to promote wider access (Raby 2001). Different permutations of these characteristics produced variations in models across the world. A global, comparative look at these models revealed notable programme variations among fifty-two countries. Of special interest to this work were three anglophone Caribbean countries, the Bahamas, Belize and

Guyana, where models showed underlying unifying characteristics, but also distinct variations (Raby 2001).

Community College Global Counterparts

In recognition of its global spread, and emerging from increased respect for and understanding of global diversity, the concept of community college global counterparts emerged. As more information on their presence and diversity was exposed through research, the discourse on community college models changed to a more nuanced dialogue about global counterparts (Raby and Valeau 2012, 2013, 2014; Raby, Friedel and Valeau 2016; Wiseman et al. 2012; Raby and Valeau 2018).

From this global perspective, their local orientation is affirmed, the options for university overflows and second chances are noted; their role as first responders to retool and respond to local workforce needs is recognized and the opportunities and accommodation provided for the majority of students are acknowledged. Their potential to provide skills that can increase economic development and social prosperity is also recognized (Raby and Valeau 2012; Elsner, Boggs and Irwin 2008, 2015; Grubb and Sweet 2005; Kintzer 1979; Strydom and Lategan 1998).

Globalization

As the global perspective took centre stage, the roots of community college counterparts have been identified in five distinct institutions. These include the Scandinavian folk high schools (Raby 1996), offering nonformal adult education (Bagley and Rust 2009); and the German *Volkhochschulen,* offering postsecondary, pre-university education and defining open access (Douglass 2000). From these bases emerged the European Polytechnic and Institute of Technology, offering alternatives to university. All of these influenced the creation of the British and Australian further-education institutions and the comprehensive US junior/community colleges (Raby and Valeau 2012). The US community college of the 1930s became associated with the "open access" mantra. This provided leverage for community college expansion in the United States and made this brand philosophically attractive and highly marketable to and sought after by the rest of the world. However, against the background of its European roots, the idea of US origin and ownership of the community college prototype lost traction.

Globalization is a process which produces a level of homogenization across the world. It connects the world through information flows, population shifts, student and scholar exchanges and technology, economic and cultural linkages (Raby and Valeau 2012). It includes the flow of ideas, technology, people, practices and cultures. The Western hegemonic pattern had been established over time and perpetuated through colonialization, the work of nongovernmental organizations and the operations of transnational corporations and development agencies (Currie 1996; Gagliano 1992; Ilon 1997; McGin 1997; Mosa 1996; Stewart 1996). Some scholars suggest that the higher education global flow has been mainly unidirectional from the developed to the developing countries, from north to south (Altbach 2011). However, more recent thought is that in general, and also in the particular case of community college counterparts, the flows have been multidirectional. The reality appears to be that there have been global flows and influence from western Europe to institutions in the United States and Canada, which modified what they received. These countries further influenced other global counterparts, which were themselves reinvented in other countries and have exerted influence all over the world (Raby and Valeau 2012).

Educational Borrowing

In its simplest form, borrowing includes someone who offers and someone who receives the gift or donation, as is. Educational borrowing often does not arise from a loan (Phillips and Ochs 2003), nor is the result simple adoption (Finegold, McFarland and Richardson 1992). Often sparks of interest are ignited, based on relevance and applicability of ideas, policies or structures which may be transmitted across geographic space (Halpin and Troyna 1995). In true borrowing, there would be passive adoption of and limited variation from the prototypes.

Educational borrowing implies the deliberate transplant of educational policy and institutional form. However, experience has shown that much variability has occurred in what has been thought to be borrowed, and this whole process has been driven largely by local economic, historical, political and cultural conditions in various contexts (Raby and Valeau 2012). This does not deny the realities of educational borrowing, which range from full transplantation, partial transplantation and rejection of the community college prototype. The full transplantation of the mission, function and form of a prototype has taken place (for example, in the borrowing of the Global Community College of Nong Khai Udon Thani in Thailand from counterparts in California; and in the establishment of the Community College of Qatar as a branch campus of the Houston Community College, Texas). The adoption of mission, form, function or a specific characteristic of an institution is a more common manifestation. Examples of this are the adoption of the American-style liberal arts educational model by some Chinese colleges and workforce training for a global economy in some Mexican community college counterparts (Laya 2009).

At the other end of the spectrum is rejection of the US community college prototype for cultural, economic or political reasons. Such was the case with Japanese community colleges, which mirrored the protoype, established during the US occupation, but which were restructured in the 1980s to become private institutions catering mainly to women's crafts and culture. Similarly, Israel effected the upgrading of regional colleges to universities to meet local needs and priorities (Yamano and Hawkins 1996).

Educational borrowing has been facilitated by globalization, which became increasingly popular from the mid-1990s. Discussions have looked at which ideas have been borrowed (Halpin and Troyna 1995), why they were borrowed (Steiner-Khamsi and Quist 2000) and which countries were involved in these processes (Raby and Valeau 2012). Acknowledging that most global flows originate in the north, the author asserts that there is also evidence of multidirectional flows, including influence from the south. Examining the politics of borrowing, including the sending and receiving of political, economic and cultural systems, it has become clear that this has not been a simple, passive or unidirectional flow, but rather that multiple countries participated in the processes (Raby 2000).

North/South Flows

Generally, north/south flows of information, technology, policies and processes operate from global counterparts in the United States and other developed countries to institutions in developing countries, which are in a dependent position. Although the United States is predominant, there are other important participants in the north/south flows, including Australia, Canada, France, Netherlands, Japan and the United Kingdom. These flows have been facilitated by international development projects which supply services targeted at purposeful development, driven either by humanitarian or profit motives (Raby and Valeau 2012). Many include bilateral linkages through student and staff exchanges. In many cases, the ideas and thoughts of the north are transmitted intact across borders (Elsner, Boggs and Irwin 2008, 2015). In the 1970s, global counterparts were developed out of the United States along these lines in Taiwan, Thailand and Suriname; and in the 1980s in Australia, Britain, British Virgin Islands, Canada, Chile, Egypt, Indonesia, Ireland, Malaysia, Mexico, New Zealand and Taiwan (Raby and Valeau 2012).

Multiple agencies were used by the United States over the past few decades to support a number of international development projects, including the American Association of Community Colleges, Rotary Student Exchange, US Agency for International Development (USAID), World Bank and World Education Services, which are well known in the Caribbean region. A well-known consortium for facilitating these flows is Community Colleges for International Development (CCID), whose membership includes counterparts in Bahamas and Barbados in the Caribbean, as well as in Australia, Canada, China, Denmark, Finland, Japan, Lithuania, Macedonia, Netherlands, Northern Ireland, Pakistan, Scotland, Singapore, Turkey, Russia, Yemen, United Kingdom and United States (Raby and Valeau 2012).

Since the 1970s, Canadian, German and Dutch agencies have been involved in international development programmes. In 2008, Canadian community college development projects had partnerships with counterparts in over sixty countries, including French technical institutes; colleges in Iran, Mexico, Senegal and Venezuela; German technical colleges and colleges in South Africa and Thailand; Netherlands upper secondary vocational educational colleges; as well as colleges in East Asia and the Middle East; Japanese junior colleges and colleges in Southeast Asia; and Australian technical and further-education (TAFE) colleges and colleges throughout Asia (Elsner, Boggs and Irwin 2008; Raby and Valeau 2009). US community college education has been stereotyped as a highly valued commodity (Humphrys and Koller 1994; King and Fersh 1992; Kintzer 1998; Raby and Tarrow 1996; Strydom and Lategan 1998). It is also accepted that the high value placed on the North American models has led to international requests for assistance by governments and institutions and development assistance by international funding agencies and nongovernmental organizations (Eskow 1998; Kintzer 1998; Humphrys and Koller 1994; King and Fersh 1992).

Membership in organizations, consultations and conferences have played a significant convergence role in defining global counterparts. Of significance is the 1971 Organisation for Economic Co-operation and Development (OECD) conference, which included delegates from Britain, France, Norway, United States and Yugoslavia, where the proceedings arrived at a cross-cultural definition for this grouping. This definition aligned with the US global counterparts. By doing so, they appear to have adopted the US characteristics as the world norm. In 1983, the Postsecondary International Network met with representatives from twenty countries to detail the OECD standards; in 1999, thirty-six European countries established the First European Community College Network to develop European community colleges that would prepare graduates for the European Union workforce and advanced study. In 1999, the World

Federation of Colleges and Polytechnics was formed (Raby and Valeau 2013). These initiatives reflect a global movement which was moving towards, but fell short of, harmonization within higher education.

South/North and South/South Flows

South/north cooperation is a framework for collaboration in which expertise and assistance flow from a developing to a developed country or a less developed to a more developed country. South/south cooperation is a framework for collaboration among developing countries in economic, social, cultural and educational areas. The cooperation may be among China, India, and countries in Latin America and the Caribbean, Africa and the Pacific, to name a few areas. Both of these may be facilitated by international agencies – an arrangement described as *triangular cooperation* (United Nations Office for South South Cooperation 2010).

Whereas internationalization was expanding through US technical assistance, it was also recognized that US models had benefitted from exposure to such elements as the UK external degrees; Norwegian attempts at decentralizing decision-making involving administration, staff and students; and Canada's performance-oriented institutional and collective bargaining. It was also acknowledged that internationalizing the curriculum was of strategic importance and could bring dividends as American institutions built multicultural components into their own curricula (Raby and Valeau 2013).

It was also observed that in 1991, World Bank vocational training policy in Asia was driven by the Japanese community college model (Anzai and Paik 2012). In the early 2000s, the United Kingdom influenced South African further-education changes. The 2003 Bologna framework influenced institutional programming throughout Europe, including the redesign of bachelor's degree programmes (Taylor et al. 2008).

Borrowing has also taken place by the United States. This was not well publicized in earlier decades, perhaps because of the infancy of the Internet, a sparsity of academic literature by non-US scholars and a predominance of US-centric models. However, by the mid-1990s, more publications were being produced, compared to earlier decades by scholars in Australian, Canadian, French, German and UK community college global counterparts, which were able to provide first-hand information on their relationship with US and other global counterparts.

Localization Contexts

One side of the coin is global dependency and the sameness of counterparts with the international community. On the other side, localization fosters independent development of community college counterparts, shaped by local realities. Adaptation in response to local realities produces uniqueness. The cases of Hawke's Bay Community College, in Taradale, New Zealand, refocusing to serve Maori local needs (Kintzer 1979) and the Hong Kong associate degree (Postiglione and Sai Kit Kwok 2015) are examples of localization effects on community college global counterparts.

Purposeful and Planned Transfer

The purposeful and planned transfer of policies and structures is a common feature of globalization and educational borrowing, often fuelled by requests from governments, leaders or institutions and frequently facilitated through international development projects. In many instances, this arrangement is driven by humanitarian considerations because the larger view is that developing the less endowed will contribute to wider socioeconomic development for the long-term benefit of all. On the other hand, some initiatives have a for-profit motive because the intent is for the host countries to pay for the expertise, experience and materials which they receive. For-profit cases reported included a CCID Intensive English Practicum in China and the Suriname Telecommunication Company Venture (Raby and Valeau 2012). Also of interest are cases between US and Canadian institutions and the British Virgin Islands (Grant-Woodham and Morris 2009).

Other planned transfers include Sri Lanka, which built six junior colleges, based on the US model, after a 1969 visit by the minister of education. In 1980, a visit from Taiwan's minister of education led to direct US linkages. A 1982 American Association of Community Colleges Paramaribo conference for Caribbean cooperative job skills acquisition, attended by participants from the United States, Canada and the Caribbean, created a foundation for global counterparts in the region (Raby and Valeau 2012).

Branch campuses are also examples of planned educational transfer. Examples include the New York and Chile Branch Community College campus (Li 2010) and Houston Community College's campus in Qatar (Raby and Valeau 2012).

Holistic and Autonomous Policy Transfer

Community college global counterparts are said to serve their local clientele in a fluid response to globalization (Raby and Valeau 2013). They respond to local needs within a global context. They are able to develop policies which align with a global trajectory, but which are responsive to local needs, priorities, values and mission, thus contributing to local social and economic development.

Recognition of the opportunity to fill a need and create a new institutional type, new certification or new job skills illustrates the holistic adoption of form. The development of new curricula by Vietnamese faculty who saw the relevance of those curricula, as they studied in the Netherlands is one example of this. Additionally, New Zealand defined and offered applied degrees to legitimize areas of study there (Raby and Valeau 2012).

Reinvention of Form

Formalized, postsecondary mass education is sponsored by more than four thousand institutions in more than 180 countries (Raby 2001), many of which are labelled *community colleges*. In the 1980s, many of these institutions were characterized as short-term, short-cycle institutions (Kerr 1994). They were later described as *nonuniversities* (Kintzer 1995). Each of these descriptors had limitations and negative connotations. The term *community college model* was introduced in this century to describe a range of institutions that offer tertiary education (Raby 2001).

Prior to that, Kerr (1994) had identified a range of tertiary education institutions including colleges of advanced education in Australia; regional colleges in Norway; comprehensive colleges and community colleges in the United States; polytechnics and colleges of further education in the United Kingdom; polytechnical institutes and specialized institutes in the former Soviet Union; technical colleges in Germany; technical and further-education colleges in Australia; technical institutes in France; universities in Italy and Sweden, junior colleges in Japan; and apprenticeships in West Germany.

While some scholars continued to study the US community college model within the US higher education context (Altbach 2011), globalization of the community college model was high on the agenda at the turn of the twenty-first century (Raby 2000; Raby and Valeau 2009). Research was elucidating the early Norwegian roots of the community college movement (Bagley and Rust 2009). Reinvention of the form of community college global counterparts began to get the attention of commonwealth countries at international conferences, as some explored the transition to another institutional form – the university college (Dennison 2000; Gallagher 2000; Holder 2000; Perriot 2000; Bethel 2000; Thayer-Scott 2000).

Over the years, community college counterparts have undergone changes in form, driven mainly by adaptation of functions, which result in a pool of varied institutions. This reinvention of form can be driven by local political, economic and cultural conditions external to the institutions, or by forces from within the institutions themselves.

Within the local environment, it is not unusual for global counterparts to experience marginalization, low status due to insufficient funding, inadequate resources generally and even labels which are limiting. Many lack legitimacy and feel intimidated as they compete with other well-established institutions like universities. Many struggle to find a niche and are faced with dilemmas such as charging fees to improve operations while simultaneously maintaining open access.

For global counterparts, change can also come from within institutions through singular or joint responses to regional or local needs. Individual institutions or groups may inspire excellence in institutional projects to counter low public expectations. Individuals, motivated by their experiences from abroad and their own dreams, can motivate groups to effect change. Sometimes change has come from rejecting irrelevant offerings. On occasion, donations of technology or programmes may not be culturally relevant. Many institutions reject them in that form, but they do adapt them to fit the local situation.

3.
The North American Community College Experience

Emerging from the 1844 German Volkshochschule, the US and Canadian junior/community colleges developed in North America at just about the beginning of the twentieth century (Greenberg 1991).

The US Experience

In the United States, higher education institutions currently include private and public research universities, comprehensive universities, liberal arts colleges and community colleges. Many earlier community college historians argued that the community college movement began in the United States, and that the antecedent of the community college in the United States was the junior college. The subsequent proliferation of two-year colleges and specialist postsecondary nonuniversity institutions can be viewed as a post–World War II phenomenon and a response to the demand for access by larger numbers and more diverse groups of students. In other words, in the context of massification and student diversity, the relatively small junior college, with a restricted curriculum, was superseded by a more open-access, multidisciplinary, community-oriented institution – the community college.

Historians (Walker 2005; Elsner, Boggs and Irwin 2008; Wiseman et al. 2012) identify the beginning of the US community college movement as the founding of the Joliet Junior College in 1901 near Chicago, under the guidance of William Rainey Harper, the president of the University of Chicago, and J. Stanley Brown, the principal of Joliet High School. In the early years, junior colleges performed a dedicated university transfer function. Around, or even before this time, some states had developed technical colleges which offered vocational training. Over time, the junior colleges took on vocational offerings and the technical colleges acquired the transfer function; and all introduced remedial courses and community service courses. Thus, all of them evolved into a large pool of comprehensive community colleges.

Day and Mellinger (1973) posit that in the 1950s and 1960s, many existing public junior colleges expanded the scope of their curricula in response to the needs of industry and business, while benefiting from the associated federal funding. Furthermore, the addition of adult and continuing education courses and community service programmes increased their complexity and diversity, transforming them into community colleges.

Birnbaum's (1983) analysis of reduction in institutional diversity bears some relevance to the discussion of the decline of junior colleges. Two theories may be relevant to this subject. The first is that of natural selection, where new comprehensive colleges emerge in the pool and survive preferentially because of their greater fitness for purpose. The second, like Day and Mellinger's (1973) position, relates to the use of strategic policy to change the existing institutional type in relation to its size, control, curriculum and student diversity to such an extent that it survives, but as a new institutional type.

Brint and Karabel (1989) suggest that the coming of the Great Depression in the 1930s brought an unexpected boost to the community college movement. Elsner, Boggs and Irwin (2008) agree that economic hard times, high unemployment among all ages and the appearance of large numbers of college-age youth led the United States to establish sixty-five public junior colleges between 1933 and 1939 to meet the demand. They also underscored the positive impact of the funding provided by the GI Bill of Rights for returning war veterans as a significant boost to community college expansion. These community colleges obviously offered access, affordability and employment opportunities.

Ratcliff (1994) traces the origin of community colleges to 1894, when the Reverend J.M. Carroll, president of Baylor University, proposed a pragmatic solution to the pressing problem of inadequate funds and insufficient students to support a large number of Baptist colleges which had emerged in Texas and Louisiana. He suggested that these small colleges should concentrate on the first two years and send their graduates to Baylor University to complete the final two years of their degree programmes. This early attempt was the result of community action to provide access to college education, and Ratcliff describes this as "community boosterism".

He also opines that self-help, rationalization of the education system, personnel changes and demands, expansion in technical and vocational education, and development of adult and continuing education contributed to the establishment of the American community college. Not surprisingly, therefore, these institutions currently provide remedial, vocational, academic transfer, and continuing and general education to persons of varying ages, social and experiential backgrounds and ethnicities (Brubacher and Ruby 1958; Ratcliff 1994).

Community college expansion peaked in the 1960s, when more than 450 new community colleges were established in the United States to meet the demand created by children of the returning world war veterans. At that time, about 45 per cent of all eighteen-year-olds enrolled in community colleges (Phillipe and Gonzalez Sullivan 2005). This expansion was funded by the Higher Education Acts, which provided for the creation and expansion of facilities, as well as direct loans and grants based on need. In 1971, the federal government extended its provision to funding for underserved groups, including Native Americans. This funding supported the creation of the Navajo Community College, for example.

As of 2006, there were 1,202 regionally accredited community colleges in the United States, including 991 public institutions, 180 independent institutions and 32 "tribal colleges". Approximately 6.6 million students take courses leading to an associate degree, and an additional 5 million take noncredit courses. Enrolment surged between 2007 and 2009 during the economic recession and levelled off subsequently. In general, around this period in the United States, the creation of new community colleges was virtually halted, but the establishment of the District of Colombia Community College was at least one exception. In 2009, President Barack Obama challenged the colleges to focus on student success in terms of programme completion and improved graduation rates, and he enacted legislation to support workforce preparation.

The American Association of Community College Statistics (2012) reveal that, of the 1,050 community colleges, there were 942 public, 73 independent and 73 tribal institutions. The degrees awarded in 2017–2018 included 852,504 associate degrees, 579,822 certificates and 19,083 bachelor's degrees. The average age of students was twenty-eight years and the median age twenty-four years. Hispanics represented 26 per cent of the student population; blacks represented 13 per cent and 45 per cent were white. Among the full-time students, 62 per cent were employed and among the part time, 72 per cent were employed. Credits by attendance was 6.8 million, including 36 per cent full-time students.

The median earnings of full-time employees by highest educational attainment was about $31,315 for those with less than high school diplomas; for those with high school diplomas – $40,510, for those with associate degrees $50,079 and $65,374 for those with bachelor's degrees.

Mission: Traditional and Contemporary

The traditional mission of the US community college is multifaceted, including access to the underserved, opportunities for transfer to universities, occupational preparation, remediation, continuing education and community outreach. In spite of the expansion of community colleges and the aspiration of students for higher education, indications are that there continue to be barriers to transfer. Challenges persist, especially for low-income students and minorities including Latinos and African Americans. Degree attainment for Latinos and African Americans is about half that of whites and Asians. US Department of Education statistics show that in 2004, about 90 per cent of 2002 high school sophomores wanted a college education; 70 per cent expected to complete four-year college but only about 62 per cent enrolled in college; and nearly half the entrants failed to return for the second year (Howe 1988; Rosenbaum 1999).

Research conducted in 2010 and published by the National Student Clearinghouse Research Center showed that 31.5 per cent (268,749) of a total of 852,439 students who first enrolled at a community college transferred to a four-year institution within six years. Approximately one-third (34 per cent) transferred after receiving a credential (either a certificate or associate degree) at the starting school. Additionally, 42 per cent of those who transferred earned a bachelor's degree within six years of starting in the community college – about 13 per cent of the original cohort.

The research also found that among those who transferred, lower- and higher-income students had similar rates of receiving a credential from the community college before their transfer (33 per cent). However, higher-income students compared to lower-income students were more likely to earn a bachelor's degree after they transferred (49 per cent versus 35 per cent).

Over the years, it became increasingly evident that transfer rates in themselves were not an accurate measure of student success since they did not take into consideration the mission of the community college, including its part-time and career and technical studies roles. In order to take a more comprehensive approach to assessment of student success, which could also identify challenges and allow for setting goals for improvement, the Voluntary Framework of Accountability was developed by more than sixty community college leaders under the American Association of Community Colleges and with funding from the Bill and Melinda Gates and Lumina Foundations. The framework was published in 2012 by the association for roll-out in 2013. The framework takes into consideration pre-collegiate preparation, developmental and adult basic education, academic progress and momentum points, completion and transfer rates and workforce outcomes for career and technical education (CTE). It uses five sets of measures: one-year programme; two-year programme; six-year outcome, CTE and student outcome post-CTE measures.

Many organizational and curricular initiatives have been instituted to create or improve pathways to success, including advanced placement, bridge programmes, college-level examination programmes, distance learning/virtual high schools and colleges, dual credit, dual enrolment and concurrent enrolment, early- and middle-college high schools, General Education Development programmes that bridge to college, international baccalaureate and tech prep and college tech programmes (Bragg and Barnett 2006).

Community colleges have been involved in some way with the delivery of the baccalaureate for quite some time. The movement towards the community college baccalaureate has been progressive and evolutionary (Floyd, Skolnik and Walker 2005). They used a four-point typology to depict how this has evolved. These include the use of the articulation model, the university centre model, the university extension model and the community college baccalaureate. The first and oldest model is the junior college "two-plus-two" articulation arrangement, which allows the transfer of lower-level college credits from the community college and the achievement of junior status at the university to complete a four-year degree in another two years.

Historically, the junior college has been involved in the delivery of the bachelor's degree, but the junior college would not take full responsibility, and universities retained control. The two-plus-two transfer function has been well documented as a form of voluntary divestment of lower-level work by the universities to allow a focus on upper-level work (Cohen and Brawer 1984; Zwerling 1976), or to offer convenient access to the place-bound student (Pederson 2000). Between 1907 and 1940, transfer enrolment represented between 60 and 70 per cent of total enrolment in the junior colleges (Eaton 1994).

With the expansion of the curriculum of community colleges to include not only academic studies, but also technical/vocational, continuing, general and remedial education needs, new associate degrees were developed, with a focus on preparation for work. These community colleges also became involved in the delivery of the bachelor's degree through new articulation arrangements, many of them negotiated and sustained by formal or informal agreements between the colleges and universities.

It is well known that one of the functions that community colleges have provided is the delivery and certification of workforce training, which usually includes general education and liberal arts courses, along with technical and vocational courses. The most popular of the latter programmes in the United States are in registered nursing, law enforcement, licensed practical nursing, radiology and computer technologies (Elsner, Boggs and Irwin 2008, 2015). The offer of noncredit courses also forms part of the portfolio of community colleges, as they strive to help with the development of the community.

Beyond the junior college two-plus-two arrangement, new articulation models enabled students to complete two years in community colleges and transfer some credits to universities which build on these credits to complete the bachelor's degree. Articulation arrangements were well established in

Florida for general education courses. California, Illinois, New York, Oklahoma, Tennessee, Texas and Washington also have intrastate agreements with possibilities for interstate cases. Transfer arrangements have been extended in some cases to "three-plus-one" arrangements. Transfer rates have varied over time, dropping in many states to well below 10 per cent in the 1960s and 1970s (Lombardi 1979) and increasing to about 20 per cent in the 1980s and 1990s (Adelman 1999; Grubb 1991; Cohen 1991; Lingenfelter 1992). As indicated earlier, more comprehensive and instructive measures of success are currently available.

Since the 1960s, the university centre model is one in which the university emerges as a joint-use site on or near the community college, where private or public universities deliver upper-level courses and confer degrees in partnership with a community college or other university. The Northwestern Michigan College University Center includes programming among eleven four-year universities and the community college to deliver baccalaureate programmes. Other centres allow the delivery of master's degrees, and some collaborate via distance education modalities. There also are instances when the community college is authorized to independently confer the degree (Lorenzo 2005).

The university extension model is similar to the university centre model, except that the off-campus site is formally an entity of the university. For example, three of Hawaii's community colleges (Honolulu, Kapi'olani and Maui) have been authorized to award the baccalaureate, and Pennsylvania State University has authorized fourteen of its seventeen branches to offer baccalaureate degrees.

There are several community colleges and related institutions that independently confer baccalaureate degrees, which have been around for some time. New York's Fashion Institute of Technology granted fashion degrees in the 1970s, and West Virginia's Parkersburg Community College obtained approval to grant the baccalaureate in the 1980s (Bragg and Barnett 2006). What has changed is the momentum of this movement.

Opponents argue that focus on the baccalaureate diverts community colleges from their central mission of remediation, transfer, community and technical education. On the other hand, proponents justify this movement based on the widening of access, affordability and response to demand. In 1999, advocates of the community college baccalaureate, including members from twenty-eight states in the United States, four Canadian provinces, Bermuda, Jamaica, research institutions, private industry and higher education institutions, formed the Community College Baccalaureate Association (Walker 2005).

Although some community colleges retain their identity as colleges, accreditation bodies reclassify the community college on the basis of its highest award in some cases. In 1993, Utah Valley Community College became Utah State College as part of its baccalaureate candidacy. In other states, baccalaureate-granting colleges are reclassified as four-year colleges. The Southern Regional Education Board has adopted the new label of *associate/baccalaureate institution* for such institutions which mainly offer associate degrees but also award other certifications.

Community College Values

American community colleges have changed considerably over the past century. Their programming has diversified and expanded to meet the interests and needs of their heterogeneous student body. However, there are values of the community college that still endure, including the focus on access to students of all ages and educational backgrounds with greater affordability and convenience of location.

There remains an unmistakable symbiotic relationship with the communities in which these colleges operate. They share close links with business and industry partners whose needs they strive to meet. They demonstrate flexibility in programming and nimble turnaround times. They enjoy propulsion by political and economic pressure and the focused vision of leaders. Unlike universities, their primary mission is not research and publication; student success and teaching and learning are their preoccupations. Community colleges have continued to be dynamic institutions, coming up with innovative ways to keep ahead of the societal developmental curve.

Operations

In the United States, community colleges are funded from different sources. In general, community colleges receive approximately 27.1 per cent from tuition, 11.4 per cent from federal funds, 33.3 per cent from state funds, 20.3 per cent from local funds and 7.9 per cent from other sources (American Association of Community College Statistics 2012).

The chief executive officer is a president, chancellor or superintendent. The institution is governed by a board of trustees, which serves to approve policies, secure funding, oversee administration, protect the interest of the community and plan for the sustainable development of future generations of students. In the United States, community colleges are required to carry out periodic self-studies and submit to peer evaluations by visiting professionals whose reports form the basis for the earning of accreditation by regional bodies, usually for periods of seven to ten years. Interim assessments and reports are used to ensure the institution's continued accreditation status. Regional accreditation is mandatory to enable students to receive federal financial aid.

Challenges for the American Community College

The community college has been experiencing increasing demand for its places, brought about by an increasing number of students who complete high school. In addition, the career aspirations and economic dreams of an increasing number of unemployed or underemployed youth and adults have been frustrated by the economic downturn, and these people also turn to these colleges. This was encouraged in 2002 data that the average lifetime earnings (over about forty years) for a high school dropout was about $1.0 million; a high school graduate with a diploma about $1.2 million; a graduate of a community college with an associate degree about $1.6 million, and a community college graduate with a bachelor's about $2.1 million (Phillippe and Gonzalez Sullivan 2005).

Demand is also being felt from students who have degrees but need retooling to survive in a knowledge-based economy and a global world. Many also turn to the community college because they cannot afford to pay for a university education. The average cost of tuition and fees at public community colleges in 2007–2008 was $2,361, compared to $6,185 at public colleges and universities (Boggs and Irwin 2015).

Amid this increasing demand is the reality of falling funding from US states, as well as increased operational costs. In an Illinois State University study, it was found that state funding dropped by nearly $584.8 million between 2003 and 2004, with thirty-two states reporting decreased funding. This problem is exacerbated by the need to pay the high costs of technology, managing faculty retention, meeting the increasing demand for remediation among students and promoting student success.

In the face of decreased state funding, partnerships with business and industry present opportunities. Collaborating with the health-care sector has offered the opportunity to expand facilities and provide clinical space. Partnering with successful information technology (IT) companies like Microsoft and AT&T has provided grants to build spaces to accommodate communication technology. There is also the potential for expanding the curriculum to cater to the interests of international students who are willing to study abroad, bringing both economic and cultural benefits to the institution.

In an effort to balance budgets, the use of adjunct faculty has become common. Often, this carries with it limited full-time engagement with students and the general cocurricular or extracurricular life of the institution. Many institutions also have retained the services of full-time faculty for years, with little succession planning in a changing environment.

As institutions are focused on widening access, there continues to be pressure to provide the necessary resources to sustain the inclusion and success of minorities, who are often disadvantaged because of ethnicity, race, sexual orientation, or physical disabilities. In addition, as the demand for and involvement with the baccalaureate increases, there is a need for managing role confusion and confronting the contention of mission creep, while advancing the cause of institutional development.

The Community College as a Contradictory Institution

There is a longstanding debate about the conflicting roles of the community college and the extent to which it achieves its stated goals (for instance, Kintzer 1982; Brint and Karabel 1989; Grubb 1991; Eaton 1994; Dougherty 1994; Rosenbaum 1999; Knapp et al. 2008). While this study does not attempt to take a position on these issues, it is useful to flag them as bases for future research.

While many scholars have argued that the community college has been a gateway to opportunity, especially for underserved students, others have suggested that it has been a protector of university selectivity and has been instrumental in maintaining the hierarchy within the higher education system. In this way, it is seen as an instrument for perpetuating inequality.

Community colleges play a major role in technical and vocational education – an area of study which has retained a stigma in many countries, especially those formerly colonized by the Europeans. Seen as a vendor of vocational education, many community and technical colleges are still seen as second class institutions. In spite of an array of articulation arrangements, traditional forces have limited the portability of community college qualifications to further study. In some cases, these barriers have limited academic advancement and led to professional stagnation. In this way, community colleges are seen as retaining a ceiling which restricts career advancement for large numbers of their graduates (Dougherty 1994).

While it cannot be disputed that community colleges have provided skilled personnel for the workforce, some critics have viewed the arrangements as more beneficial to business, industry and governments. These stakeholders are perceived as benefiting from low-cost training for their workers in an environment where governments also have been able to get more training for less funding from the state. However, to achieve this, the institutions are often underresourced.

Other critics have taken the position that the community college has struggled with juggling the different components of its mission. When it focuses on sound academics to promote student transfers to a university and even offers its own bachelor's degrees, it may place less emphasis on remediation. In optimizing its capacity for vocational training and human resource development, it limits its capacity to provide a baccalaureate-level education. In keeping costs down for public- and private-sector funders and for the students themselves, it limits the infrastructure development and comprehensive services which would promote retention and student success. Additional research is needed to interrogate these assertions not only in the United States, but also in the wider Caribbean, including Barbados.

The Community College Global Counterpart in Canada

Canada is a federation of provinces with no national education system. However, the federal government influences and even steers the development of postsecondary education through economic policy. Higher education in Canada is viewed as a collection of different provincial/territorial systems operating in parallel (Jones 1997). Universities have been in existence there for centuries. The nonuniversity, postsecondary sector includes technical institutes; colleges of arts, science and technology; and community colleges. A few were created prior to the 1960s. However, from the 1960s to the early 1970s, the majority of provinces created college systems with very definite mandates, governance, funding and programming arrangements. Among them is the St Clair College of Applied Arts and Technology, which is of particular significance to this study.

Federal grants established the colleges, but the provinces share operational costs. Only a few are designated as community colleges and of these, two are multicampus systems. They include Northwest Community College, Vancouver Community College, New Brunswick Community College, Nova Scotia Community College and Sprott-Shaw Community College. About a dozen are designated institutes. The majority do not award associate degrees.

Ontario's community colleges can be traced from the Mechanics Institutes of 1830 (Smyth 1970). Victoria College, founded in 1903, has been identified as the first junior college, associated with McGill University (Campbell 1971). Lethbridge Junior College in Alberta, established in 1957, and Lakehead College of Arts, Science and Technology in Ontario, established in 1956 out of the Lakehead Technical Institute, are other pioneers in the field. By 1958–1959, Canada had forty-nine junior colleges, with more than half in Quebec; forty of these schools are controlled by churches (Campbell 1971).

Factors which have promoted expansion of the colleges include projected expansion in the pool of secondary school graduates, adoption of human capital theory and its acceptance of the high rate of returns for postsecondary education, the need for more affordable training and the need for preparation for university entry (Dennison and Gallagher 1986).

Across the provinces, four models of college development have been identified. In Ontario and Prince Edward Island, colleges were established as distinct entities from the universities and were not involved in transfer arrangements, focusing exclusively on workforce training. Of particular interest is the Western Ontario Institute of Technology, which in 1958 admitted 104 male students to four three-year programmes in electronics, electrical technology, mechanics and chemistry. This facility was housed in an 1890 elementary school building. The institution grew, and by a bill passed in 1965 by the Provincial Legislature, was established as one of the Colleges of Applied Arts and Technology (CAATs) in Windsor, Ontario. The college admitted its first three hundred students in 1967, and during the first few years, it was involved in a significant twinning partnership with the Barbados Community College.

The second provincial college model was that obtained in Alberta and British Columbia (BC). There, they combined transfer and technical vocational training and, in the case of British Columbia, added second-chance opportunities for adults. The third model was more widespread, operating in Manitoba, New Brunswick, Newfoundland, the Yukon and Northern Territories. There was no university transfer arrangement; instead, a focus on technical vocational training with an emphasis on short, work-entry training programmes. Newfoundland later introduced university transfer education.

The fourth model was practised in Saskatchewan and included a combination of colleges without walls in rural areas and technical institutes in urban areas. This evolved into the Saskatchewan Institute of Applied Science and Technology, with rural colleges providing brokering for educational services. The Quebec model, Model Five, mirrored the European experience. In the later stages of high school, students entered the three-year career prep stream or a two-year university prep stream.

Nova Scotia had several universities and did not create a college system initially, but a number of institutions already existed, including two institutes of technology, a land-surveying institution, an agricultural college and a junior college. In 1974, the Junior College Campus of St Francis merged with Xavier University. In 1988, Nova Scotia Community College was established, comprising nineteen campuses in fourteen communities.

For the Yukon, although the Whitehorse Vocational Training School was established in 1963, the 1960s and 1970s were periods of aspiration. Realization of postsecondary education can best relate to the establishment of the Yukon Vocational and Technical Training Centre and its successor, Yukon College.

In 2004–2005, there were 150 colleges in Canada, with about 40 per cent of those attending being postsecondary students. The colleges are responding to diversity, globalization, partnerships with industry and applied research; some offer bachelor's degrees. They experience the challenge of balancing sometimes-competing missions of being engines of economic growth by training skilled workers and providing opportunities for changing society through more general education.

Due to divergence in the establishment forces and differences in institutional form and labels and mission priorities, Canada appears to have adapted the community college concept to its own context. These colleges can be accommodated within the framework of global community college counterparts. Interestingly, it was St Clair College of Applied Arts and Technology that served as an effective mentor to the developing Barbados Community College.

Conclusion

The anglophone Caribbean countries have strong links with the United Kingdom, the United States and Canada, as well as among themselves. The ties to Britain are historical, strong colonial ones which left a legacy of systems and policies which often did not necessarily reflect local realities. The links with the United States and Canada are facilitated by geography and a shared language. In the case of Canada, there is also a relationship through Commonwealth membership.

There is a long history of migration from the Caribbean for work and study, coupled with a pattern of north/south flows of consultants, technical assistance, aid and remuneration from Caribbean nationals abroad. There are also significant north/south flows of goods and services, as well as technology and telecommunication. All these facilitate north/south global flows in trade, aid and information, as well as educational borrowing. Through relationships with the American Association of Community Colleges, Canadian Association of Community Colleges, British Association of Colleges, numerous funding agencies and multinational corporations, globalization and educational borrowing have been facilitated over the years.

In the ensuing chapters, the discussion will continue to examine the extent to which globalization and educational borrowing have influenced the emergence and development of community college counterparts globally, as well as in the wider anglophone Caribbean and in Barbados.

4.

The Global Movement and Community College Counterparts

The Literature on Global Counterparts

An early history of the American community college is well told by Brubacher and Rudy (1958), with some additional attention given to their origins in discussing the uses of the university (Kerr 1963). The junior/community colleges expanded in the United States and their counterparts were established in Canada (Campbell 1971; Dennison and Gallagher 1986; Skolnik 2015). During the 1970s, such countries as Australia (Flint 1978; Barnaart 2015), Norway (Hanisch 1978), New Zealand (Harre 1978) and Brazil (Gershwin 2015) also became involved. At that time, US institutions, in the main, were inward-looking, grappling with local issues. There was limited engagement with others, and very little academic discourse on the nature and similarities of these institutions in other countries. However, growing technology and changing communication patterns transformed this (Raby and Valeau 2013).

It was the increasing multiculturalism and internationalization in the US setting and the growing "outward look", as well as the gradual maturing of international scholars outside the United States and their "outward look" which caused the fields of vision to converge, shedding light on emerging and existing patterns. This exposure and growing awareness led to the realization of commonality and uniqueness among a diverse pool of counterparts. Scholars began to show interest in world adaptations of the community college concept (Kintzer 1979). Tertiary education was being advanced as a radical approach to higher education (Cotterell and Haley 1981). The first generation of global community college counterparts commenced in 1971 (Raby and Valeau 2013).

During the 1980s and early 1990s, American authors continued to emphasise community colleges in the United States – particularly their function and continued development (Cohen and Brawer 1984; Ratcliff 1994; Madden 2010), including the collegiate function (Cohen and Brawer 1987), articulation and transfer functions (Kintzer 1982; Kintzer and Wattenberger 1985; Cohen 1991; Eaton 1994; Grubb 1991; Lingenfelter 1992), completion rates and financing.

The history, mission and management of community colleges in the United States was still engaging academics, and the streams of their historical development were articulated (Ratcliff 1994).

The 1990s ushered in a new international orientation, with a look at reform and quality assurance in the United States and Britain (Burgos-Sasscer and Collins 1996); humanitarian-driven, self-help international development projects (Cook 1996); a search for new international partnerships (Humphrys and Koller 1994); developing two-year colleges abroad; and for-profit partnerships (Harris 1996; Raby and Tarrow 1996; Schugurensky and Higins 1996). It was also a time of grappling with a meaningful and comprehensive definition of community college and community college–like institutions, while thought was also given to exporting the community college concept (Greenberg 1991; Kintzer 1998; Kintzer and Bryant 1998).

Short-cycle higher education emerged as a classification for these institutions (Kintzer 1993) and the nonuniversity terminology also came into use (Neave 1991). Scholars questioned the conflicting impacts and futures of the community college (Dougherty 1994). The Caribbean began to look at the emergence of its own community, state and national colleges in the Organisation of the Eastern Caribbean States (OECS) member-states (Peters 1993). Non-American authors were examining their tertiary education realities and needs and were also assessing the extent to which the US community college construct could be accommodated in their specific context. The community college global counterparts were also assessed and established in South Africa (Strydom and Lategan 1998), Japan (Yamanon and Hawkins 1996) and Yemen (Alsohybe 2015), while experimentation continued in Latin America (Madden 2010). The second generation of research into global community college counterparts, with a focus on the merits of collaboration, was in progress (Raby and Valeau 2013).

A move to document the higher education environment of the Caribbean was afoot, leading to a number of national reports on higher education (Bobb-Smith 2007; Gittens 2007; Roberts 2006a, 2006b; Fielding and Gibbons 2007). The associate degree in the Caribbean struggled to gain recognition for advanced placement in local and regional universities, as well as in North America and the United Kingdom. Formal articulation arrangements were negotiated to facilitate university transfer (Roberts 1999, 2000a, 2000b, 2000c, 2001, 2003a, 2003b, 2003c, 2006a, 2006b, 2006c).

The discourse on educational borrowing was getting exposure, and the practice became more widespread (Raby and Valeau 2013). Countries were adopting, adapting or rejecting global counterpart models from the north, and there was ongoing evidence of emerging south/south and south/north flows.

Research was being conducted widely on the community college counterparts, and comparisons were being made across the world. Counterparts were planning and establishing new networks of community colleges in China (Lin-Liu 2001; Postiglione, Wang and Watkins 2015), evolving two-year colleges in Korea (Ryoo in Raby and Valeau 2013), establishing the Higher Colleges of Technology in the United Arab Emirates (Drummond and Hartley 2015), examining vocational and continuing higher education in Brazil (Gershwin 2015) and writing about Spain's vocational education system (De Bresser and Martinez 2015; Wiseman et al. 2012). This period of research into community college counterparts represented the documentation generation (Raby and Valeau 2013).

The Pool of Global Counterparts

After more than 120 years in the United States and 50 years in the Caribbean, community colleges with various labels have emerged as protean institutions, created, developed, shaped and sustained by the needs and wants of their communities, continually rejuvenated by their agility and responsiveness to the desires and aspirations of their communities, sponsors, learners and beneficiaries.

In their mature form, even though they are under the auspices of or sponsored by the state because they are accepted as contributing to the public good, they utilize multiple sources of funding. They are multidisciplinary in scope, as evidenced by a broad curriculum which is continually expanding to cater to society's needs. They are multifunctional, providing pathways for transfer to universities, as well as preparing workers for various careers and occupations, thus developing a larger middle class. They are developmental in orientation, creating lifelong learning opportunities which cater to remedial, adult and continuing education, as well as leisure needs. They are beacons of innovation which use partnerships with industry and civil society to maximize their utility. Many use multiple modes of learning to widen access and reach out to the underserved (Raby and Valeau 2012; Brint and Karabel 1989; Wiseman et al. 2012).

Notwithstanding the variations, these institutions are enabled by political, socioeconomic, technological, human resources and globalization forces and seem to be sustained by periodic strategic repositioning. Politically, they are sponsored and enabled by leaders who have bought into human capital theory and seek to use education to capitalize on both the obvious private returns to the individual and the public returns to the state. Economically, by training the unemployed and the midcareer and displaced worker, these institutions promote employment, reskilling and entrepreneurship. Socially, by engaging a broad spectrum of youth and adults, they divert persons from hopelessness, crime, violence and other dysfunctional behaviour.

The use of information and communication technology allows the underserved, separated by geographical distance, to have access to learning resources. Their flexibility permits asynchronous offerings and agile responses to requests and needs, and their relevant modes of delivery cater to the differences in learning styles of a wide cross section of learners. Globalization forces have called for greater transparency in operations and enabled wider cooperation and networking across boundaries, creating new opportunities for strategic repositioning through partnerships.

In addition, community colleges offer five basic kinds of programmes: transfer, technical and occupational, continuing education or lifelong learning, remedial education and workforce development (Wiseman et al. 2012). Some distinguishing features of community college counterparts include their relevance to their local environment, options for university overflows and second chancers, first responders for retooling workers, and opportunities for many diverse students (Raby and Valeau 2012).

The point being made here is that the role which is filled in the United States by the community colleges is filled in other countries by community college counterparts, many of which carry different labels but perform similar functions. In considering the global community college movement, Elsner, Boggs and Irwin (2008) have reported much activity and influence since the 1960s. Community colleges (junior colleges) in both name and nature were reported to have been established in the United States around 1900; Canada in the 1960s (Skolnik 2015); Jamaica in 1974 (Adamson 2015); Thailand in 2002 (Cissell and Tanom Inkhamnert 2015); Vietnam in the 1960s and starting again in 2000 (Oliver, Engel and Scorsone 2015); New Zealand in the 1970s and 1980s (Doyle 2015); India in the 1990s (Raby and and Valeau 2014); China in 1998 (Postiglione and Chen 2015); Yemen in 1999 (Alsohybe 2015); Georgia in 2005 (Halder 2015); and the Dominican Republic in 2006 (Halder 2015). This movement is ongoing in other countries as well, such as Tunisia (Hagedorn and Mezghani 2013).

Global counterparts have also spread to French West Africa; South Africa, in its Further Education Technical Colleges (1998); Chile, in its Technical Training Centers (1981); Hong Kong, through its associate degree offerings (2001); Japan, through its junior colleges and colleges of technology; Singapore, by way of its Institute for Technical Education (1992); Turkey in its two-year vocational schools; and United Arab Emirates, in their Higher Colleges of Technology (1998).

Some of the community college functions are served by colleges of further education or baccalaureate programmes in England, Denmark, Ireland, Netherlands, and Spain, as well as by Australia's TAFE institutions. There are clear aspirations towards and discussions about the establishment, re-establishment or maintenance of community college counterparts by Brazil, Colombia, Indonesia, Qatar, India, Dominican Republic and Georgia.

Globally, the conceptualization and sometimes the establishment of community college counterparts became widespread in the 1960s and 1970s, influenced by north/south flows. However, the form and functions of these counterparts were also influenced by regional currents (developed countries other than the United States and Canada) and by local socioeconomic and political realities. Many local adaptations took place to enable local responses to prevailing needs.

Community College Counterparts in Eastern Countries

A look at some Eastern countries may serve to illustrate these trends. These include China, Thailand, Vietnam, Yemen, India, United Arab Emirates, Japan and Hong Kong.

In China, the 1980s showed increased attention to postsecondary nonuniversity education, driven by rapid local socioeconomic change, the attendant need for trained workers and exposure to global trends. This led to the establishment of community-oriented junior colleges which delivered full- and part-time workforce training and adult and continuing education. Technical/vocational colleges were established and delivered two- to three-year degrees in cooperation with universities. Ideas would have been borrowed from the United States, and community colleges were established, culminating in 1998 with affiliation arrangements through the American Association of Community Colleges, with more than eighty US community colleges. At the same time, there were other regional currents, evidenced by China's networking with Germany's technical and dual system, Australia's TAFE system, and models in France, South Korea and Japan (Postiglione, Wang and Watkins 2015).

There was also evidence of community college activity in Thailand from the 1970s, in a push to improve access to higher education and allow local control and governance in rural areas. Evidence of this was an aborted effort to convert teachers' colleges to community colleges in the early 1980s. However, teachers' colleges were allowed to extend their curriculum. Between 1987 and 1989, Thailand introduced central government–controlled, single-discipline colleges. Work with USAID to establish community colleges in 1994 failed due to inadequate funding. However, in 2002, starting with ten institutions, a system of community colleges was launched, offering associate degrees. The Office of Community Colleges became a division within the Higher Education Ministry in 2008 (Cissell and Tanom Inkhamnert 2015).

After the Vietnam War, there was a need to train demobilized military personnel for civilian jobs. In 1971, the decision was taken to convert redundant military installations and underused educational facilities in Vietnam into colleges, providing both transfer and career development. By 1987, there were twenty-eight colleges, registering approximately 38 per cent of higher education students. The Soviet model was adopted in 1993, but it was soon discontinued. The Ministry of Education worked with Canadian and US colleges to restructure the system. The ministry renamed pedagogical colleges *junior colleges* and established community colleges. In 1995, Vietnam National University was established from a merger of nine independent universities, and this new institution ran a pilot community college in three rural remote areas to improve access. Ministry of Education certification was withheld because of the lack of articulation of qualifications within a European-style university system.

In 2001, the system gained momentum from work between the Canadian International Development Agency and American Association of Community Colleges. Faculty exchanges took place, allowing for some north/south collaboration. In 2008, the Vietnam Association of Community Colleges was formed, and in 2009, there were 226 colleges (Oliver, Engel and Scorsone 2015).

Faced with the issue of preparing persons for jobs in a young population, in 1996, the Government of Yemen passed the Community College Legislation, outlining the mission, mandate and structures of a community college system. In 1997, the project was initiated and in 1998, the Sana'a Community College was established and became operational in 2001, along with the Aden Community College. They offer three-year diplomas with general education in year one and specialization in years two and three. In 2005, they were able to establish a governance framework which was funded by the World Bank. Between 2008 and 2012, these colleges were able to establish a number of international partnerships (Alsohybe 2015).

There have been CCID-sponsored delegations to India, Fulbright exchanges, development workshops and working partnerships for over twenty-five years. In the early-to-mid-1990s, colleges for the people were established. By 2006, 160 colleges have been brought by the government under the higher education system (Halder 2015).

In 2000, a more structured community college programme was piloted in Indonesia, enabling vocational schools and polytechnics to develop one- and two-year certificate programmes, in partnership with industry. Approximately 105 vocational secondary schools and 10 polytechnics took part. However, a master plan has been developed which calls for the establishment of 497 community colleges by 2020 (Cissell and Harris Iskandar 2015).

In the United Arab Emirates, there are specialized vocational schools and the Higher Colleges of Technology, as part of the government's response to the need to create a larger pool of nationals for the workforce and a larger pool of educated women. In 1988, the first four campuses were opened in Abu Dhabi and Dubai. Only emirate nationals could attend, and they admit high school graduates, including many women. There are also government-licenced private institutions. Since 2008, there have been three national, federally supported higher education institutions – the Higher Colleges of Technology, Zayne University and United Arab Emirates University (Drummond and Hartley 2015).

Japan does not have community colleges, but it does have institutions which serve similar functions, including junior colleges, professional training colleges and colleges of technology. Junior colleges granting associate degrees were established in 1950, first on a provisional basis and then given permanent status in 1960. These institutions are losing their popularity because four-year institutions have become more open and vocationally more appealing (Tsunoda and Iida 2015).

With a British educational system in operation, Hong Kong was returned to China in 1997. Since 2000, Hong Kong has decided to use the community college associate degree model to double its higher education enrolment. They offered self-financing associate degree programmes in nonprofit community colleges and were able to double their 2010 enrolment targets. The associate degree is a stand-alone exit qualification for employment at the para-professional level and has raised some controversy, having not proved to be very successful in terms of transferral to public universities.

Community college functions, specifically the conferral of associate degrees, are carried out by several institutions, including the University of Hong Kong, the Chinese University of Hong Kong, the Hong Kong Baptist University, the Open University of Hong Kong, the Hong Kong Polytechnic University, the City University of Hong Kong, the Hong Kong Institute of Education, the Vocational Training Council and Lingnam University (Postiglione and Kit Kwok 2015).

There are no community colleges in Turkey, but vocational schools of higher education perform similar functions. The higher education system includes four-year universities and two-year vocational schools, many operating within the university system.

In 1911, the Ministry of Public Works opened a vocational school, and in 1952, the technician school system expanded to deliver three-year programmes. In 1965, two higher-level schools were established, which helped students transfer to four-year universities, but they soon closed. In 1972, six higher technical schools were established and by the mid-1970s, universities began to establish their own two-year schools for full-time students. The Ministry of Education established a parallel system of twenty-four two-year schools, but with the first year using the distance education mode and with no focus on university transfer. By 1979, graduates could not find jobs, and the schools soon closed. By 1981, the majority of the vocational schools of higher education were under the Ministry of Education or part of the university system. Their degree programmes and administration have been legally defined (Aypay 2015).

Community College Counterparts in Africa

There are no community colleges in French West Africa, but there is a new focus on technical vocational education, and technical and vocational schools are assuming a similar role to that of the community college. One example is the Institut Universitaire de Technologie in Senegal, which confers a two-year degree in business and administration. This movement was driven in the 1980s by increased student output from secondary schools, high unemployment, and the vision of the UNESCO-UNEVOC International Centre for Technical and Vocational Education and Training that technical vocational education and training (TVET) would provide the opportunity for national development.

The revitalizing of technical vocational education and training has continued to be seen as a matter of national security and economic urgency. However, the development of this training is hampered by the colonial legacy of its inferior status and national cultural issues, as well as by governance and funding (Sawadogo 2015).

Postsecondary education in South Africa has been influenced by the US and Canadian community college models. Their Further Education and Training Colleges have some similarities to the North American community college and the UK further-education colleges. The TVET system dates back to 1884, when programmes were introduced in mining engineering to support development needs. The Apprenticeship Act of 1922 offered training for whites, a few Indians and coloureds. The technical colleges were autonomous, flexible and responsive, and they established linkages with employers and the community.

In 1948, under the apartheid regime and centralized control, including the use of the Afrikaans language, state funding fell off and a shortage of skilled labour persisted. The Advanced Technical Education Act of 1967 established colleges for advanced technical education. There was much discussion in the 1990s about skills development in general, and for African blacks in particular, from the perspective of the African National Congress.

The US community college concept has been supported in South Africa since the 1980s. In the late 1980s and early 1990s, South Africa's National Institute for Community Education promoted the establishment of community colleges, with support from United States Agency for International Development. In 1994, shortly before the end of the apartheid era, and in search of more affordable education, an education renewal system was introduced to embrace "edukons", which would function as US community colleges. However, the education renewal system was criticized by educators, workers and organizations as a way of preserving the status quo.

Under the Further Education and Training Act of 1998, South Africa's technical colleges were renamed *FET colleges*. In 2005, the government committed 1.9 billion rand in capital funding to the FET colleges for 2006–2008. There has been a recapitalization of the system and the establishment of a new national department of higher education and training, giving the central government direct control over the sector. It is envisaged that these colleges will prepare youth for employment. The FET college is poised for improved delivery of vocational and continuing education (Fisher and Scott 2015).

Community College Counterparts in South America

As the world's sixth-largest economy, with a rapidly expanding middle class but a glaring skills deficit, Brazil presents itself as a country whose transformation is crying out for improved education. From a position of an illiteracy rate of 50 per cent in the 1950s, a primary school completion rate of less than 40 per cent in the 1990s, and 38 per cent enrolment in high school, Brazil moved in 2012 to a situation where a six-year-old child from a low-income bracket had a good chance of attaining more than twice the number of years of education as his or her parents in the 1980s.

Higher-income families are very interested in postsecondary education and normally opt for private schooling. In this environment, much interest was shown in US community college education in 2008, evidenced by consultations with Highland Community College in Washington State and the Community College of the District of Houston, Texas. In 2014, more than two hundred community college students travelled to Brazil through US–Brazil Connect, which hosted the Brazilian Leadership Connect Program (Gershwin 2015).

In Chile, technical training began in 1797, and the first technical institute, the Commercial Institute of Santiago, was established in 1898. In 1920, only 4.5 per cent of the population had received technical education. In 1932, two technical schools were merged to form Frederico–Santa Maria Technical University, which offered three-year technical programmes. Technical education became a government priority, driven by the industrialization thrust. In 1947, there was a merger of engineering schools and technical pedagogic institutes which created the Universidad Tecnica del Estado. Up until the 1970s, the higher education system included nine universities – seven private and two state owned. Educational reform took place in 1981. Currently, there are three types of institutions – universities, professional institutions and technical training centres. Chile has a de facto binary system (Gershwin et al. 2015).

Colombia is interested in the community college, as demonstrated by its presence at the CCID conferences. Specific interest was shown in the Arizona Tribal Community College and Arizona State University. Colombia is also interested in technical colleges and further-education development (Elsner and Sanchez 2015).

Community College Counterparts in Europe

The European Group, including Denmark, England, Ireland, Netherlands and Spain, do not host community colleges, per se, but in some of their institutions, some features of the community college movement are apparent. In Denmark, by 1959, skilled labour was in great demand, and in 1977, the Vocational Education Act was passed in response to rising unemployment, mandating one year of school-based vocational training, followed by an apprenticeship.

In 1995, two Danish colleges attended the ongoing alliance of Southern Community Colleges, evolving into the Transatlantic Technical and Training Alliance, ushering in a period of bilateral cooperation. In 2003, the Stepwise in Qualification Plan has offered increased flexibility for individual vocational and technical education, including the incorporation of prior learning. Driven by its Globalisation Strategy of 2007, Denmark has made remarkable progress in student technical training and student success (Rosenfeld, Liston and Shapiro 2015).

In England, the newer universities were established in the nineteenth and twentieth centuries. In the 1950s, there was greater demand than there was supply of higher education. In the 1970s, the demand became even greater, because of not only increased population, but also the secondary school reforms brought about by the Education Acts and an expanding pool of secondary school graduates. Before the Report on Higher Education (1963) by the Committee on Higher Education appointed by the prime minister and chaired by Lord Robbins, there were about fifty-two universities on the University Funding Council and eighty-two polytechnics and colleges. The number of full-time students increased to over 600,000, with 350 part-timers. There were approximately 55 per cent of British higher education enrolment in the polytechnics, 9 per cent in the Open University system and 36 per cent in universities.

Since the late 1980s, a consensus was reached that a high-skills, high-technology paradigm was essential for achieving growth in a globalizing world (Whitley in Elsner, Boggs and Irwin 2008, 2015) and the universities were not geared towards the production of low- and intermediate-level skills at an affordable price. It became necessary to reform technical and vocational education.

There was also a deliberate expansion of the further-education sector. By 1987, the polytechnics were authorized to award their own degrees, and by 1992, the Further and Higher Education Act abolished the binary system and cleared the way for polytechnics to become universities. Mergers took place between universities and colleges and several further-education colleges entered into partnership with universities through franchise, validation and outreach activities. These events blurred the further- and higher education boundaries and advanced the move to a unitary system.

A National Committee on Enquiry into Higher Education in 1997, chaired by Don Dearing, recommended continued expansion of higher education, but with a focus on lifelong learning, quality and diversity, and with this expansion taking place mainly at the subdegree level and with the promotion of access to underrepresented groups. In early 2003, there was a wave of skills development led by the Department of Children, Schools and Families and the Department of Innovation, Universities and Skills. A number of plans addressed interorganizational linkages and market responsiveness (David and Hall 2015).

Ireland does not have community colleges. Early technical education was conducted in five specialist colleges, such as one founded in Dublin in 1887. These offered science and technology, art, commerce, music and women's work (dressmaking courses, cooking and laundry). In the 1930s, technical vocational education accelerated, and in 1941, a sixth college was added. These were later merged to form the Dublin Institute of Technology. A number of second-level technical schools emerged and produced postsecondary programmes. These are located in the further-education sector, which was boosted in 1970 by the National Institute of Higher Education in Limerick and by twelve regional technical colleges offering a range of two-year national certificate and diploma programmes in engineering, science and business/humanities. A National Qualifications Authority has served to integrate and coordinate all academic and technical vocational awards (McMahon 2015).

The Netherlands has a highly developed, university-based higher education system. Colleges of senior secondary education and training are comparable to the English further-education system. The Netherlands has launched the Learning Village, which embraces a new concept of individual learning which allows for development of the self. There are forty-six colleges of further education, which provide innovative learning experiences. The Koning Willem I College has been described as the nation's only community college, but it actually provides education from kindergarten through community college (Free 2015).

There are no community colleges in Spain. After completing compulsory secondary education, students have the option of entering a two-year baccalaureate or a vocational education programme. The baccalaureate allows continuation at a university (de Bresser and Martinez 2014).

Community College Counterparts in Oceania

Australia's TAFE colleges share the nature, though not the name, of community colleges. In the 1970s, many changes took place in the technical vocational sector in Australia, driven by the changing profile of the workforce arising from the transition from manufacturing to service industries. In 1974, the Kangan Technical and Further Education Report laid the groundwork for educational change. Since 1992, vocational education and training is delivered by TAFE colleges – public or private institutions or government-recognized providers, including secondary schools, community organizations and universities (Barnaart 2015).

New Zealand has a polytechnic system which emerged from technical high schools. After World War II, in response to the growing demand, the Technical Correspondence Institute (now the Open Polytechnic of New Zealand) was opened to provide distance education. In the 1960s, technical institutes were established. In 1974, the government passed legislation to establish community colleges, which would offer both vocational and continuing education programmes. Nine community colleges were established in the 1970s and eight in the 1980s, creating a total pool of twenty-five technical institutes and community colleges. In the mid-1980s, the majority were renamed *polytechnics,* and more recently, many have been designated institutes of technology (Doyle 2015).

Direct North/South Collaboration

In the Dominican Republic, establishing community colleges was the vision of Leonel Fernández, who had studied and worked in the United States. He ran for the presidency and advocated for "Colleges of the People" as a way of matching people's skills to employment opportunities. He signed an agreement with the Daytona Beach Community College in Florida, and later with the

Tompkins Courtland Community College in New York and Portland Community College in Oregon. The first college opened in 2006, and plans were made to establish four community colleges, partnered with different US colleges (Halder 2015).

Beginning in 2005, visits took place from Georgia to four US community colleges – Kirkwood Community College and Eastern Iowa Community College in Iowa; Waukesha County Technical College in Wisconsin and Moraine Valley Community College in Chicago. In 2006, educators attended the CCID thirtieth anniversary conference in Jacksonville, Florida. The Community Colleges for International Development and the Georgian government signed a memorandum of understanding, piloted by the US ambassador. This arrangement gained government support. In 2008, the community college building was opened on the campus of Gori University for career education and professional and continuing education (Raby and Valeau 2014).

Conclusion: Something Old, Something Borrowed, Something New

As can be seen from the review given in this chapter, the concepts of technical vocational education in schools and under apprenticeship go back for centuries. Similarly, elite university education was an ancient practice. However, beginning in the 1960s, the worldwide wave of expansion of postsecondary technical vocational education, the growing need for trained human resources and the improvement in and expansion of secondary education gave wings to the community college movement. As the socioeconomic and political climate set the stage in host countries, globalization has fuelled the establishment of community college counterparts throughout the world. Scholars are documenting their own experiences, which can be useful case studies for practitioners in the field.

So far, the global trend which has been established is that many countries have had something old – universities, postsecondary specialist institutions and secondary schools offering technical education. However, within the context of the local realities commencing in the 1960s, these institutions were unable to meet the human resource needs and achieve the shifting targets set for the creation of knowledge societies. Technical vocational education reform has been taking place since then. Through spontaneous mirroring or even subliminally, ideas have been deliberately borrowed from North America through north/south flows, but also from other regions, including Europe, Oceania and Asia. Old institutions have been reformed and new institutions created. These new, emerging institutions are not necessarily called *community colleges,* but many reflect some of the features and ethos of the US community college. It is evident, therefore, that globalization and educational borrowing have influenced the emergence and development of community college counterparts across the world, but also that local conditions have customized the community college counterparts. Here, too, there is evidence of thinking globally, networking regionally and acting locally.

5.

The Community College in the English-Speaking Caribbean

Location

The countries of the English-speaking Caribbean include Belize in Central America, the Bahamas and the Turks and Caicos, located off the southeast coast of Florida, and a chain of islands running from the Cayman Islands and Jamaica in the northwest to Trinidad and Tobago in the south. The chain comprises the Leeward Islands – Anguilla, the British Virgin Islands, St Kitts/Nevis, Antigua and Barbuda, Montserrat and the Windward Islands, including Dominica, St Lucia, St Vincent and the Grenadines and Grenada. Barbados is the easternmost, and Trinidad and Tobago the southernmost islands. Guyana, in South America, is also included in this group (Ferguson 1999).

Anguilla, the Cayman Islands, Montserrat, the Turks and Caicos and the British Virgin Islands are still British overseas territories, but all the others are states which gained their independence, commencing with Jamaica in 1962 and following through to the 1980s. The Leeward and Windward Islands are members of the Organisation of Eastern Caribbean States and use a common currency, the Eastern Caribbean dollar. As a subgroup, they have also attempted to coordinate their education systems through initiatives undertaken by the Organisation of the Eastern Caribbean States, as well by collaboration with the wider Caribbean group under the larger umbrella of the Caribbean Community (CARICOM). Regional professional associations such as the Association of Caribbean Tertiary Institutions have also played a leadership and coordinating role.

The anglophone Caribbean states share a common history of first settlement by indigenous people, European colonization – some by the French and/or the Spanish, but all by the British at some point. They have all experienced the enforced migration of African slaves for the growing of agricultural crops, and many have been a part of the later migration of East Indians as indentured servants. The Chinese, Syrians and Lebanese also settled as traders and businesspeople in some countries. Not surprisingly, the official language is English, but there are also dialects which have developed through French, Spanish or African influences. The societies are multiracial, with the majority of the population being of African descent, except in the case of Trinidad and Tobago and Guyana, where there may be a slight East Indian majority (Ferguson 1999; Roberts 2003b).

Bermuda is a British overseas territory located in the North Atlantic Ocean. Its gross domestic product per capita ranks among the highest in the world. Its economy is based on offshore insurance, reinsurance and tourism. It is an associate member of the Caribbean Community and a contributing country to the University of the West Indies. Bermuda is discussed here because it shares a strong tie with the anglophone Caribbean through its membership in the Association of Caribbean Tertiary Institutions, in which its college's president, Dr Durinda Green, serves as the association's vice-president.

The Caribbean countries are geographically close to and sociologically linked with the United States, but the long history of British colonization has created and sustained strong cultural ties, including the structure and patterns which are still evident in the higher education system. Although the community college has existed in the United States for more than a century, it was only fifty years ago that the first of these institutions was established in the English-speaking Caribbean, in Barbados.

The earliest higher education institution in the region, Codrington College, was established in Barbados. During the nineteenth century, the predominant institutions for the education of adults were teachers' and theological colleges. In the early decades of the twentieth century, technical colleges and nursing schools were added to the institutional pool. The establishment of the University College of the West Indies in 1948 ushered in the University of the West Indies in 1962, followed by the establishment of national universities in Guyana (1962) and, more recently, in Jamaica (the University of Technology), and Trinidad and Tobago (the University of Trinidad and Tobago) (Peters 1993; Roberts 1999).

Over the past decades, new local private universities with religious affiliations (Northern Caribbean University in Jamaica and University of the Southern Caribbean in Trinidad and Tobago) have emerged; foreign universities have been established in the region, such as in Grenada (St George's University) and new institutions such as university colleges (University College of the Cayman Islands and University College of the Caribbean) have been added to the pool. Many countries also play host to several offshore universities, offering mainly medical sciences and business (Howe 2003).

The late onset, slow growth and limited diversity in the higher education system allowed accommodation to new institutional types and fairly easy

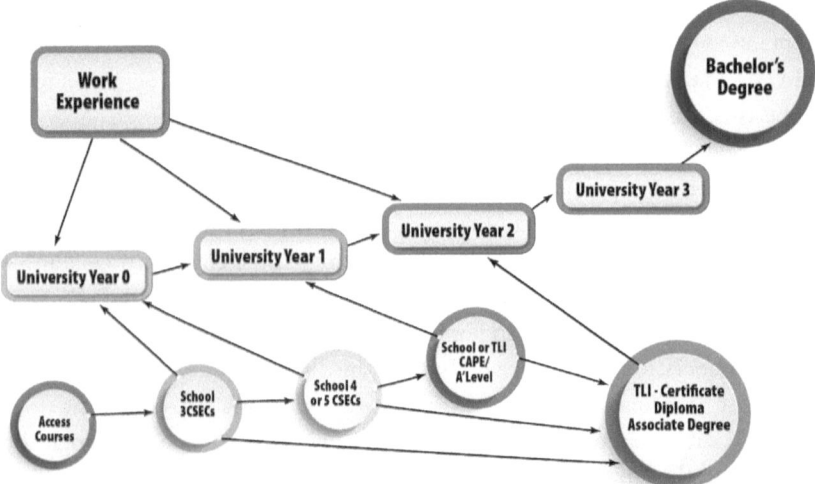

Figure 5.1. Alternative pathways to and through tertiary education in the anglophone Caribbean

rationalization of roles among them. The traditional pathway to university was the secondary or high school, where a relatively small number of students completed University of Cambridge or London University O-level examinations, and later the Caribbean Examinations Council's (CXC) Caribbean Secondary Education Certificate (CSEC). From that group, the best performers in the examinations were selected to go on to complete the A-level examinations or later, the Caribbean Examinations Council's Caribbean Advanced Proficiency Examinations (CAPE) for entry to universities. As soon as the University of the West Indies was established, the teachers' and theological colleges established educational linkages with it and these arrangements created new and alternative pathways to university education. Technical colleges also forged linkages. Figure 5.1 is a representation of some pathways which have evolved over time (Roberts and Brissett 2003).

Traditionally, students spend five years in secondary or high school from first to fifth forms. By the end of that period, they would have taken the Caribbean Secondary School Examinations set by the Caribbean Examinations Council. The diagram shows five different routes for students:

1. Access courses (no Caribbean Secondary School Certificates)
2. Three Caribbean Secondary School Certificates
3. Four or five Caribbean Secondary School Certificates
4. CAPE units or A levels
5. Associate degrees or TLI certificates

Some students who leave secondary school at the end of fifth form may proceed to a university which offers four-year degrees, or to a teachers' college or community college. Others may gain access to part-time study or preliminary science courses at the University of the West Indies, where the majority of students would normally be accepted to a three-year bachelor's degree or professional programme, having successfully completed sixth-form or community college studies.

Through articulation agreements, students may also proceed to the University of the West Indies from teachers' colleges or community colleges and earn normal entry or advanced placement. Mature students may qualify to enter several institutions based on prior learning. The community college can be credited with the creation of new pathways among higher education institutions in the Caribbean.

The community college represents not a linear but a jigsaw puzzle piece in the higher education landscape. However, that piece did not easily fit into the pre-existing picture. It seemed to some to be a hybrid institution reaching into the upper levels of the secondary school, up into the lower levels of the university and across into the world of work. Some embraced it as an effective instrument for widening access to higher education. Others endorsed it as a means of rapidly responding to community training needs. Yet others criticized it as a misfit which would lower the academic quality of tertiary education.

Features of the Caribbean Community College

Like the US community colleges, those in the Caribbean offer associate degrees, but these are not identical in nature. In 1993, the Association of Caribbean Tertiary Institutions established guidelines for associate degree programmes and defined the associate degree as "a postsecondary qualification awarded to students who successfully complete a specified number of courses in full-time or part-time study". The association stipulated further that associate degrees should have three identifiable components – specialized or career-oriented majors, a general education core and courses chosen by students as electives. The package should include not less than sixty credits. The minimum stipulated entry requirements are four subjects at CXC General Proficiency Grade I or II or their equivalent, but with special consideration given to mature students, in light of their life and work experiences. It is understood that programmes may have specific requirements in addition to these general entry requirements (Roberts 1999).

In the United States, associate degrees may have either an academic/university transfer focus or an occupational focus, although the latter may also be used for university transfer. The academic/university transfer programme embodies the principles of a broad, liberal education and as such, mirrors the structure and content of the lower division of a four-year liberal arts bachelor's degree in the United States. It emphasizes a broad general education component but allows some emphasis on a declared major, together with the pursuit of elective subjects in an area of interest, outside the area of specialization.

The divergence in structure of the associate degrees has a historical basis. Up until the 1960s and 1970s, Caribbean secondary school students followed the syllabi of and sat British external examinations at both Ordinary and Advanced levels. The system was one which required specialization at Advanced level (the last two years of secondary school), where students would study two or three subjects in depth and sit a less consequential general paper. Students would choose subjects within blocks: classics, sciences, the arts or business, for example. This focused choice would provide a seamless transfer into British universities to pursue three-year bachelor's degrees.

The Caribbean associate of arts and science degrees can be regarded as a hybrid qualification, adapted to enable some transfer to the University of the West Indies and British universities, more so through the worth of their majors; but also to facilitate transfer to American universities, more so on the merits of their general education component. The applied associate degrees are more homegrown, influenced by the occupational and professional needs of the local environment, but incorporating sufficient general education to also allow university transfer.

Caribbean community colleges find common ground with those in the United States and among themselves in their missions, even though there may be slight variations in emphasis. They cater to a wide cross section of the society, undertake holistic development of their students, are responsive to occupational needs, provide academic and adult education, share a commitment to community service and renewal, and vary in their commitment to and practice of applied research (Alleyne 1995).

They are all statutory bodies, governed by councils, boards of governors, managers or directors and are not under the direct control of governments. However, because these are in sovereign states, there are variations in how college governance is experienced from one country to another. These differences emerge from the formal and informal networks within small countries, the details in the acts themselves and the powers of the ministers of education. Governance affects academic freedom, staff appointments and promotions, student selection and certification, academic programme development, response time to requests, security of tenure, quality assurance and ultimately staff engagement and student success.

Academic and senior administrative staff profiles show variations across countries. However, in general, doctorates would average below 10 per cent, certificates and associate degrees below 5 per cent and master's degrees below 30 per cent, with the majority having bachelor's degrees and some teaching qualifications. In many Caribbean colleges, as with US colleges, there are increasing targets for faculty and staff to earn terminal degrees. With more community colleges offering bachelor's degrees, the age differential and the average age of students have increased in recent years.

Community College Development Models in the Anglophone Caribbean

In spite of its detractors, the community college or some related entity has existed or still exists in Anguilla, Antigua and Barbuda, the Bahamas, Barbados, Bermuda, Belize, British Virgin Islands, Cayman Islands, Dominica, Grenada, Jamaica, Montserrat, St Kitts and Nevis, St Lucia, St Vincent and the Grenadines, Trinidad and Tobago and the Turks and Caicos. There are no community colleges in Guyana. Belize has established junior colleges.

It is true to say, however, that there is not a single model of the community college in the Caribbean. These colleges are united in their public ownership or state support, commitment to access, affordability, comprehensiveness in the range of programmes, flexibility in programming, focus on teaching over research and their responsiveness to the needs of their communities and students. However, the variation in their origins, governance arrangements, funding and levels of offerings point to several models. Viewed as community college counterparts, as was seen in the global pool presented in chapter 4, there is evidence of "something old, something borrowed and something new".

In this region, the first community college was established in Barbados in 1968. In the Caribbean, community college antecedents include specialist institutions such as teachers' colleges, theological colleges, nursing schools, technical colleges, a few junior colleges and universities. By virtue of their long-term existence and operation in communities, the structure, position and purpose of the older institutions such as the universities and teachers colleges were well articulated and clearly understood. However, the emergence of community colleges complicated the tertiary educational landscape. They were different from the specialist colleges due to their diversified curricula. Like universities, they were comprehensive in scope; but unlike them, they were much more open in access and more vocational in orientation – more focused on teaching and less on research.

In the case of Jamaica, there is much convergence with the US community college in name, mission, features and partnerships, but the existence of differences suggests that adaptation has taken place. Unlike Latin America, over time Puerto Rico has established both junior colleges and community colleges.

Prior to Jamaica's independence in 1962, a number of specialist colleges and the University College of the West Indies were already in existence. Established in 1948, the University College of the West Indies had become the university for the entire English-speaking Caribbean by 1962, with its first campus in Kingston, Jamaica. The pre-existing colleges included Mico Teachers College (1836), Calabar Theological College (1846), Bethlehem Teachers College (1861), Shortwood Teachers College (1885), St Joseph's Teachers College (1887), West Indies College (1919), West Indies School of Public Health (1945), Caribbean Nazarene Theological College (1951), the College of Arts, Science and Technology (1958) and the Jamaica School of Music (1961). These were followed by Church's Teachers College (1965), United Theological College (1966) and Moneague Teachers College (1972).

In 1974, the first community college, Excelsior Community College, was established. Over the next thirty years, Knox, Brown's Town and Montego Bay community colleges were established in 1975, and Portmore Community College in 1992. Moneague Teachers College and Bethlehem Teachers College expanded their range of offerings beyond the discipline of education to become like community colleges in 1993 and 2004, respectively. The College of Arts, Science and Education became a community college–type institution through the merger of the Teachers College with the School of Agriculture in 1995.

There are other tertiary institutions which performed some community college functions in the course of their development, but their evolution followed a different path. These include private institutions which tend to focus on business. One such school is the University College of the Caribbean, formed in 2004 from a merger of the former Institute of Management and Production and the Institute of Management Sciences.

The West Indian Training College evolved from a small school founded in 1907 to become a multidisciplinary junior college called the West Indian Training College in 1919. This transitioned to the West Indies College, a baccalaureate institution in the 1950s, offering bachelor's degrees in theology. Since then, it has expanded and upgraded its offerings to become the Northern Caribbean University, a liberal arts, private, Seventh-Day Adventist university which has been officially recognized by the Jamaican government as a university since 1999, and its programmes are accredited by the University Council of Jamaica.

The College of Arts, Science and Technology was never a junior college or community college, although it has always been a postsecondary public institution with an emphasis on access. It became the University of Technology, a public, national university, in 1964.

Jamaica's first community college, Excelsior, was introduced in 1974 in response to access, labour market needs and the need to increase transfers to universities. Currently, there are five community colleges and three multidisciplinary colleges in Jamaica: Bethlehem Moravian College, College of Agriculture, Science and Education (CASE), and Moneague College, founded in 1998 but derived from the teachers' college of 1948.

The Council of Community Colleges of Jamaica was established in 2001 as a statutory agency under the Ministry of Education to supervise and coordinate the work of the colleges. The organization is governed by a council composed of members from education, business and industry. Anguilla Community College and the Turks and Caicos Community College are affiliated members.

The Caribbean Community College Models

In trying to understand the Caribbean community college models, one needs to consider the following:

1. Their origins relating to when and how they came to be; the access and opportunities which they opened up for the underserved; the players involved in their initiation, establishment, popular mobilization, operation and sustainability; and the part played by the community, government, insiders, universities, business and industry.

2. Their place in the tertiary education system and on the tertiary education landscape, including any overlap with secondary and other postsecondary institutions, as well as with local and international universities.

3. Their mission and purpose – that is, whether they see themselves as vocational or academic, as well as the extent to which they promote equity or perpetuate inequity.

4. Their organizational structure and characteristics created through flat and agile arrangements, as well as the dynamics existing among students, faculty, governance, finances, instruction, general education, social role, community involvement and career education. Consideration also needs to be given to the idea of whether they facilitate, prolong or inhibit the earning of the bachelor's degree.

5. Their culture and ethos and how others see them in their bid to widen access, their appeal to nontraditional students and the reality of the journey (whether cul de sac or gateway).

6. The forces and challenges which shape their operations, as well as their adaptation to local, national, regional and international developments, including the proliferation of foreign tertiary educational providers; legislation,

regulations and international treaties; accreditation processes and requirements; the impact of professional associations; competition which they experience and competitive advantage which they acquire; and any public accountability demanded by their multiple stakeholders.

Origins

Across the region, community colleges were established as public institutions, mostly soon after their countries gained national independence. The prevailing rationale was to provide the education and training of human resources for middle management and technical positions to meet the needs of these newly independent countries. The regional university would provide for the top tier. However, changes sometimes were made through the amalgamation of middle-tier institutions like teachers' and technical colleges; in many cases, these would be merged to create state, national or community colleges. Table 5.1 summarizes the institutions, countries and dates for each country's independence and each institution's establishment.

Table 5.1. Establishment Date of Community and Other Relevant Colleges by Country

Name	Country	Year of Country's Independence	Year of Establishment	Status of College
Barbados Community College	Barbados	1966	1968	Public
College of the Bahamas	Bahamas	1973	1974	Public
Bermuda College	Bermuda	N/A	1974	Public
Excelsior Community College	Jamaica	1962	1974	Public, with religious ties
Knox Community College	Jamaica	1962	1975	Public, with religious ties
Brown's Town Community College	Jamaica	1962	1975	Public
Montego Bay Community College	Jamaica	1962	1975	Public
Antigua State College	Antigua and Barbuda	1981	1977	Public
Clifton Dupigny Community College (now Dominica State College)	Dominica	1978	1983/2002	Public

(Continued)

Table 5.1. (*continued*)

Name	Country	Year of Country's Independence	Year of Establishment	Status of College
Sir Arthur Lewis Community College	St Lucia	1979	1985	Public
Community College of the Cayman Islands (now University College of the Cayman Islands)	Cayman Islands	N/A	1985/2004	Public
Clarence Fitzroy College	St Kitts and Nevis	1983	1988	Public
H. Lavity Stoutt Community College	British Virgin Islands	N/A	1990	Public
Portmore Community College	Jamaica	1962	1992	Public
Moneague College (formerly Moneague Teachers' College)	Jamaica	1962	1993/1958	Public
Bahamas Baptist Community College	Bahamas	1973	1995	Private
Turks and Caicos Community College	Turks and Caicos Islands	N/A	1994	Public
College of Agriculture, Science and Education	Jamaica	1962	1995	Public
T.A. Marryshow Community College	Grenada	1974	1996/1998	Public
St Vincent and the Grenadines Community College	St Vincent and the Grenadines	1979	1997/2004	Public
Bethlehem Moravian College	Jamaica	1962	2004/1861	Private
Anguilla Community College	Anguilla	N/A	2009	Public
Montserrat Community College	Montserrat	N/A	2003	Public
College of Science, Technology and Applied Arts of Trinidad and Tobago	Trinidad and Tobago	1962	1984	Public

Table 5.2. Classification of Institutions into Community Colleges and Other Colleges

Community Colleges in Both Name and Function	Community Colleges in Many Functions, Though Not in Name
Anguilla Community College	Antigua State College
Bahamas Baptist Community College	Bermuda College
Barbados Community College	Bethlehem Moravian College
Brown's Town Community College	Clarence Fitzroy College
Community College of the Cayman Islands (now University College of the Cayman Islands)	College of Agriculture, Science and Education
Excelsior Community College, Jamaica	College of Science, Technology and Applied Arts of Trinidad and Tobago
H. Lavity Stoutt Community College, British Virgin Islands	College of the Bahamas (graduated to University of the Bahamas)
Knox Community College, Jamaica	Dominica State College
Montego Bay Community College, Jamaica	Moneague College
Montserrat Community College	
Portmore Community College, Jamaica	
Sir Arthur Lewis Community College, St Lucia	
T.A. Marryshow Community College, Grenada	
Turks and Caicos Community College	
St Vincent and the Grenadines Community College	

Table 5.2 differentiates the institutions which are labelled community colleges from those which have community college functions but have different names.

The emergence of the Caribbean community colleges can be viewed as following five paths or models. First, there are those which resulted from the amalgamation of different types of specialist institutions, often technical schools, teachers' colleges, agricultural schools and other types of institutions. This group includes Sir Arthur Lewis Community College, Antigua State College, Dominica State College, St Vincent and the Grenadines Community College, T.A. Marryshow Community College, Clarence Fitzroy Bryant College, Montserrat Community College and the Cayman Islands Community College. Although not strictly community colleges, the College of the Bahamas (now University of the Bahamas), Jamaica's College of Agriculture,

Science and Education, Bermuda College, and Trinidad and Tobago's College of Science Technology and Applied Arts share some similarity in their historical development.

Second, there are those which derive from the amalgamation of similar sections of multiple institutions, such as the sixth forms of multiple secondary schools in a parish. This was the case with the Montego Bay and the Brown's Town community colleges.

Third, there is the case of the adaptation and upgrade of upper levels of a single secondary institution, such as Knox and Excelsior community colleges in Jamaica. The merged sixth forms and secretarial classes of Knox High School evolved into the community college of that name. The teacher training, nursing education and business education (including secretarial studies) sections of Excelsior High School were separated and upgraded to become that community college.

Fourth, there are new institutions created from scratch, often to meet unmet demands for postsecondary education in a region. Examples include the Portmore, H. Lavity Stoutt, Turks and Caicos and Barbados community colleges. In the case of the last example, other institutions or sections were later incorporated into it.

Fifth, there are those which expanded their specialist discipline by adding general education areas, such as Moneague College and Bethlehem Moravian College, both former teachers' colleges.

Whatever the pathway, the end result of these developments was the creation of multidisciplinary institutions which continually responded to the wide-ranging academic and workforce needs of their diverse clientele.

Model 1 Colleges: Amalgamation of Pre-existing Specialist Institutions

Table 5.3 lists community colleges that were created by the amalgamation of pre-existing institutions of learning.

Antigua State College

During the late 1970s, public opinion was pointing towards the establishment of a comprehensive college in Antigua, and this movement was encouraged by a strong recommendation made by Alister Francis in his doctoral thesis (1975), which underscored the demand and provided a blueprint for establishing a multipurpose college, mainly through a merger of existing postsecondary, specialist institutions. He became the first principal of the college that was formed.

Table 5.3. Community Colleges Formed through Amalgamation of Pre-existing Institutions

Country	Colleges Amalgamated	Institution Formed	Date of Establishment
Antigua and Barbuda	Leeward Islands Teachers' Training College	Antigua State College	1977
	Golden Grove Technical College		
	A' Level College		
Bahamas	Bahamas Teachers' College	College of the Bahamas	1974
	San Salvador Teachers' College		
	C.R. Walker Technical College		
	Sixth Form Programmes		
	School of Nursing	College of the Bahamas	Later additions
	The Research Unit		
	Bahamas Hotel Training School		
Bermuda	Bermuda Technical Institute	Bermuda College	1974
	Bermuda Hotel and Catering College		
	Academic Sixth Form Centre		
Cayman Islands	Trade School	Community College of the Cayman Islands	1985
	Hotel School		
	Marine School		
Dominica	A' Level College	Clifton Dupigny Community College	1983
	Technical College		
Dominica	Clifton Dupigny Community College	Dominica State College	2002
	Dominica Teachers' College		
	Princess Margaret School of Nursing		

(*Continued*)

Table 5.3. (*continued*)

Country	Colleges Amalgamated	Institution Formed	Date of Establishment
Grenada	Grenada Teachers' College	Grenada National College	1988
	Grenada Technical and Vocational Institute		
	Institute of Further Education		
	National Institute of Handicraft		
	Mirabeau Agricultural Training School		
	Domestic Arts Institute		
	Continuing Education Programme		
	Pharmacy School	Renamed T.A. Marryshow Community College	1995
Jamaica	College of Agriculture (formerly Farm School, then Jamaica School of Agriculture)	College of Arts, Science and Education	1997
	Passley Gardens Teachers College		
Montserrat	Montserrat Technical College (closed 1995)	Montserrat Community College	Enacted 2003, commenced 2004
	Glendon Hospital School of Nursing (closed 1995)		
	A-level programmes of Montserrat Secondary School		
St Kitts and Nevis	Teachers' College	Clarence Fitzroy Bryant College	1988
	Technical College		
	School of Nursing		
	A' Level Programme		

(*Continued*)

62 | THE BARBADOS COMMUNITY COLLEGE EXPERIENCE

Table 5.3. (*continued*)

Country	Colleges Amalgamated	Institution Formed	Date of Establishment
St Lucia	St Lucia Teachers' College	Sir Arthur Lewis Community College	1986
	Morne Fortune Technical College		
	St Lucia A' Level College		
	Victoria Hospital School of Nursing		
St Vincent and the Grenadines	St Vincent Teachers' College	St Vincent and the Grenadines Community College	Commenced 1996; established 2005
	Technical College		
	A' Level College		
	School of Nursing		
Trinidad and Tobago	College of Health Sciences	College of Science, Technology and Applied Arts of Trinidad and Tobago	2000
	College of Nursing		
	School of Languages		
	College of General Education		

Antigua State College, which had a brief existence as the Island College in 1976, was established at Golden Grove in 1977 through the merger of the Leeward Islands Teacher Training College (formerly the Spring Garden Moravian Teachers College) with the Golden Grove Technical College. The college was established as a national institution, but one of its antecedents, the Teachers College, was a subregional institution catering to all the Leeward Islands, as well as Barbados and the Turks and Caicos. Under the Canada Training Awards Programme, students came to Antigua State College from Cayman Islands, Montserrat, Anguilla and St Kitts and Nevis.

The technical college included three departments: Hotel and Catering, the Commercial Department and the Engineering and Construction Department. Antigua State College therefore began its operations with four departments: these three and Teacher Training. In 1978, the sixth-form programmes of the secondary schools were discontinued at the schools and transferred to the college, adding a fifth department, the Advanced-Level Department. In

1981, the Hotel and Catering Department was transferred from the college and became the Hotel Training Centre, under the management of the Ministry of Tourism. It was relocated to Dutchman's Bay.

The college's concern about validation was met by the external examinations of the Advanced-Level Division and the endorsement of teacher education by the Joint Board arrangement with the University of the West Indies. In 1988, like the Sir Arthur Lewis Community College, it negotiated a franchise arrangement to deliver UWI Level 1 arts, natural science and social science programmes at Antigua State College. Under this arrangement, the facilities and teachers were approved, course outlines were supplied and examinations set and certified by the University of the West Indies. Students could transfer to the University of the West Indies to complete the relevant bachelor's degrees. In 1995, Antigua State College added geography and computer science to the suite of courses, and in 1998, it added UWI Level 2 programmes in social sciences and a jointly delivered, UWI-certified hospitality management bachelor's degree programme.

Designated a Centre of Excellence in Business in 1988, Antigua State College brokered an arrangement with the College of Arts, Science and Technology in Jamaica to accept Antigua State College graduates with a diploma in business studies to complete their bachelor's degrees in business teacher education in one year. The college also pursued the franchise of a two-year paralegal programme from Barbados Community College under a UWI/USAID project. This lasted for four years.

Like a community college, the publicly funded Antigua State College continued to expand into new areas. It offered a diploma in nursing, recognized by the local and regional nursing body, and a diploma in pharmacy which was soon articulated with the programme of the University of Technology, Jamaica.

Antigua State College delivers CAPE programmes, primarily for transfer students; engineering craft programmes originally certified by the City and Guilds of London, chiefly for training the workforce; diplomas in nursing and pharmacy for professionals; and the first two levels of UWI bachelor's degrees. It also delivers an associate degree in teacher education and developed its own associate degree in business studies.

Student diversity, programme relevance and community responsiveness are features of Antigua State College. There is evidence of some adult and continuing education, and the institution exudes the aura of a community college. However, its aspirations are in other directions because interest has been expressed from time to time in becoming a college or campus of the University of the West Indies, or even an independent University of Antigua. In fact, it has become a campus of the University of the West Indies.

Bermuda College

Bermuda College was established in 1974 by an act of Parliament. It was formed from the amalgamation of three pre-existing institutions: the Technical Institute (1956), the Bermuda Hotel and Catering College (1965), and the Academic Sixth Form Centre (1967). It offers a variety of academic, technical and professional programmes at certificate, diploma, and associate degree levels and offers professional and noncredit training and certification. It is organized into four divisions: Applied Science and Technology; Business Administration and Hospitality; Liberal Arts and Centre for Professional and Career Education. Its campus began construction in 1979, with its last buildings completed in 1996. The Stonington Beach Hotel, opened in 1980, is the hotel training facility.

The college is led by twelve governors, and its governance is patterned after that of state-funded colleges in the United States and Canada. The arrangement protects the college from direct political influence. In essence, Bermuda College is a community college which offers university-parallel programmes that allow students to transfer to universities in the United States, United Kingdom, Canada and the Caribbean. There are articulation arrangements with Georgia State University, Miami University and Mount St Vincent University. Transfer agreements exist with about fourteen universities.

Bermuda College is accredited by the New England Association of Schools and Colleges through its Commission on Institutions in Higher Education. It is also accredited by the Commission of the American Culinary Federation Education Foundation to offer the associate of applied science degree (culinary arts) and a diploma in culinary arts.

The college describes itself as a community college which is dedicated to the highest standards and which is highly student centred, focusing on learning and student success. It has an Institutional Research and Planning Centre and is headed by a president and two vice-presidents – one for academic affairs and the other for finance and operations.

Clarence Fitzroy Bryant College, St Kitts and Nevis

The 1960s and early 1970s were very vibrant periods in the development of postsecondary institutions in St Kitts and Nevis. The School of Nursing was established in 1966 under the Ministry of Health, for the training of general nurses and midwives. The minister of education at that time, Clarence Fitzroy Bryant, had a vision and expressed the view that the training of teachers was critical for national development. The Teachers College was established in 1967, with an initial focus of providing training for primary and secondary schoolteachers who were already employed. The Technical College was established in 1971 for the training of school leavers at the craft and tradesman levels.

In 1988, the sixth forms of the Basseterre High School in St Kitts and the Charlestown Secondary School in Nevis were discontinued, and they became part of the College of Further Education. This college was established out of the amalgamation of the Teachers College, which became the Division of Teacher Education; the Technical College, which became the Division of Technical and Vocational Education; and the School of Nursing, which grew into the Division of Health Sciences. The combined sixth forms became the Division of Arts, Sciences and General Studies; and the Division of Adult and Continuing Education was added to fulfil the institution's mission. This college, headed by Dr Bertram Ross, provided the opportunity to accelerate the training of local persons for leadership positions and to meet the needs of an expanding workforce.

In 1996, all the divisions were consolidated in one location at Burdon Street, Basseterre, and the institution was renamed the Clarence Fitzroy Bryant College. In 1998, the college joined Antigua and St Lucia in offering their college students the UWI Level 1 bachelor's degree programmes in arts and sciences. Soon afterwards, the college introduced the UWI School of Education's associate degree in education, as well as associate degrees in other areas.

In response to pressure from applications from offshore universities, St Kitts and Nevis introduced the St Christopher and Nevis Accreditation of Institutions Act 1999 and established a board to regulate the tertiary education sector and process applications for registration. By this action, it was well ahead of the other OECS countries.

Like a community college, Clarence Fitzroy Bryant College proudly asserts its philosophy; it sees itself as one which caters to all ages and all needs of learners and contributes to the advancement of the country.

College of Agriculture, Science and Education, Jamaica

The College of Agriculture, Science and Education resulted from the merger of Passley Gardens Teachers College, founded in 1981, with the College of Agriculture, which has had a longer history. It had its beginnings in 1910 as the Farm School, located in Kingston on the site now occupied by the University of Technology. In spite of its small size, it had the distinction of producing one of Jamaica's leading animal scientists, Dr D.P. Lecky. In 1942, the institution was relocated to Twickenham Park in Spanish Town and renamed the Jamaica School of Agriculture, which soon allowed women to enrol.

By an act of Parliament in 1981, the Jamaica School of Agriculture was closed and the College of Agriculture established, this time at Passley Gardens, Portland. It was charged with carrying out teaching, research and extension services. In the same year, to provide training for teachers in Portland and neighbouring parishes, the Passley Gardens Teachers College was established. It joined the other teachers' colleges in preparing students initially for the Joint Board of Teacher Education primary and secondary teachers' diplomas, but with an emphasis on science, mathematics and computer science. The college went on to offer the postcertificate diploma in education and an early childhood training programme.

In 1995, in response to the recommendations of a commissioned report by Sir Philip Sherlock, the institutions, already located in proximity, merged to become the College of Agriculture, Science and Education. In 1997, the first associate degree in natural science was launched, and this gained recognition by and articulation with bachelor's degree programmes at both the University of Technology and the University of the West Indies in 2000 and Northern Caribbean University in 2001. The College of Agriculture, Science and Education launched a suite of community college programmes in 2000 and its first bachelor's degree in technology, in 2002.

The College of Agriculture, Science and Education shares features of the community college but has the distinctiveness of a primary focus on agriculture, science, technology and education.

College of the Bahamas/University of the Bahamas

Bahamas has had a number of teachers' colleges: Oates Field Teachers College, Bahamas Teachers College and the San Salvador Teachers College. The Nassau Technical College opened in 1962 and was renamed the Technical Institute in 1966. In 1968, the Nassau Technical Centre was established; it merged in 1971 with the Technical Institute to create the C.R. Walker Technical College.

After 1967, there was an active thrust by successive governments to train Bahamians to fill skilled, professional, middle and top management positions in the country, which were held by non-nationals at the time. This boosted the demand for higher education. At first, local higher education was limited to three years of teacher training at the two colleges certified by the UWI Institute of Education. Technical training took place at the C.R. Walker Technical College on a day-release basis. Courses ranged from cosmetology, hotel training and plumbing. Many of the courses were locally certified, but certification for boiler operators was done by an Ontario-based certification board.

The College of the Bahamas was established as a public, multidisciplinary institution in 1974 through the amalgamation of four institutions: Bahamas Teachers College, San Salvador Teachers College, C.R. Walker Technical College and the Sixth-Form Programme. At first, it offered A-level studies, certificates and diplomas. In the early 1990s, it introduced bachelor's degrees in business, education, science and nursing.

In 1992, the Research Unit was introduced. Beginning in 1996, it was expanded and active overtures were made to conduct research with international agencies such as the United Nations Development Fund for Women, International Labour Organization and the Caribbean Agricultural Research and Development Institute. In 1995, the College of the Bahamas was granted full autonomy to become a corporate entity, change its structure and seek private funding. In 1997, a strategic planning team was established to plan the college's transition to a university. It underwent major restructuring in 1998. The nomenclature of a university was introduced, including *professor* and *associate professor*. Generous study leave was also given to facilitate the rapid upgrading of staff qualifications. The prime minister presented a development plan in Parliament, including the college's transition to a university.

The infrastructural costs were steep but were met by some government funding, but the majority of the money came from the private sector, including banks and foundations. In 2000, the Bahamas Hotel Training Centre amalgamated with the college to form the Hospitality Institute. The institution accelerated its bachelor's degree offerings to include a bachelor's degree in law with the University of the West Indies and a bachelor's degree in pharmacy in conjunction with the University of Technology in Jamaica. It launched its first postgraduate programme in 2001 with Kent State University in Ohio. Over the next few years, it launched master's degree programmes with a number of US colleges, such as Ashford University in San Diego, University of South Florida, Kent State and Wheelock College in Boston. Its first independent graduate degree was a master's in business administration, launched in 2006.

An ad hoc committee continued to work on the transition, and the long-awaited Charter Day came on 16 November 2016. At the time of the transition, there were five bachelor's degrees in about fifty-five majors. At last, the institution had ceased to be like a community college and had become a university, with its stated mission as "to advance and expand access to higher education, promote academic freedom, drive national development and build character through teaching, learning, research, scholarship and service".

College of Science, Technology and Applied Arts of Trinidad and Tobago

Trinidad and Tobago has had a number of tertiary education institutions during its history, including the Imperial College of Tropical Agriculture (1921), which formed the nucleus of the UWI St Augustine campus. Established later were the Caribbean Union College (1927), now the University of the Southern Caribbean; Eastern Caribbean Institute of Agriculture and Forestry (1954); UWI, St Augustine (1960); John Donaldson Technical Institute (1962); San Fernando Technical Institute (1980); and the Trinidad and Tobago Hotel School (1990).

By an act of Parliament in 1984, the National Institute of Higher Education, Research, Science and Technology was established as a statutory body with a mandate to promote the development of science, technology and higher education, as well as to enhance innovation and creativity in the wider society. Shortly after its establishment, a number of entities were established to promote higher education in health sciences and modern languages. The following institutions were established under its purview: College of Health Sciences, College of Nursing, General Education and School of Languages.

The decision was taken in the 1990s to reorganize tertiary education in Trinidad and Tobago and to amalgamate some institutions into a comprehensive college. The College of Science, Technology and Applied Arts of Trinidad and Tobago was established by an act of Parliament in 2000 from several pre-existing institutions, including the four colleges of the National Institute of Higher Education, Research, Science and Technology. The College of Science, Technology and Applied Arts of Trinidad and Tobago offers arts and sciences, radiography, medical laboratory technology, nursing, business and library studies. The School of Language is an official provider of translation and interpreting services.

As a newly created institution, the College of Science, Technology and Applied Arts of Trinidad and Tobago adopted the credit-based system of instruction and the associate degree qualification, both features of a community college. The University of Trinidad and Tobago, established in 2004, assimilated some other pre-existing, specialist, postsecondary institutions such as the San Fernando Technical Institute and Eastern Caribbean Institute of Agriculture and Forestry.

University College of the Cayman Islands (formerly Community College of the Cayman Islands)

The years 1976–1981 were critical for postsecondary education development in the Cayman Islands. Within that five-year period, the Trade School, the Hotel School and the Marine School were launched. In 1985, the three institutions were amalgamated to create the Community College of the Cayman Islands, a part-time institution which attracted faculty from all over the world.

By an act of Parliament in 2004, the institution was upgraded and renamed the University College of the Cayman Islands. It offers technical/vocational education, workforce training, associate degrees in numerous disciplines, bachelor's degrees in business administration, computer science, natural and social sciences and education. It also offers an executive master's degree in business administration and a master's in public administration. It has formed strategic alliances with local and overseas corporations and educational institutions. It has articulation arrangements with regional universities, as well as universities in the United Kingdom and the United States.

In 2014, the UK-based Accreditation Service for International Schools, Colleges and Universities accredited the University College of the Cayman Islands and designated it as a Premier institution. Although it has graduated from community college status, its practices indicate that it still embodies the values which it originally embraced.

Dominica State College

Prior to being named Dominica State College, the national college bore the name of a pioneer of universal education in Dominica, Clifton Dupigny. The Dominica Teachers Institute was inaugurated in 1973 and later became the Dominica Teachers Training College, established to increase the pool of trained teachers for primary and secondary schools. The Sixth-Form College emerged in the late 1970s, offering A-level programmes in preparation for university studies. In response to the 1984 recommendations made by the Inter-Governmental Committee on Caribbean University Education, the Teachers College and the Sixth-Form College were merged to become the Clifton Dupigny College, headed by Henry Volney. The Technical College was established in 1972, and its principal was Merrill Matthew.

The Dominica State College Act of 2002 created the Dominica State College out of the amalgamation of the institutions mentioned earlier, as well as the School of Nursing. The first president was Bernard Yankee. The transition from Clifton Dupigny was informed by stakeholder consultations and assisted by transition teams led by Hilroy Thomas, who was assisted by Donald Peters, who later became principal. In the new arrangement in the Dominica State College, the Clifton Dupigny Academic Division became the Faculty of Arts and Sciences, the Technical Division became the Faculty of Applied Sciences, the Teachers Training College became the Faculty of Education and Human Development and the School of Nursing became the Faculty of Nursing and Health Sciences.

Dominica State College delivers certificates and associate degrees, as well as a bachelor's degree in nursing. The college has established links with the University of the West Indies, the University of Technology in Jamaica and universities in the United States, including Wheelock College.

Montserrat Community College

The idea of the community college was first broached by the Government of Montserrat in the early 1990s, in the context of its subregional commitment to expanding postsecondary education opportunities. Prior to this, A-level studies were offered at the Montserrat Secondary School; craft-level training was offered by the Montserrat Technical College and nursing education and training were given at the Glendon Hospital. A feasibility study conducted in 1992 recommended that the technical college be upgraded to a community college. Volcanic activity on the island in 1995 resulted in the closure of the postsecondary institutions and the temporary abandonment of the community college idea.

Once the volcanic activity subsided, the need for the college as part of the rebuilding effort was given priority, and the act was proclaimed in 2003. With funding under the OECS/HRD/Tertiary-Level Programme EDF VII Project, construction of the site for the college began in 2003. In 2004, a board of governors was installed; an interim head and mainly part-time staff were appointed. The first cohort of full-time students was admitted to A-level studies, and part-time students to Office Administration and Principles of Business. The new premises were opened officially on 28 August 2005.

The college prepares students for CSEC and CAPE. It also offers technical and vocational education in such areas as cosmetology, building and adult and continuing education. Although the range and levels of programmes are limited, this represents a significant step in local tertiary education.

Sir Arthur Lewis Community College, St Lucia

Morne Fortune in St Lucia, otherwise known as "the Morne", is an historic and picturesque, elevated site which hosted many battles over the centuries. With assistance from the British, the ruins at the Morne were restored to provide accommodation for educational institutions. The St Lucia Teachers College was established in 1963 in another location but was later transferred to the Morne in 1968. Morne Fortune Technical College was opened in 1970, and the St Lucia A' Level College was launched in 1974. From as early as 1971, thought was given to erecting shared facilities for these separate institutions. A science block was constructed.

In 1983, the Ministry of Education established a task force to explore integration of the facilities. Its report recommended the establishment of a comprehensive tertiary education institution, formed from the amalgamation of the Teachers, Technical and A' Level colleges. It should be a community college named in honour of a renowned scholar and educator, Sir Arthur Lewis, who later became St Lucia's first Nobel laureate (in economics).

The college was established by an act of Parliament (number 8, of 1985) which authorized it to offer education and training in agriculture, arts, science and general studies, health sciences, teacher education and educational administration, technical education and management studies. The entry requirements of the divisions of these institutions and their levels of operation were different and had to be carefully managed to conform with the various standards.

The college saw itself as a dynamic institution for the acceleration of human resource development through catering to the diverse educational needs and interests of a heterogeneous student body – many taking craft-level courses for job skills; some preparing for middle professional and middle management positions; others preparing for university transfer and yet others pursuing special interests, either on a part- or full-time basis.

Initially, the college delivered A-level courses and local certificates in teaching and technical studies. In the absence of formal quality assurance bodies, the college was careful to obtain validation through external examinations from recognized bodies and form links with the regional university. It validated its teacher education certification through its arrangement with the UWI Joint Board for Teacher Education.

In 1988, it entered into an agreement for the delivery of Year 1 of the UWI bachelor's degrees under a franchise arrangement with the university. The areas of study were arts and natural and social sciences. In 1992, the college was able to deliver the UWI full bachelor's degree in education, and the UWI Level 2 in social sciences in 1999. It also had articulation arrangements with the University of Technology in Jamaica and later established links with Munroe College in New York.

Associate degrees came later. The associate degree in agriculture was the first one developed by the college and recognized by the University of the West Indies for advanced placement. The University of the West Indies worked with the OECS colleges to develop an associate degree in education, which enabled completing the bachelor's degree in St Lucia in two additional years. In 2006, a two-plus-two arrangement was worked out between the University of the West Indies for the Sir Arthur Lewis Community College associate degree in hospitality and tourism. The design and development of this degree was facilitated by the Caribbean Tourism Organization, with technical assistance by Bernice Critchlow-Earle of the Barbados Community College.

The relationship between the Barbados Community College and Sir Arthur Lewis Community College dates back to the early 1980s, when the principal designate, Leighton Thomas, based in Barbados in the environs of the Barbados Community College, did formal and informal consultations with the college administration. The relationship with the University of the West Indies was even stronger, leading at times to discussion about becoming a University College of the University of the West Indies, a direction which never gained overwhelming or consistent traction. Consistent with its community college status, its value placed on accessibility, affordability, diversity in clientele, relevance of offerings and responsiveness to community needs are all reflected in the mandate and purpose of this College.

St Vincent and the Grenadines Community College

During the 1960s and 1970s, there was renewed interest and activity relating to the tertiary education sector, and St Vincent and the Grenadines was no exception. The St Vincent Teachers College was established in 1964, the Technical College in 1971, the School of Nursing in 1977 and the A' Level College in 1996.

The A' Level College was seen as the first division of the anticipated community college, and very early, the minister of education, John Horne, was exploring a franchise of programmes from the University of the West Indies. The four institutions existed separately, but with the understanding that they would become one. Policy documents were drafted to obtain funding, and prospective staff looked for opportunities to upgrade their qualifications.

In 1998, a master plan for the development of the college was drawn up by the Ministry of Education, Culture and Women's Affairs. Funds were procured for a building. In 2001, there was a consultation by Roosevelt Williams, whose recommendation of a task force was honoured. In 2002, a Ministry of Education Sector Development Plan was prepared. A director of the college, Veronica Marks, was appointed in 2004. The draft bill was completed, and the recently appointed management committee came up with twenty-five comprehensive goals.

The four divisions were officially amalgamated in 2005, and the college became operational under Joel Warrican. It offers associate degrees in teacher education, hospitality, psychology, paralegal studies, business, information technology, performing arts and media studies, fine arts design and cultural communication, and even cybersecurity. Articulation arrangements exist with the University of the West Indies; University of Technology, Jamaica; St George's University, Grenada; and Munroe College in New York. There are franchise arrangements with Jamaica Theological Seminary, the University of the West Indies and University of Technology, Jamaica.

It was a nine-year journey from establishment of the A-level college to the enactment of the community college, which was officially registered in 2013 in preparation for accreditation. Reportedly, the college has been approached by the University of the West Indies with an invitation to consider becoming a college of the university. In the meantime, though, it continues to be a comprehensive, multidisciplinary, multifunctional, innovative, flexible, responsive and accessible institution – consistent with its community college label.

T.A. Marryshow Community College, Grenada

In the 1960s and 1970s, Grenada undertook the establishment of a number of postsecondary and tertiary institutions. In 1988, the government decided to create the Grenada National College from the amalgamation of the Grenada Teachers College, the Grenada Technical and Vocational Institute, the Institute of Further Education, the National Institute of Handicraft, the Mirabeau Agricultural Training School, the Domestic Arts Institute, the Continuing Education Programme and the Pharmacy School.

The first principal, Dr James Pitt, and several others worked to integrate the college. In 1995, by an act of Parliament, the institution was renamed T.A. Marryshow Community College, in honour of one of Grenada's most outstanding citizens. Theophilus A. Marryshow was a self-educated journalist, author, political activist and orator who became known as the "Father of West Indies Federation". The act was amended in 1996 to support the delivery of certificates, diplomas and bachelor's degrees. In 2004, the college phased out many certificates and began to offer associate degrees.

Reflective of the community college values, the mission of T.A. Marryshow Community College stated that it would provide "accessible, quality, educational and training opportunities to help individuals achieve their personal and professional goals and to cater to the changing needs of the labour market in our developing society". Its flexibility is demonstrated in its provision of full- and part-time, night and weekend classes.

There are three campuses and three schools: Arts, Science and Professional Studies; Applied Arts and Teaching; and Continuing Education. The chief executive of the college is the president. Schools are led by deans and associate deans, and departments are supervised by chairs and programme coordinators. Students include high school graduates and working adults in business, industry and the public sector, as well as retirees.

T.A. Marryshow Community College has strong participatory links with the National Science and Technology Centre. It offers a wide range of associate degree programmes, as well as competency-based programmes in the School of Continuing Education. In its early stages of development, Barbados Community College staff offered technical and training assistance. T.A. Marryshow Community College has articulation arrangements with St George's University, the University of the West Indies and University of Technology, Jamaica. In 2011, it signed a memorandum of understanding to partner with the University College of the Caribbean, Jamaica, for the delivery of bachelor's degrees in business administration, information technology, human resource management, and marketing, as well as a master's in business administration. It is noteworthy that the college offers both the bachelor's degree and the executive master's degree.

Model 2 Colleges: Adaptation of Upper Levels of Sixth-Form Schools

Excelsior Community College, Jamaica

Excelsior Community College which is located in Kingston, evolved from a secondary school founded by the Reverend A. Wesley Powell and acquired by the Methodist Church in the Caribbean and the Americas in 1950. By the 1970s, the school had an enrolment of almost 2,000 and was comprehensive in its offerings, including the training of secondary school teachers in 1971. This blossomed into the evening division of the institution.

In 1974, led by Thomas Edward (Ted) Dwyer, the secretarial, teaching and nursing departments of the school were combined with the pre-university studies, inclusive of sixth-form offerings, to launch Excelsior Community College. There are reports of visits and consultations with the Barbados Community College on this venture.

In 1985, teacher training and nursing were discontinued but later restored. The college offers programmes in the humanities and education, business, computer science and engineering, pure and applied sciences, performing arts and hospitality and tourism. It offered its first bachelor's degree in computer science in 2001 and offers a bachelor of nursing degree, on franchise from the University of the West Indies.

Excelsior Community College has some parallels with the Barbados Community College, including its range of offerings, associate and bachelor's degrees, the offer of day and evening programmes and its multicampus operations.

Knox Community College, Jamaica

Knox Community College, located in Spalding, in the parish of Clarendon, with operational campuses in Cobbla, Mandeville and May Pen, receives grants from the Government of Jamaica, but it is an institution of the United Church of Jamaica and the Cayman Islands. Its similarity to Excelsior resides not only in its year of establishment, multicampus layout and affiliation with the church, but also in the way that they were formed. In this case, the secretarial studies, farm management and sixth-form classes were sectioned off from the rest of the high school to become the community college. Their offerings expanded into more than fifty programmes at all levels, including certificates, diplomas and associate and bachelor's degrees. There are three bachelor's programmes in education, business studies and environmental studies.

Model 3 Colleges: Amalgamation of Similar Sections of Multiple Institutions

Brown's Town Community College, Jamaica

In 1975, it was the idea of educator Glen Owen, the Ministry of Education and Archdeacon Trevor Thomas to consolidate A-level education and create one sixth-form institution in Brown's Town, Jamaica. Neighbouring high schools in the parish of St Ann – St Hilda's, York Castle, Westwood and Ferncourt – would be feeder schools. Burchell Whiteman became the first principal of Brown's Town Community College.

This college was host to the UWI Distance Education Centre and a broker for the University of Technology programmes. In time, it established two-plus-two arrangements with University of Technology for the bachelor's degree in food science management and franchised other bachelor's degrees in business administration and hospitality and tourism. In collaboration with the Council of Community Colleges of Jamaica, if offers bachelor's degrees in business studies and hospitality and tourism. It offers associate degrees in arts and sciences, as well as others in vocational areas. Professional degrees in business and accounting are also on offer.

Montego Bay Community College, Jamaica

Montego Bay Community College had secular origins. Having observed a community college in Puerto Rico in the 1950s, the governor general, His Excellency the Most Honourable Howard Cooke, was instrumental in advocating the merging of the sixth forms of three schools in Montego Bay: Cornwall College, Mount Alvernia and Montego Bay High School. In 1975, this merger resulted in the establishment of the community college initially as an A-level college, with each location offering a different specialty in arts, business or science.

The first principal was Olive Lewis, and the college was managed by a board of directors. Over time, the college expanded its offerings to include associate degrees in a wide cross section of disciplines. It also offers five bachelor's degrees in collaboration with the Council of Community Colleges of Jamaica in hospitality, entertainment and tourism; information systems and business studies. The college partners with many other tertiary institutions and private-sector organizations to achieve relevance and efficiency.

Model 4 Colleges: Creation of New Entities

Anguilla Community College

The Anguilla Community College had hospitality as its launching pad. It started in 2006 as the Community College Development Unit, targeting the training of workers in the hospitality industry. The project was headed by a three-member team, with Dawn Reid as director, and it was located in a two-room facility. The Community College Act was passed in 2009, and a new facility opened comprising office space, computer laboratories and five classrooms. There was also a café for food and beverage training, as well as for providing catering services.

The first principal, Delroy Louden, was appointed in 2010, and he was succeeded in 2018 by Carl Dawson. Interestingly, the first board of directors included Bernice Crichlow-Earle, director of the Hospitality Institute of the Barbados Community College.

The Anguilla Community College offers sixth-form technical courses, instruction for the Caribbean Secondary School Certificate and the Caribbean Advanced Proficiency Examinations and business and hospitality diplomas and degrees. It is an associate member of the Council of Community Colleges of Jamaica and has access to its degree offerings. In 2014, the college signed a memorandum of understanding with the University of the Virgin Islands to allow easy transfer of credits by its graduates, as well as for the earning of University of the Virgin Islands degrees on site. There are also special arrangements with the Barbados Community College for hospitality training.

H. Lavity Stoutt Community College, British Virgin Islands

The H. Lavity Stoutt Community College is named in honour of its first and longest-serving chief minister, who was also the first chairman of the school's board of directors. His passion for education is said to have been sharpened by his own limited formal education. He floated the idea of the college as early as 1982, before his government lost power, and revived the idea when he returned to power in 1986. The occurrence of Hurricane Hugo in 1989 delayed the plans for the college. However, the ground-breaking ceremony took place in September 1989 at Paraquita Bay. Theodore Provost was appointed president. The college was originally established in 1990 as the BVI Community College under the College Act.

In the interim, facilities were rented in the Omar Hodge building in Road Town, and classes were held with the assistance of mainly part-time teachers. A task force, chaired by Jennie Wheatley, identified training needs in the areas of business, hospitality and personal development. Consultants with community college experience were engaged, and the board appointed an executive committee to manage the daily operations of the college.

Eileene Parsons was appointed as project manager, and a focus committee was put in place to sensitize the community and get feedback on the feasibility of a college in that small community. After two and a half years, the well-appointed, three-storey building was completed, opened on 15 August 1993 and renamed H. Lavity Stoutt Community College with Charles Wheatley as president. The college extended its offerings to Virgin Gorda in 1996.

Over the years, the college has offered certificate, diploma and associate degree programmes in arts and sciences; business, tourism and information technology; technical and marine studies; and education and community programmes. In 2000, it launched a culinary programme with the New England Culinary Institute and added its own associate degree offering in 2012. To support its critical financial services sector, H. Lavity Stoutt Community College introduced the Financial Services Institute in 2002, offering a diploma in offshore finance and administration and international finance and administration. The college has also delivered the qualifications of the United Kingdom's Chartered Management Centre for supervisors and junior managers, up to the highest level of the executive diploma in management.

In 2006, the college offered training for Seafarers, a requirement for the certification of ferry boat operators between the British and US Virgin Islands. H. Lavity Stoutt Community College also offers an associate degree in marine studies. In that year, the Learning Resource Centre was opened as well, unlocking opportunities for research, computer access and expanded library services. In 2011, the college added a 416-seat auditorium which, among other ventures, has been used to accommodate the Performing Arts Series, instituted by former president Michael O' Neal.

The community college was accredited by the Middle States Commission on Higher Education in June 2015. It also has articulation and partnership arrangements with the University of the Virgin Islands, Wright State University, Missouri Southern State University and the State University of New York, as well as with the University of the West Indies.

Portmore Community College, Jamaica

Portmore is one of the largest urban areas in the parish of St Catherine, twenty-four kilometres from Jamaica's capital, Kingston. To open up Portmore for development and provide housing in proximity to Kingston, a causeway was built in the 1960s and a number of housing schemes developed in the area. In anticipation of the development boom, the Government of Jamaica established Portmore Community College, starting with only thirty-eight students and seven teachers. Nine years later, the college had grown to the extent that a new campus was necessary. It started with A-level offerings and one associate degree programme but soon expanded into the delivery of CAPE and bachelor's degree programmes, the latter in collaboration with the Council of Community Colleges of Jamaica. It also franchises certificate programmes from the University of the West Indies.

Turks and Caicos Islands Community College

In 1992, Chief Minister Charles Wesley Misick of Turks and Caicos publicly broached the idea of establishing a community college. Following this, the minister of education, the Honourable Arabella Smith, set up a task force which considered the matter and obtained community feedback. A feasibility study was conducted in 1993, and a follow-up was done by educator Jacob Bynoe. The president of the University of Technology of Jamaica, Alfred Sangster, was consulted, and he recommended the establishment of a college with its primary centre in Grand Turk and secondary campus in Provenciales.

The ordinance establishing the college came into effect in 1994, and the Turks and Caicos Islands Community College opened in the H.J. Robinson High School in Grand Turk and the Clement Howell High School in Provenciales. The college officially opened in 1995, and its first principal was Jacob Bynoe. Further consultations were had with experienced community college principals: Keva Bethell, College of the Bahamas; Norma Holder, Barbados Community College; and Leighton Thomas, Sir Arthur Lewis Community College. They advised that the Provenciales campus be dedicated to hospitality and other technical vocational studies.

The college's facilities at Lighthouse Road were completed in June 2001 and dedicated in 2002. The college offers certificates and associate degrees and has established links with a number of North American colleges. It is an associate member of the Council of Community Colleges of Jamaica and offers bachelor's degrees.

Model 5 Colleges: Expansion of Specialist Tertiary Institutions

Bahamas Baptist Community College

Bahamas Baptist Community College is a private institution with religious roots. It is the tertiary education arm of the Baptist Educational System in the Bahamas. It was established in 1995 under the leadership of the Reverend Dr C W Saunders, and Dr Baltron Bethell was its first president. Initially, its focus was on the Bahamas General Certificate of Secondary Education (BGCSE) and on adult and continuing education. It established a strong partnership with the College of the Bahamas, for which it offered a college prep programme. It has expanded its offerings to include over thirty associate of arts majors and numerous certificate programmes. Its mandate includes the delivery of distance education programmes in the island of Eleuthera. It has established articulation arrangements and memoranda of understanding with the College of the Bahamas, the University of the West Indies, University of Michigan, University of Detroit, Florida Memorial College, Florida Atlantic University, Northwestern College, Mars Hill College in North Carolina and Berkeley College, New York.

Bethlehem College, Jamaica

In 1861, there were several Moravian primary schools in Jamaica. Bethlehem Moravian College was founded in that year by the Jamaica Province of the Moravian Church as a training school for teachers of those schools. It was first located at Bethabra, Newport, in the parish of Manchester; started with three pupils and continued for some time as a female-only institution. It was devoted not only to intellectual, but also to spiritual development. For several years, the minister of the church was the principal of the college, and this proved to be a demanding job, leading to overwork and illness in some cases.

The college later moved to Malvern, in the parish of St Elizabeth, and takes pride in the contribution that it has made to the development of the Malvern community through employment and continuing education. It provides continuing schooling for high school repeaters, career advancement programmes, continuing education programmes and short courses for skills upgrades in areas such as cake baking and decorating and computer repair.

Since the 1960s, it has worked with the Joint Board for Teacher Education to provide teacher education and currently works under the auspices of the Council of Community Colleges of Jamaica. In 1994, it added associate degrees in business education and computing and hospitality. In 1997, in collaboration with the Consortium of Institutions for Tertiary Education, the college partnered with the University of Wisconsin–Whitewater to offer bachelor's degrees in primary and secondary education. It has forged links with institutions in Canada, United States and the United Kingdom.

In 2004, it became Bethlehem College, a multidisciplinary college reflecting the community college ethos.

Moneague College, Jamaica

Moneague Teachers' College, located in the parish of St Ann, was established in 1956 for the training of experienced teachers for the primary education system. It later ventured out into other areas for basic, all age and secondary teachers.

In 1987, it provided a one-year, in-service, professional upgrade certificate. Following the recommendations from a review in 1993, the college embarked on a journey to achieve multidisciplinary status. It retained teacher training as its main niche but expanded into business, commerce, tourism and hospitality and computer studies. It offers day and evening courses and short-term skills training for the workforce.

It works under the auspices of the Joint Board of Teacher Education and the Council of Community Colleges of Jamaica, and it embodies the values of the community college.

Table 5.4 presents five models for Caribbean community college development and lists the colleges under each model type.

Table 5.4. Five Models for Anglophone Caribbean Community College Development

Model 1: Amalgamation of Pre-existing Specialist Institutions	Model 2: Adaptation of Upper Levels of Sixth-Form Schools	Model 3: Amalgamation of Similar Sections of Multiple Institutions	Model 4: Creation of New Entities	Model 5: Expansion of Specialist Tertiary Institutions
Antigua State College	Excelsior Community College, Jamaica	Brown's Town Community College, Jamaica	Anguilla Community College	Bahamas Baptist Community College
Bermuda College	Knox Community College, Jamaica	Montego Bay Community College, Jamaica	Barbados Community College	Bethlehem College, Jamaica
Clarence Fitzroy Bryant College, St Kitts and Nevis			H. Lavity Stoutt Community College, British Virgin Islands	Moneague College, Jamaica
College of Agriculture, Science and Education, Jamaica				
College of the Bahamas				
College of Science, Technology and Applied Arts of Trinidad and Tobago				
Community College of the Cayman Islands			Portmore Community College, Jamaica	
Dominica State College				
Montserrat Community College			Turks and Caicos Islands Community College	
Sir Arthur Lewis Community College, St Lucia				
St Vincent and the Grenadines Community College				
T.A. Marryshow Community College, Grenada				

Tracking Community College Movement Regionally and Globally

Figure 5.2 tracks the movement of the community college across different Caribbean countries. Although linear establishment dates are presented, the real situation is a matrix development, with all these entities linked to the global network.

Figure 5.2. Tracking the community college movement in the anglophone Caribbean

Conclusion: Something Old, Something Borrowed, Something New

As mentioned at the outset, the establishment paths of the Caribbean community colleges vary, but the majority involve building on something old: twelve from the amalgamation of pre-existing specialist institutions; two from merging similar sections of multiple pre-existing institutions; two from adapting upper levels of pre-existing sixth-form schools and three from expanding pre-existing specialist institutions. Only five colleges were created as brand-new institutions. In all these cases, their establishment was propelled by the human resource needs of newly independent countries; expansion of secondary education output; adaptation of expanding educational systems; and accommodation of a new level or type of institution within an educational system. The Caribbean was experiencing a global wave of mass education and a local political and educational thrust for the development of these local community college counterparts.

In some instances, the church played a critical role, as in the case of Excelsior and Knox community colleges and Bethlehem College in Jamaica. Mention also must be made of the Bahamas Baptist Community College, which is unique not only because of its church connection, but also because it is private. All the others are government owned, aided or sponsored. Also uncommon is the case of the Community College of the Cayman Islands, which started with only part-time offerings.

The primary mission of the community colleges in the Caribbean has evolved over time. Many institutions started as A-level colleges with mainly a transfer function. To establish their credibility, in their early years, they safeguarded their entry requirements at the expense of open admission, but some provided bridging courses and alternative entry requirements. The initial incorporation of technical/vocational institutions, or the later assimilation of them, provided the opportunity for workforce training. As the institutions established themselves, they were able to put a greater emphasis on adult and continuing education, thus fulfilling their commitment to community development and lifelong learning while improving their financial viability.

Initially, quality assurance was achieved by many institutions through the endorsement and validation of their programmes by established universities. Hence, the Teacher Education programmes were certified by the Joint Board of Teacher Education, led by the University of the West Indies. In addition, Antigua State College, Sir Arthur Lewis Community College and Clarence Fitzroy Bryant College negotiated franchise arrangements with the University of the West Indies, and over time, almost all community colleges established articulation arrangements with the University of the West Indies. The H. Lavity Stoutt Community College benefited from arrangements with the neighbouring University of the Virgin Islands, but also with universities on the mainland United States. Outreach to and partnerships with the United States, Canada and the United Kingdom became common practice for community colleges in the region.

Networking within the Association of Caribbean Tertiary Institutions, American Community College Association and the Canadian Association of Community Colleges was critical to community college development. The umbrella of the Council of Community Colleges of Jamaica provided a coordinating body for joint action, resulting in improved efficiency and enhanced quality for the small colleges in Jamaica, as well as on other islands.

Of note is the fact that the community colleges in the Caribbean emerged in the 1960s, 1970s and 1980s under the umbrella of the various countries' ministries of education, which, in the absence of national accreditation bodies, oversaw standards. As mentioned earlier, quality assurance for associate degrees and other college qualifications was also initially achieved through the legitimization offered by the validation and acceptance of college qualifications by reputable universities (Roberts 2003a). This is in contrast to the US environment, where since the late nineteenth century, accreditation in higher education involved a peer review process, coordinated by accreditation commissions and member institutions.

An examination of the steps which were taken specifically in the southern states of the United States to articulate and protect standards for junior colleges may provide important insights into accreditation generally in the United States. It is reported that in 1895, the Association of Colleges and Secondary Schools of the Southern States oversaw the development of degree-granting institutions by coordinating their activities, elevating their standards of practice, promoting uniformity of entrance requirements and setting boundaries that would define these institutions. By 1915, that association passed a bylaw outlining requirements for the recognition of junior colleges (Day and Mellinger 1973).

Standards for junior colleges had been adopted in 1921 by the American Association of Junior Colleges, and in 1924 by the National Committee on College Standards under the auspices of the American Council on Education. This comprehensive range of standards encompassed entrance requirements, requirements for graduation, degrees, the number of college departments, training of faculty, the number of classroom hours for teachers, financial resources, a library, laboratories, separation of college and preparatory classes, the ratio of college students to the whole student body, a general statement concerning equipment, extracurricular activities, inspection and filing an application triennially (Day and Mellinger 1973).

The expansion of the junior college curriculum, diversification of its programmes and duration of its offerings made it necessary to revise the accreditation standards and processes and build in greater flexibility in 1950. A self-study programme with follow-up by a visiting committee was approved and introduced in 1960.

Since the 1950s, community college quality assurance in the United States has been achieved mainly from a regional peer review system which benefits from federal oversight. In that setting, national accreditation bodies have less oversight, but they do accredit institutions and programmes across the country and internationally.

Since the 1970s, there has been some convergence of the US and Caribbean systems. With the emergence of national accreditation systems in the Caribbean, Ministries of Education play only an indirect quality assurance role through the regulation and monitoring of their national accreditation bodies. Regional (Caribbean-wide) accreditation bodies in the Caribbean play a limited role in relation to some professional programmes, including nursing, engineering, law and medical sciences (Roberts 2003a).

Through creativity and effort, the early two-year colleges in the Caribbean developed from their humble beginnings beyond the targets and limits which were set for them. Gradually, many extended their offerings to include franchised, joint and eventually their own bachelor's degrees. The College of the Bahamas, in a country where there was no national university, gradually upgraded its resources and capacity to successfully transition to university status; and the Cayman Islands Community College also underwent the metamorphosis to a university college.

As increasing numbers of community colleges offer the baccalaureate degree and partner in offering post-baccalaureate and other graduate qualifications, some are seeking to restructure and upgrade as well as change their mission and status. However, for small islands with small populations, which are dependent on public funding in a competitive environment and a global world, for many, this transition has remained an aspiration. The community college movement in the region began with the establishment of the first college in 1968 and continued until the establishment of Anguilla Community College in 2009. In their emergence, they have thought globally, networked regionally and acted locally – benefiting from global educational borrowing, but customizing their forms and functions, based on local realities.

Note: The preceding discussion of the Caribbean Community College did not include the Barbados Community College. The next chapters take an in-depth look at its establishment and evolution from its inception in 1968 to its golden anniversary in 2018.

Figure 5.3. Montego Bay Community College, Jamaica

Figure 5.4. Excelsior Community College, Jamaica

Figure 5.5. Portmore Community College, Jamaica

Figure 5.6. Moneague College, Jamaica

Figure 5.7. University College of the Cayman Islands

Figure 5.8. Anguilla Community College

Figure 5.9. H. Lavity Stoutt Community College, British Virgin Islands

Figure 5.10. Sir Arthur Lewis Community College, St Lucia

Figure 5.11. Dominica State College

Figure 5.12. St Vincent and the Grenadines Community College

6.

The Barbados Community College
The Establishment Year, 1968

In 1968, some sixty-eight years after the first junior college was established in the United States, eighteen years after one was established in Puerto Rico, and only a few years after the community college became popular in the United States, the idea of establishing a community college could be considered quite unusual – even premature – in the English-speaking Caribbean. However, in the newly independent, traditional Barbadian context, it would have to be regarded as no less than revolutionary. And yet, in this unlikely place and ahead of its time, amid strong political opposition and significant industrial unrest, the idea managed to take root. In 1969, the Barbados Community College became a reality and began admitting students.

Erskine Sandiford has admitted that before 1968, he had never visited a community college. He explained further that before he went into government, he was very much concerned with the development of education in Barbados and was looking carefully at the problems involved. He thought that the college would be a solution to those problems. He had no research studies done. Some may say that he had a dream, and he may say that he had a vision. In any event, he seemed pretty certain that he wanted the Barbados Community College to be neither a hybrid nor a transplant, and he took some time to explain what he wanted it to be and do.

Using the 20/20 vision of hindsight, one may conclude that the Barbados Community College was a homegrown adaptation – a plant germinating from a seed in the mind of a reflective educator, a seed that may have been dispersed later throughout the Caribbean from a plant which has successfully germinated and blossomed across the seas for over fifty years. Contemporary colleagues in the Ministry of Education attest to the founder's struggle with the challenges of a vibrant and growing primary education sector; an expanding secondary education sector, itself energized by free secondary education; and an increasing demand for tertiary education provision. For Erskine Sandiford, the challenges were real, the risks enormous and the opportunities compelling. He was fortunate to be in the right places at the right times to articulate his ideas and enable their implementation; but it was never without opposition and resistance.

Controversial Beginnings – Political

Perhaps the first formal mention of this concept was in the 1966 manifesto of the Democratic Labour Party, which alluded to a "Junior College to provide specialist education at sixth form level for suitably qualified pupils of all schools". At that time, the pillars of the economy continued to be agriculture (mainly sugar cane), tourism and industry. Each had its challenges and opportunities. The newly independent country of Barbados required more trained human resources to provide top and middle managers, as well as skilled workers to support growth in those sectors. It was recognized that the education system was vital to meeting these pressing needs and required reorganization, if not transformation, so it could respond urgently to them.

Historically, Barbados has always placed a high value on education, hosting the oldest tertiary education institution in the region, Codrington College, first established in 1745 as a school and later as a college in 1829. Barbados's grammar schools date back as early as the seventeenth century (Combermere School established in 1695; Harrison College in 1733; the Lodge School in 1745; and Queens College for Girls in 1883). During the 1960s, the sector was being expanded to include comprehensive schools such as West St Joseph, St George Secondary, Garrison Secondary and St Lucy Secondary. (Except for St George Secondary, all of these have been renamed.) At that time, the number of public secondary schools was twenty-four, but only four had sixth forms. With greater access to free secondary education but with a fixed number of places available in these four sixth-form schools, there was a bottleneck in the system concerning advanced studies. Limited postsecondary educational opportunities were also available at the UWI Extramural Department, but that too was inadequate.

At the opening ceremony of the Barbados Community College in 1969, the Honourable Lloyd Erskine Sandiford, minister of education, pointed to the rapid developments in the fields of banking, manufacturing, business and commerce, tourism, transportation and construction, as well as to the shared view that urgent and sustained training was required to support these developments. What was unsettled, however, was the appropriate and preferred training option. He proceeded to highlight four answers to this question.

The first was increasing the number of places at the four sixth-form schools, but he dismissed that as merely maintaining the status quo. The second was the introduction of sixth forms in other schools. However, these had resource limitations, especially human resources to cover the wide range of disciplines needed. The third was to retain the four sixth-form schools, with their academic focus, and make provisions in another institution specifically for technical and vocational training. However, mindful of the perceived status difference between the academic and the technical institutions, he thought that this approach would perpetuate that dichotomy and therefore be inimical to the development of an integrated and harmonious society. The fourth option being pursued was that of the coexistence of sixth-form schools alongside the establishment of community colleges. Sandiford (1969) argued that this option would do all of the following:

- Provide terminal education for secondary school graduates to groom them for the world of work
- Prepare secondary school graduates for higher education at colleges and universities
- Meet the needs of adults and youth for continuing education

This launch had been preceded by stormy discussion and widespread dissent by the members of the opposition Barbados Labour Party in Parliament. The disagreement was about the education minister's real intentions, the timing of the proposal and its stated priorities (Barbados 1968, 1836–40).

The announcement of the college also had been met with outrage from the teachers' union, the Association of Assistant Teachers in Secondary Schools, which was concerned about equity in salaries across the system ("Teachers Body Raps Statutory Board Role", *Advocate News*, 14 August 1968). It was also viewed with scepticism by some members of the public. However, the initiative had been lauded by members of the governing Democratic Labour Party and by individuals from the public whose educational needs appeared to have been considered and were being addressed ("Education Stands at Crossroads", *Advocate News*, 18 August 1968).

It was interesting to note that much forethought and planning went into this innovation. There had been a broad-based advisory committee on the establishment of the Barbados Community College, including representatives of the University of the West Indies, the Association of Headmasters and Headmistresses, the Association of Assistant Teachers in Secondary Schools, the Independent Schools Association, the Comprehensive Schools, the Barbados Workers Union, the Chamber of Commerce, and the Barbados Manufacturers Association. The chairman was Ralph Johnson, chief education officer. These key stakeholders undoubtedly were invited to bring differing perspectives from the schools, university, workers and employers. There was also a planning committee in the Ministry of Education which is said to have spent over two years preparing a comprehensive cabinet paper. Colin Kirton, an education officer who was involved with the planning, also became the interim principal to get the administration of the college initiated (interview with Colin Kirton, December 2016).

Discussions in Cabinet Leading to the BCC Act of Parliament – Act 1968-23

Many of us, at a distance, will admit to finding debates in the British Parliament colourful, entertaining, often hard hitting and even harsh. However, closer to home, where individuals are known to us, the discourse may seem more unsettling and much less funny. Sometimes it requires careful analysis and a patient look beyond the apparent acrimony and beneath the humour to find the substance of the disagreement and to arrive at the key points of divergence. The parliamentary debate in Barbados in July 1968 was a good example.

The bill was introduced by the Honourable James Cameron Tudor. He highlighted the immediate demand by some two hundred qualified students who could not find places in the four sixth-form schools. He looked at the option of creating more sixth-form schools but thought that ill-advised. He proposed an institution to accommodate about 350 students – the current 200 and an additional 150 persons who were already out of school. As if in anticipation of the arguments to follow, he pointed to the matter of the teachers' union. He argued that the minister of education was entitled to the authority of his position and pleaded for quick action to meet these immediate needs instead of doing a time-consuming, comprehensive enquiry into the entire education system (Barbados 1968, 1836–40).

The Honourable Bernard St John, in his rebuttal, argued against what he saw as a move to abolish sixth-form schools. First, he challenged the government: "Come clean; come openly; if you feel that it is in the best interest of education in Barbados that there be no Sixth Form education in these schools, come out and say so. Argue it out on that basis." Second, he posited that it would be better to utilize the facilities of the Evening Institute and Extramural Department of the University of the West Indies for academic training. Third, he suggested that providing an improved primary school system and expanding technical and vocational education (secretarial, for example) were of higher priority than providing academic education. Fourth, he expressed suspicions about the power which would reside in the minister of education, stating that although he was not afraid to give ministers power, he did object to the minister having the power to change the college's scheme of governance and the teachers' conditions of service without parliamentary approval. Fifth, he alluded to the inequities in salary – staff at the college would earn higher salaries. He stated: "They can only get them away by drawing them away from our existing schools. They are going to draw them away – the staff first, and then the pupils will follow the staff. That is the intention" (Barbados 1968, 1840–42).

The Honourable Louis Lynch echoed many of the objections advanced by St John, pointing out that "what is needed in our small community is a thorough investigation of our educational system, and not the addition of a small appendage . . . 9,000 of the children who failed the exams would not be able to avail themselves of Community College education". He felt that a better approach would be to address the problem in the sixth-form schools. He also prioritized expanding the Trades Training Centre over spending money on a community college. He too was concerned about the power of the minister, especially in relation to the dismissal of the principal (Barbados 1968, 1843).

The Honourable Burton Hinds, junior member for the parish of St Peter, underscored the need to review the entire education programme instead of proceeding piecemeal, in light of the financial constraints, evidenced by the half-day schedule imposed on some schools. He was concerned about the power of the minister in setting entry qualifications, as well as the unnecessary duplication of courses offered by sixth-form schools. He also feared that because the college would be drawing on students who could not get into the sixth-form schools, it would itself become an inferior institution (Barbados 1968, 1846–50).

Sir Grantley Adams, leader of the opposition, was one of the harshest critics; he characterized the bill as dishonest in its entirety. He warned that Sandiford intended to become the principal, and he strongly advocated that the debate on the principle of the college should be separate from the discussion of financing. He commented that "only a fool would vote for that bill. . . . Mussolini could not act worse than the Prime Minister of this island. Sir, this is totalitarianism." He described the proponent of the idea as a liar and a black sheep, and labelled the idea itself as hypocrisy, double-dealing and squeezing people. He noted that the bill would pass, based on the majority party's dominance, but he warned that it would be an issue in the next election. He emphasized that "it was sheer hypocrisy to try to pretend that this [bill] had anything to do with abolishing Sixth Forms when all of his [leader of the House] arguments led to that. . . . We all know that the Minister wanted to start a Sixth Form College. . . . We all know that the PM was opposed to that idea and this is a compromise – not just a Compromise Bill but a compromise of conscience" (Barbados 1968, 1867–68).

The Honourable Lionel Craigg supported the position of the previous opposition speakers. He remarked, "I am confident that this Community College will be a drain on the other secondary schools in this country" (Barbados 1968, 1878).

Jameson B. Springer, on the other hand, supported the bill. Lauding the free education system in Barbados, he stated: "I do not worry about cost; cost of education to me has never been a problem. A Government has to be able to afford education, and the price could never be too high. . . . If a Community College means meeting the vacuum and creating the atmosphere in which 300 school leavers who walk down Broad Street for eighteen months before either the Law picks them up or they go to Canada and do some menial work – if the establishment of the Community College means destroying the Sixth Form Schools at those schools and finding employment for those people to keep them in school, then I say 'Destroy the Sixth Forms'." Regarding power, he added: "If a politician has an idea – and it is said to be Sandiford's idea – the power should be concentrated in him" (Barbados 1968, 1880–81).

The vote was taken. It was carried, and the bill was read a second time and put into committee. Each clause was voted on, and the bill, as amended, was passed. Some members of the public were unhappy, as indicated in this anonymous letter to the editor in the *Advocate* newspaper: "The indecent haste with which this exercise has been carried out must now give plausibility to the fairly common belief that the desire was more to destroy the sixth form schools than to establish a meaningful and well-planned institution catering to the needs of the country" ("Opening of New College Put Back", *Advocate News*, 27 September 1968). On 29 July 1968, the act of Parliament was passed, establishing the Barbados Community College.

This ambivalence about competition with the sixth-form schools was evident among government ministers, teachers and the general public. It is interesting that, supported by an economic argument, Principal Clyde Best himself openly asserted that sixth-form education should be removed from the schools and be absorbed by the college. When the college opened its doors, he proposed, "We have more modern laboratories and a great variety and more modern equipment because there is only one location which the government must provide for". He also pointed to the value of part- and full-time study. It is noteworthy that this thread of ambivalence may have waned in intensity, but has been strong enough to survive for fifty years.

Educational: Teachers' Union Concerns

The bill was passed in July 1968. Conditions of service were drawn up and recruitment of teachers started shortly afterwards. Although the Association of Assistant Teachers of Secondary Schools was represented on the Advisory Committee, once the recruitment of community college teachers began from among the ranks and the conditions of employment were being discussed, the union began to express deep concerns. These included luring teachers away from the sixth-form schools and perhaps more importantly, the inequity which was being created by the offer of higher salaries to community college teachers. A senior teacher in a sixth-form school was paid a maximum of $690 per month, and a new teacher at the Barbados Community College was to be paid a maximum of $710 per month; the salary for an assistant tutor at Barbados Community College began at $580 per month, as opposed to $360 per month for the sixth-form school ("Teachers Upset about Their Pay", *Advocate News,* 23 September 1968).

The union was dissatisfied with the inequity which they saw. The government argued that community college teachers would have to be compensated for working both day and evening. The union saw this requirement as merely balancing the wider scope of the work in sixth-form schools. Negotiations broke down between the union and the government, and the teachers went on strike, demanding equitable pay for the teachers in all secondary schools and community college. The strike started in November 1968, and other unions were considering supporting the action of the Association of Assistant Teachers. Senator Nigel Barrow supported the strike, arguing that the teacher in a secondary school who taught at different levels and carried a greater workload also deserved better pay ("Teachers Upset about Their Pay").

The Association of Assistant Teachers of Secondary Schools announced the settlement of the strike on 28 December. The government resolution, effective January 1969, increased secondary school teachers' salary and conceded that salaries should be based on experience and qualifications. The gap between the assistant tutor at the college and secondary school teachers was reduced from $220 per month to only $60 per month. All pension rights were preserved, and teachers were paid 50 per cent of their salaries for the period of the strike. Initially, the majority of teachers came from the Combermere School. The governing bodies of this and other sixth-form schools appeared to have been sympathetic to the union, perhaps in consideration of their own loss of teachers and the negative impact that could have on students preparing for A-level examinations in just a few months.

Conclusion

After much opposition by the government, the teachers' union and even the public, the act was passed, the institution established and the stage set for the launch of a new institution in Barbados, Barbados Community College. The words "Community College" in the name signalled links with and some may say "borrowing from" the United States. In addition, although this was a new institution, it was temporarily housed in old buildings – the refurbished Sherbourne House and the formerly repurposed harbour site vacated by the University of the West Indies. It was, therefore, a product of the old, the borrowed and the new.

Figure 6.1. Eric Armstrong, first chair of the Barbados Community College, 1969–1971

Figure 6.2. Sir Keith Hunte, chair, 1971–1977

Figure 6.3. Dr Leonard Shorey, chair, 1977–1986

Figure 6.4. Colin Kirton, chair, 1986–1995

Figure 6.5. Professor Trevor Hassell, chair, 1995–2000

Figure 6.6. Lolita Applewaite, chair, 2000–2003

Figure 6.7. Dr Asquith Thompson, chair, 2003–2006

Figure 6.8. Desmond Critchlow, chair, 2006–2008

Figure 6.9. Bertram Carter, chair, 2008–2011

Figure 6.10. Stephen Broome, chair, 2011–2018

7.

The Establishment Years under Clyde Best, 1969–1976

Looked at closely, the evolution of many colleges would represent a phase of initiation where the idea is broached and incubated; a phase of actual establishment, both legally and physically; an implementation phase of earning credibility and gaining legitimization; a stage of expansion and consolidation; and a period of strategic realignment, followed by further growth and development and ensuing strategic realignment over time. In this and the remaining chapters in this book, the information presented is gleaned from the relevant Barbados Community College annual reports, unless otherwise stated.

We have already discussed the incubation of the idea of the college over a five-year period, as well as its legal establishment in the form of the Education Act. The next seven years of the Barbados Community College, 1969–1976, show evidence of the following phases:

- The physical establishment of the college
- Earning the credibility of and legitimization by a sceptical society over a seven-year journey
- Infrastructural development at the Eyrie campus (the ground-breaking of which took place in 1970)
- The establishment of three initial divisions (Liberal Arts, Science and Commerce) and three additional divisions (Technology, 1973, and Fine Arts and Health Sciences, 1974); expansion into new disciplines for increasing numbers and a growing diversity of students pursuing academic, vocational and continuing education, as well as venturing into targeted community development
- Growing academic strength and validation through improved performance in external examinations, as well as the establishment and implementation of new policies, processes and practices
- The acquisition of a growing pool of more qualified staff and their motivation and renewal through professional development
- The first articulation agreement with Penn State University, in 1977
- Self-evaluation, external reports of relevance and strategic realignment

Physical Establishment, 1969–1972

The years 1969–1972 represent a period of planning for a permanent home and providing varying programmes for a growing student body. It is a little-known fact that in 1968, the Barbados Community College had an interim principal, the senior education officer Colin Kirton, who was appointed to carry out the legal establishment functions, including the appointment of the first official principal, Clyde Best (popularly known as Charlie Best). He too had been an education officer in the Ministry of Education, having taught at three primary and two secondary schools and having been a head teacher at one of these schools. He had also recently returned from serving as the head of the education administration in the Turks and Caicos Islands. This experience in education and educational administration was undoubtedly valuable, but it did not prepare him specifically for his new assignment.

Shortly after his appointment, Best visited eleven community colleges in the United States, funded by a fellowship. He regarded the Barbados Community College as a unique institution where incoming staff had the opportunity and responsibility to design timetables for students from age sixteen to sixty, in optional day and night classes, for fifty-two weeks of the year. Best spoke about the challenge of acquiring sophisticated equipment and specialist supplies, and striving to provide purpose-built and adequate accommodations, albeit initially in temporary facilities at Sherbourne and the Harbour (Barbados Community College Annual Report 1969).

There was also the challenge of living with initial opposition. To support this, he recounted that an unsuccessful contender for the post of principal wrote to him (quoting from Titus Lucretius Carus, c. 99 BC–55 BC from *De Rerum Natura*), "Pleasant it is when the winds are troubling the waters in a mighty sea, to witness from the land another man's great toil; not because it is a delight to behold anyone's tribulation, but because it is sweet to see from what evils you yourself are free."

Eric Armstrong was the first chairman of the nine-member board of management of the Barbados Community College. The official opening of the college took place on 5 January 1969, by Lady Scott, wife of Governor General Sir Winston Scott. The feature address was given by the minister of education (and senator), the Honourable Erskine Sandiford.

The college opened in old facilities at two locations four miles apart, in the parish of St Michael – Sherbourne and Deep Water Harbour. In the Sherbourne house, there were eleven lecture rooms, a library with about two thousand volumes of books, the principal's office, an office for the registrar/bursar, a staff common room, a supervisor's office, a room for groundsmen and maids and a set of lavatory and toilet facilities. Two of the lecture rooms were specially equipped: one for geography and the other with machines for commerce.

At the Harbour site, which had been recently vacated by the University of the West Indies, there were two laboratories with preparation rooms, one lecture room, two small rooms for administrative staff and two sets of lavatory and toilet facilities. Timetabling was done in a way that reduced the need for commuting between the two locations on a daily basis. Nigel Bradshaw remembers timetabling mathematics in the morning at Sherbourne so that students could commute to the Harbour site in the afternoon for science laboratories.

There was a roll of 300 students in three divisions: 55 full-time and 245 part-time evening students. There was an academic staff establishment of twenty two, including one principal, two senior tutors, six tutors and thirteen assistant tutors. However, at the outset, only nineteen of these teaching posts were filled, distributed among the three divisions: Liberal Arts, Science and Commerce. The teachers, eleven men and eight women, were all timetabled to carry a teaching workload of twenty hours a week. Seven had master's degrees, and twelve had bachelor's degrees; some had specialist teaching qualifications, but all had at least some teaching experience.

There were Arthur Sealy (MA), who taught Latin; C. William Wickham (MA), who taught Spanish; and Adele Lynch (BA) and Robert Belgrave (MA), both of whom were qualified to teach French. In science, there were Alvin Barnett (BSc), whose specialty was physics; Norma J Holder (MA), for mathematics and chemistry; Edgar Manifold (BSc), qualified in chemistry and zoology; Nigel Bradshaw (BSc), specializing in mathematics; and Marilyn Light (MSc), in biology and botany. Grace Cohen (MA), Lucene Bishop (BA) and Anne Hewitt (BA) taught English and Use of English courses. S Ebisemiju (MSc) and Edward King (BA) were geographers; Calvin Yard (BA and DipEd) was a teacher of history and Marcina Haynes (BA) and Andrew Bend (BA) taught history and civics. Hubert Bynoe (BA) was a teacher of economics and statistics.

Students were prepared in specific subjects for external examinations at Cambridge Advanced Level, London Chamber of Commerce (LCC) Associated Examination Board Advanced Higher Stage and for professional examinations set by the Chartered Institute of Secretaries and Association of the Institute of Bankers (AIB). Students were also prepared for internally examined general courses: Civics, Use of English, and Man and the World of Science. Special sessions were organized to address such areas as social welfare and physical well-being, drama and musical appreciation.

To make their studies more relevant, geography students took field trips to local factories and the McGill Weather Station; history students toured

St Vincent and the Grenadines, and civics students visited such locations as the Grazettes Industrial Park and the Legislative Assembly. Student discipline was good: attendance was excellent among day students, averaging about 86 per cent; and good in the case of evening students, reaching an average of 76 per cent.

By the end of the first period, January–August 1969, it was recognized that there was a need for a deputy principal, particularly to help with the part-time programming and evening students. Full-time staff members were needed for Spanish, and part-time staff for a number of courses, including Law, Accounting, Typing, Shorthand, Office Procedures, and Operating of Business Machines. Overall, accommodation was very limited and became increasingly so as the student body grew.

The complement of administrative staff was seven, comprising the registrar/bursar, Ambrose Stoute; stenographers Juel King and Heather Hood; supervisor B. Walcott; clerical officer O. Jessamy and library assistants David Trotman and M. Harewood. The number of part-time teaching staff had grown by five, and John A. Clarke was newly employed as a full-time physics teacher.

Community relationships were strengthened through guest lectures from members of the community and the mounting of fashion shows, concerts and other cultural collaborative activities by the college, including seminars, institutes and conferences, as well as through participation of students on radio and television shows. Student activities extended beyond Barbados to include study tours to Martinique by students studying French. As part of the learning activities in the general courses, there was an essay competition in the areas of Use of English, Social Anthropology, Civics, Caribbean History and World of Science. The winners of the first competition were R.A. Skeete, first prize; L.J. Springer, second; and Rosemary Alleyne, third.

There were active proposals and plans for establishing, at the permanent site at Eyrie, accommodation for the three operational divisions (commerce, liberal arts and science), as well as for the future divisions of technology, fine arts and agriculture. Together, these divisions would offer advanced training at the technical, middle management and pre-university levels to a previously underserved student population. The student body was to be different, having no age limit but the stipulated academic qualifications.

On 23 November 1970, the ground-breaking ceremony for the Eyrie campus took place, moving closer to the establishment of a permanent site at Eyrie, Howells Cross Roads, to house the divisions of Technology, Science, Liberal Arts and Commerce and the administrative buildings. In 1970, Aurea Kirton, the Springer Memorial Principal, won the competition to design the college's crest and motto.

During the first year, a theatre workshop was put on by regional experts under the auspices of the Extramural Department of the University of the West Indies for eighty participants. The new science tutor widened the student experience by conducting School of Yoga activities on Saturday afternoons. Students ventured into playing cricket at Blenheim and taking part in table tennis, drafts and bridge. Staff worked with the Students Council to organize the Photography Club, Inter-School Christian Fellowship, the Geography Society and Cercle Français. On 5 January 1971, the college held its first graduation ceremony, and based on performance in the A-level examinations, ten of its first graduates transferred to university (six of them to the University of the West Indies).

The technology block was completed and officially opened on 4 April 1973 by Sandiford, who had seen the realization of a vision which he shared in his public address. The facility included one large workshop each for mechanical engineering and building and civil engineering, one medium-sized workshop for electrical engineering, an engineering laboratory, three drawing offices, six lecture rooms, changing rooms and offices.

There was a spirit of optimism as the college looked forward to the liberal arts three-storey block, which would also house the Division of Commerce. In addition, they were looking forward to the two-storey administration block and the impressive L-shaped science block, which would be made up of fifteen lecture rooms, one large and one small lecture theatre and six laboratories: two each for biology, chemistry and physics. Staff talked about the planned student centre, with commons, games room and staff facilities including a conference room and a sick bay. Everyone looked forward to having an adequate library. However, the divisions of fine arts and agriculture were still a somewhat distant dream.

During the academic year 1972–1973, the principal was pleased about the opportunities that were being provided by the college for the society. He sought at that stage to articulate not only its purpose in relation to the individual student, but also its intention to continue on an expansion path.

Expansion Phase, 1973–1976

Division of Technology

In 1973, The Division of Technology had acquired not only new buildings, but also eleven full-time staff members. Only some positions were filled, including that of the senior tutor, Otho St Hill; two overseas tutors, a UK technical assistant, Dr A. Kovaleik, attached through Canadian University Services Overseas, and a West German technical assistant, K. Weber; and three full-time local instructors. There were also thirteen part-time instructors initially. Ninety-three students were being prepared for the City and Guilds of London Institute ordinary technician diplomas in mechanical and electrical engineering and in building and civil engineering.

A technical academic board was established for the division, setting a precedent which others would follow, and a partnership with government and industry had begun. The Barbados Land Surveyors' Board and the Ministry of Lands accepted a proposal for a land-surveying programme to commence in January 1974. This would lead to the Barbados Land Surveyors' Licence. Cooperation was also secured from the Ministry of Communications and Works to organize training for technicians of the Waterworks Division within the framework of the World Health Organization (WHO) standards.

The college received equipment under the UK Technical Assistance Project and government-purchased supplies to the tune of Bds$78,990. The division acquired a 250T concrete compression testing machine for the Civil Engineering programme, and this would prove very useful for partnering with industry. The Technical Teachers Certificate programme was designed for secondary teachers, using facilities and teachers from the Division of Science in the areas of mathematics, physics and chemistry. The technical teacher training was launched for thirteen industrial arts teachers, and short courses were offered to the staff of the Engineering sections of government departments.

As part of establishing the credibility of the institution, the programmes were rigorous and included not only technical subjects, but also a fair amount of general education and scientific content. The programmes attracted a range of students, some of whom had strong technical, but weak language and science background, and included some that had come through the Craft programme from Samuel Jackman Prescod Polytechnic (SJPP).

To assist students with qualification deficits, the division added bridging courses in mathematics and physics for those who had not successfully completed these subjects at the General Certificate of Education (GCE) O level. In spite of this effort, the failure rates were high in these science subjects. On the other hand, the division was encouraged by the teaching support given by the Barbados Association of Professional Engineers, Barbados Society of Architects and the Barbados Society of Land Surveyors.

At the outset, the equipment ranged from adequate in a few areas, deficient in most, poor in some and nonexistent in others. However, the staff were creative. They secured the SJPP machine shop for some classes. The polytechnic also loaned foot-operated metal shears. Even the St George Secondary School was pressed to lend a power saw to the college.

In 1975, the first five students took the final internal examinations of the college for mechanical and technical engineering, and all were successful. Frederick Adamson was recommended for a National Development Scholarship to Penn State University. Forty students were being prepared to write the next examination. The college was concerned about quality and legitimacy and was pleased that a team of engineers from Penn State University visited to evaluate the quality of training. They were impressed and recommended that graduates of the programme be admitted to the third year at Penn State, to complete the bachelor's degree in two years. This was the college's first articulation arrangement, which was established in July 1975.

Division of Commerce

The Division of Commerce, headed by Henry Moe, started with accounting, commerce, banking, economics, shorthand, secretarial practice, statistics and typing. In 1972, The Division of Commerce was the largest division, with 346 students enrolled in A-level studies, as well as in professional studies including secretarial science. Final-year student secretaries were getting practice in business houses, and thought was being given by the division to training bilingual secretaries and expanding into hotel management training.

In 1973, in the arena of secretarial studies, a workweek experience was introduced that saw students placed at the Barbados Telephone Company, DaCosta and Musson, Barclays Bank International, Plantations Ltd, Bank of America and Barbados Light and Power Company. In 1974, this continued to be the largest division, and it appeared to have been affecting the country's development in business as the demand for places continued to grow. It was sobering that more than fifty qualified applicants were refused admission because of accommodation constraints.

As Henry Moe went on study leave, Hubert Bynoe acted as senior tutor. The division saw improvement in the performance of the A-level students in economics – twenty-five entered, thirteen earned grade A's and eleven O-level passes – 53 per cent success. Of twenty-five evening students, only three were successful. In accounting, of thirty-one who sat, seven gained A-level certificates and twelve gained O levels.

Division of Liberal Arts

Meanwhile, the Division of Liberal Arts, with its 276 students, was contemplating a Language Centre and expanding the general education core offerings beyond civics and English for communication. The division featured highly in the 1973 Barbados Arts Festival in music, dance and literary work. The Drama Group staged an original play, *The Night Before,* showcasing the talent of students Nancy Ferguson, Elizabeth Clarke and Lionel Sealy, the latter two not only acting in but also directing the play, which was performed at Combermere School on 15 February. Elizabeth Clarke, who was also head of the Writers' Club, staged public readings of her poetry.

In 1973, there were 96 day students and 115 evening students, totalling 221; 68 dropped out that year: 20 from the day and 48 from the evening group. Adele Lynch returned from studying in Jamaica to a department with a vibrant French option, which was favoured by the students over Spanish. The evidence was that while 28 students were entered for A-level French, only 9 were enrolled in Spanish, and even fewer studied Latin. English was the largest department in the division, and the history department was engaged with the changeover from European to West Indian history. Overall, the A-level results were disappointing – only 38.5 per cent for day students, and 10 per cent for evening students. English and geography students were the best performers. Nevertheless, the momentum in staff development continued, as Robert Belgrave left for Canada to pursue his PhD.

During the 1974–1975 academic year, the enthusiasm and team spirit of staff continued unabated, although examination results fell short of projections based on student performance in mock examinations. In addition, only four students enrolled in Latin, and two withdrew after the first year. The English department boosted its morale by converting a classroom into an English room with added audiovisual materials and appropriate decor. Students' interest also peaked in 1975, as Hispanic Society students visited Venezuela and geography students visited St Vincent and the Grenadines.

Reflection

Lucene Bishop, who was one of the initial teaching recruits from Combermere School, explained that she regretted leaving behind at that school the camaraderie in the staffroom with Stanton Gittens, Charlie Pilgrim, Gloria Blackman, Dorian Pile and others, but she chose the Barbados Community College because her salary was higher and there were prospects on the horizon for exciting changes. At Barbados Community College, it was a close-knit group, with Grace Cohen as head of English, Arthur Sealy as head of the division and Anne Hewitt as a colleague in English. Calvin Yard was across the way in history, and Adele Lynch in French. In the beginning, there was no staff room that was large enough, but staff found ways to interact anyway, including entertaining groups at home at the end of each term.

Lucene Bishop's students continue to speak of her prowess with Shakespeare to this day, and she cherishes their enlightenment and achievement as she watched them grasp the treasured themes in *Macbeth* and *The Merchant of Venice*. She remembers especially such students as Irene Sandiford-Garner and Kerrie Simmons, now politicians; Rosemary Alleyne, a media personality, Esther Philips, a former senior tutor and prize-winning poet; and Joseph Inniss, a community college tutor and curriculum development officer.

Hewitt was one of the first assistant tutors who joined the staff in 1968; she taught English literature, specializing in Chaucer. She enjoyed a good relationship with the small staff, which included Bishop and Cohen. Principal Best offered the freedom to grow, and later Principal Barnett was very supportive as well. But she recounted that it was during Sealy's tenure as acting principal that she had a most painful experience which resulted from her misunderstanding of procedure and her enthusiasm to problem solve on her own. The results for the Cambridge examinations had been sent to the acting principal, Sealy, at the college from the Ministry of Education on Friday, for release on the following Monday. Based on her knowledge of the past performance of the students in mock examinations, she found the grades disappointing. She raised the matter with Sealy and advised that a query should be sent to Cambridge. When this did not seem immediately forthcoming, she showed her displeasure to the principal and sent the query to Cambridge herself. The normal route for such an investigation should have been from teacher to principal, through the ministry to the University of Cambridge Examination Board.

The Ministry of Education was very displeased about the breach of that procedure. Sealy was upset as well, and Hewitt herself had mixed feelings. She regretted her "obvious misbehaviour," which she labelled as the worst moment for her at the Barbados Community College. Needless to say, this was countered by the pleasure she enjoyed when she received an apology from the Cambridge Examination Board, and even more so by an upward adjustment of the grades for thirty-three of the forty-four students. For her, this was a significant achievement because her assessment of her students was validated; the board had admitted its error; and thirty-three students were the beneficiaries of her intervention.

As a young staff member (in her late twenties), Hewitt was able to identify with her creative, lively and even unorthodox students. She remembers the yearly pageant at Sherbourne and her decision one year to dye her valued white wedding dress green in order to provide a Victorian costume for her students. She recalled also the in-depth study of the Cambridge curricula and how, in spite of the foreign context, students were able to master the texts and their themes.

She acknowledged that the Barbados Community College encouraged staff development and she had the opportunity to benefit from the diploma in education at the University of the West Indies. She was also given the opportunity under Principal Barnett to begin to develop General Education programmes. She left the college with mixed feelings in 1981 to take up the position of job training manager at Barbados Shipping and Training.

Division of Science

The first head of the Division of Science was Alvin Barnett, who had joined the Barbados Community College from Harrison College. In January 1969, the day class in science included five men and six women, and in the evening, eighty-five men and forty-five women were enrolled, studying such subjects as biology, botany, chemistry, mathematics, physics and zoology.

In 1972, the Division of Science had 208 students who were still housed in inadequate accommodation at the Deep Water Harbour site. This did not dull their enthusiasm, though, which drove them to conduct research on the distribution of flora and fauna in a gully five hundred yards northwest of St Thomas Church, on Highway 2. They hosted the Barbados Association of Science Exhibition and mounted a display which covered 120 square feet of wall space. The entry, entitled "The World of Algae", was deemed quite meritorious (winning second prize).

In 1973, The Division of Science was looking towards its planned facility alongside the Division of Technology at Eyrie. In the meantime, two temporary laboratory assistants, Hugh Stanford and Hamilton Boxill, were confirmed in their positions. There was no written dress code for students, but there was the understanding that there would be "no wearing of shirts with inscriptions or unusual or unsuitable headgear". Students took the initiative to successfully establish and operate a lending library for science books and continued to participate, albeit less enthusiastically, in the Photographic Society.

The dropout rates were alarmingly high, especially for the part-time students in mathematics, chemistry and biology. This was attributed to a number of factors, including large class size, adjustment challenges of students who had been out of school for a while, managing work and study, poor attendance, home responsibilities and even teacher inexperience in dealing with adult students. Absenteeism was high for mock examinations, and examination performance was not acceptable. To address these problems, a policy was drafted to allow students to extend the two-year programme of study over three years.

In 1975, there was an increase in staff morale, student performance and student enrolment. This was due to the growing popularity of the college, reduced student attrition, final-year students spending a third year for better grades, and marked improvement in the performance of students in mock examinations, in spite of the increased passing percentage from 40 per cent to

45 per cent. There was also a decrease in absenteeism from examinations due to observance of a stricter policy. The earning of the first Barbados scholarship, by Brenda Shorey in 1975, capped that year's achievements.

At around the same time, as a result of the expansion of the project to the Deep Water Harbour, the Division of Science laboratories and classrooms had to be removed. Temporary accommodations were found at Sherbourne, and the completion of the facilities at Eyrie became even more urgent.

Division of Fine Arts

Joyce Daniel had heard that the request for art courses had been growing since 1969. Full of excitement and enthusiasm, she joined the Barbados Community College Staff in 1973. The Department of Fine Arts was established in January 1974, and she became the first tutor. The college's stated mission was to assist the Barbados Industrial Development Corporation in providing training to advance the development of the handicraft industry.

There was sparse accommodation and very limited equipment. The physical environment was very deficient. The fine arts department was assigned a single room in the Technology division, with no running water – the students had to bring buckets of water to the classroom. In spite of those conditions, morale was high and the students worked hard. Initially, the department focused on painting, print making, drawing and art history. Daniel had a vision for the delivery of graphic art, sculpting and applied arts and metal craft courses to follow. Initially, seventeen students were enrolled for A levels, and ten were successful; five received passes in the subject at the O level, and two failed. Happily, many of these students went to the United Kingdom to continue their studies.

This department was upgraded to a division on 1 January 1974, offering drawing, painting, design, printmaking and history of art. There were nineteen day students and thirteen evening students, totalling thirty-two. The single full-time tutor, Daniel, was fully engaged, but she was also making recommendations for noncertificated courses for adults in drawing, painting, commercial art, interior design, sculpture or ceramics, and fabric design.

In 1975, fifty students were enrolled – twenty-eight in year 1 and twenty-two in year 2. They moved from the Division of Technology to two rooms in the Eyrie House, where the project office was also located. The lighting was much better and there was running water, but the floors were old and many of the floorboards were rotting, and bat droppings were commonly seen. However, Principal Best was encouraging and supportive.

During 1976 to 1977, UNICEF gave the division a grant for a kiln, a printing press, screen-printing materials and inks. The tutor had a very heavy workload, assisted by part-time teachers in the areas of advertising art and history of art. Twelve students were entered for A levels, eight passed at the A level, and four at the O level. Of the eight, one went on to England and the others to the Barbados Teaching Service. Students won awards in the National Independence Festival for Creative Arts (NIFCA) and mounted an excellent exhibition at the Barbados Hilton Gallery. In October 1975, the division started the in-service teacher training course for teachers of art in all-age schools; twelve teachers registered, and ten graduated.

Division of Health Sciences

In 1971, the Ministry of Health prepared a cabinet paper pointing out the shortage of trained health personnel. In response, plans emerged for the establishment of a School of Health Sciences, using the Tercentenary School of Nursing Building. A Steering Committee was set up, chaired by Carlisle Burton, permanent secretary for special assignments in the Office of the Prime Minister. The college was represented by Barnett of the Division of Science. At the commencement, the board established the posts of tutor and clerk-typist.

Three years later, the Division of Health Sciences was established in November 1974, in response to the implementation of a decision taken by the Caribbean health ministers to provide regional training in the paramedical professions as part of a seventeen-government regional project, funded by the United Nations Development Programme (UNDP) and UNICEF, with the Pan American Health Organization (PAHO) as the executing agency.

Initially, there was a challenge in finding a senior tutor externally, so Barnett was asked to launch this division. As was the case for the Division of Technology, a number of potential students in the allied health disciplines did not have the full complement of O-level qualifications in science and general education, even though they would have had some relevant experience. To open up the training opportunity for these areas, a bridging certificate course was developed. This was called the Pre-Health Sciences course, and it included what was considered to be the O-level equivalents of biology, chemistry, physics, English and mathematics. In late 1974, this was the first divisional offering.

The division formally opened in November 1975 with forty students in the Pre-Health Sciences Programme. After years of planning, the division was now a part of the training project for allied health sciences in the Caribbean. Accommodation was a challenge involving the conversion of the old pathology laboratories at Jemmotts Lane to science laboratories, as well as the refurbishment of a room at the psychiatric hospital as a workshop for occupational therapy assistants.

In May 1975, I joined the division as the first assistant tutor for chemistry and biology. Later, Hinkitch Bell was employed as a public health instructor and was assisted by Tom Kirby, who was sponsored by Project HOPE in the United States. They developed a programme to train public health inspectors. The Ministry of Health and the Caribbean Food and Nutrition Institute had conducted training for three cohorts of food service supervisors. In 1975, the fourth was transferred to the Barbados Community College, under the leadership of Rosie Jackman and Arlene Erceg. As part of its publicity and recruitment campaign, the division worked with the Ministry of Education to conduct workshops for school leavers, sharing information about the Allied Health vocations.

Completion of the laboratories in the Old Hospital Laboratory was delayed. However, at the end of August 1975, there were four lecture rooms, two laboratories and one room for the Pre-Health Sciences Programme. The Ministry of Education installed partitions to increase the number of rooms to six. The Pan American Health Organization contributed equipment and textbooks; Project HOPE donated furniture, instructional materials and teachers; the Ministry of Education contributed laboratory equipment and supplies; the Canadian High Commission donated occupational therapy supplies; and the Barbados Pharmaceutical Society donated books.

The first Pre-Health Sciences Programme, which commenced in late 1974, concluded in December 1975. In August 1975, the Food Service Supervisors course commenced, and it finished in December 1975. The Public Health Inspector's Programme, which started in February 1975, concluded in December 1975. In January 1976, the new programmes included Occupational Therapy Assistants, headed by Hilary Bethell; Pharmacy, headed by David Fitts; and Medical Laboratory Technology (MLT), headed by Anthony Johnson. There was also the second cohort of public health inspectors. In 1976, there were ninety-two students, including sixteen non-Barbadians. That was evidence that the college was making a regional impact.

Division of Community Services

A Community Services Programme had been implemented, and under its aegis, there was a Human Potential Programme for sixty persons, including youth, senior citizens, priests and laypeople who met on Saturday afternoons. Group sessions covered such topics as Leadership Training, Building a Greater Sense of Self-Worth, Personal Growth, the Discovery of Meaning through Inner Dialogue, Transactional Analysis, Planning Life Goals and Development of Inner Awareness. There were also plans to offer certificate and diploma programmes in Recreation Leadership, but with lower entry requirements for students in this division.

This unit was expected to offer training to all the other divisions of the college, as well as to reach out to foster links with the wider community. The launch of the first formal programme of the division, Recreational Leadership, was planned for October 1974. It was an ambitious, one-year certificate programme including courses in Communication, Community Recreation, History of the Caribbean, Health Science, Civics, Special Activities, and Field Work. The entry qualifications for the certificate were lower than the usual college requirements, pitched at the level of the Barbados School Leaving Certificate.

In 1974–1975, the college was still very interested in making a stronger mark on the community and supported the delivery of youth leadership training programmes. A tutor was seconded from the government to revise the existing year 1 course outlines and prepare a paper on the role of the division; interview prospective staff and students; explore assistance from nongovernmental organizations such as the YMCA, the Caribbean Epidemiology Centre and the UWI Extramural Department; submit memoranda; and report to the principal. Twenty-three students enrolled in Recreational Leadership, four of whom dropped out. The first year was completed, and planning was on the way for the second year.

A name change was recommended, and the Division of Community Services was officially established to offer short courses, services, workshops, lectures, consultations, concerts, community studies and social action programmes. There was also the plan to offer future degree and certificate programmes. In the first year, twenty-three evening students registered. There were three part-time staff members and visiting lecturers, as well as a qualified officer from the Ministry of Education. The staff was augmented in the second year by a full-time tutor, Lomar Alleyne. This division encountered multiple problems. Its scope was scaled down, and the division itself was eventually discontinued in 1976.

Students

Student Roll

In September 1969, the student enrolment had risen to 497, including 300 second-year and 197 first-year students. The student roll for September 1971–1972 rose to 825, with 252 full-time day students and 573 part-time evening students, and with 469 men and 356 women. The attrition rate was considerable for the part-time students, indicated by 105 of them dropping out by the end of Year 1. The roll increased over the five years between 1969 and 1973 annually, rising from 300 to 497 to 600 to 825, and finally to 980. The higher ratio of men to women and evening to day students persisted from the beginning.

Extracurricular Activities

In the first years, the Literary, Debating and Dramatic Society produced the college magazine. Esther Inniss (now Phillips) remembers activities by the Debating Society and interesting hikes. Creative dancing was also conducted by a local specialist from the community and the Camera Club was also established during the first year. Summer courses were offered by staff who volunteered their time to help with remediation. In the 1970 academic year, the Students' Council was formally established, as well as the Literary Society, the Inter-School Christian Fellowship, Geography Society and Cercle Français.

Reflection-First Students

Inniss was one of the first students at the college, from 1969 to 1971, and served as the first guild president. Others in the group included Raymond Maughan, Ronald Williams, Charles Burnett, William Layne, Wismore Greaves and Joseph Inniss. Esther Inniss vaguely remembers the principal in the background, but she recalls that he made an effort to relate to the students. The tutors were also very attentive and invited students home. For her and many of the other students, the atmosphere was one of optimism and appreciation of the opportunity to do A levels because her school, St Michael's Girls, did not have a sixth form. The BCC principal, Clyde Best, corroborated this, as he remarked that many of the students, both because of their numbers and lower qualifications, would not have been able to gain access to the four sixth-form secondary schools.

Like Esther Inniss, Joseph Inniss, former Barbados Community College tutor and curriculum development officer, and multiple times the president of the Staff Association, remembers the family atmosphere which existed at the college in the early years. In those years, young teachers and students formed a very close bond.

Examination Results

The 1971–1972 Cambridge A-level results were modest to poor. For the Cambridge A-level examinations, 188 students took 305 subjects; 160 wrote 280 papers; and 28 students were absent for 45 papers; 80 A-level certificates were gained, 108 O-level passes were returned and there were 108 outright failures. Of the twenty-one candidates who took the Associated Examination Board, seven passed; all three candidates who took the London Chamber of Commerce examinations passed; for the Association of International Accountants, the two candidates who were entered passed but only two of the four who took section 2 succeeded. The single candidate who took the Admiralty Interview Board exam succeeded, and one of the two who sat for the Private Secretary's Course passed (Annual Report 1972).

Staff

In 1968, there were nineteen teachers. The number increased to twenty-one with the addition of a new zoology tutor, Mohammed Muhajari, in the Division of Science; and Mildred Pincott, in the Division of Commerce. By the next academic year, the staff had grown to twenty-two full-time teachers with the addition of Andrew Lewis in Commerce.

Continuing Education of Staff

From as early as 1970, the Barbados Community College encouraged and facilitated staff development. In this regard, M. King and Marcina Haynes obtained the diploma in education at the University of the West Indies, Mona, Jamaica. Mohammed Muhajiri and Nigel Bradshaw attended summer courses in molecular biology and in probability, statistics and computer-oriented mathematics, respectively, sponsored by the Organization of American States (OAS).

Staff development continued apace in 1971, with Adele Lynch pursuing the diploma in education and Andrew Lewis pursuing a master's degree in economics. When Adele returned to the French department in 1973, Robert Belgrave took leave to go to Canada to pursue a PhD. As was the pattern for previous years, staff development continued in 1974. Three members of the teaching staff – Anne Hewitt, Nigel Bradshaw and Frederick Inniss – went on to pursue the newly established in-service diploma in education at Cave Hill. In the next academic year, Lucene Bishop, Jeanette Springer, Norma Holder and I went on to Cave Hill, at which Alvin Barnett was a teacher, to obtain the diploma in education.

Barnett was using the knowledge and skills which he had received in his education programme in England in his teaching. He was awarded a PAHO/WHO fellowship of one-month duration to study organization and management of divisions of health sciences at McMaster University and the Mohawk College of Applied Arts and Technology.

Establishing Credibility

During this period, the Barbados Community College experienced severe criticism from teachers in other institutions (and even teachers within the college), politicians in the Barbados Labour Party, and the general public. On the other hand, it also received praise from educators, other politicians and the public. Principal Best spoke of "asperities of many awkward reports that were partisan, inaccurate, imaginary and scurrilous".

In this period of establishing credibility and legitimacy, the college focused on such metrics as student attendance, attrition, examination results, throughput to universities, programmes, staff development and job placement. Needless to say, there were both successes and failures. Student enrolment almost quadrupled, from 300 in 1969 to 1,190 in 1974. The college had moderate success with external examinations, fairly good transfer rates to universities and strong evidence of persons getting job upgrades as a result of their acquiring new skills and competencies. A number of technician engineers, accountants and land surveyors had been trained. There was a projection that thousands of others would receive diverse postsecondary experience in the near future.

Specific successes included some improvement in and good prospects for accommodation; establishment of three new divisions – Technology, Health Sciences and Fine Arts; expansion of the curriculum; leadership and innovation by the principal; growing numbers of highly motivated academic and administrative staff; the first Barbados Scholarship; a national development scholar; and validation of quality, as indicated by the first international articulation arrangement and improved performance on external examinations. In addition, there was an improving profile of technical studies in the country; improving articulation and establishment of policies; strong relationship with professional associations; increasing visibility in the region; the presence of overseas students; and sustained student transfers to the University of the West Indies and other universities.

Some of the challenges included shrinking interest in Latin as a language; the fall-off in enrolment in the Community Services Division; limited community links and continuing education programmes; and failure to hire a deputy principal. The college continued to be concerned about its credibility; and not surprisingly, the board accepted a proposal submitted by staff for the establishment of a committee to evaluate the performance of the college. A draft survey was designed and submitted for use from September to December 1974.

During this phase of the college's development, career guidance was limited to gathering information to compile student profiles and expressed needs; giving lectures and discussions to students preparing for graduation; offering conflict resolution and problem-solving seminars; and building networks with secondary schools. There was the need for detailed and documented policies, procedures and guidelines, as well as evaluation of teaching programmes. The disciplines of accounting and engineering were still heavily reliant on part-time staff.

In 1973–1974, the *Shorey Report*, prepared by a prominent educator and publicized in the press, stoked controversy by advocating the phasing out of sixth-form schools and the abolition of the Common Entrance examinations. Principal Best supported those recommendations.

Evaluation

Voices of the People

Interviews of Calvin Yard on the inside, and newspaper reports from Principal Aurelius Smith of the Lodge School, statements by the Honourable Louis Tull and Honourable Lionel Craigg and others, illustrated the diversity of the prevailing views. The Lodge School principal questioned the quality of the Barbados Community College, citing the fact that students with poorer academic qualifications attended the college. He criticized the A-level results thus: "In fact, it is so low that an investigation into this expensive piece of educational window dressing is most certainly required." However, a student responded: "It is accepted that the results of the community college's A-level examinations were satisfactory, when one considers the circumstances" (*Advocate News*, 17 September 1970).

Three areas of criticism in the *Advocate News* of 20 February 1978 are instructive. The minister of education, the Honourable Louis Tull, stated that "he had inherited problems at the Community College and was desperately trying to straighten them out". He thought that the institution was not staffed "by the right people", and that it needed "much more than a Deputy Principal". Bradshaw thought that "there were too many acting positions in which staff could not give of their best and some of the permanent appointees needed training themselves". Teachers at the college, like Neville Badenock, an earlier opponent of the college's establishment but then a staff member, felt that the college was not truly a community college because it did not have enough engagement with the community. Some parents were not happy with student discipline because unlike in the school setting, students could leave the college when not attending classes ("Community College Move Over", *Nation News*, 18 January 1978).

On the other hand, supportive voices like Earl Glasgow, a former opponent but later assistant tutor at the Barbados Community College, commented, "As far as I am concerned, BCC is satisfying the needs of the community – we are producing pupils who can find a job in the community – especially on the technical side. People from the secondary schools are switching over to the community college and are pursuing courses in the technical areas. This is showing people that there is no disgrace in working manually" ("Educator: No Regrets", *Barbados Advocate*, 3 September 1986).

In addition, Eva Thompson affirmed, "This college is the most forward-looking institution in the Caribbean area. . . . A student at the college could pursue A-level subjects in almost any combination." She maintained that the island "had a different and better institution created for an adult student population" (ibid.).

As an indication of public perception, the *Advocate* also commented ("Community College an Added Opportunity", 7 January 1971): "The Community College is obviously offering opportunity to those who desire Advanced level coaching and are unable to get this at the sixth form schools. It also offers a number of subjects on its curriculum not offered in the sixth form schools. Furthermore it must seem to be a godsend to those who had to rely on correspondence courses in their quest for higher education."

Evaluation by the Principal

In his annual reports, Principal Best recalled his efforts publicizing the work of the Barbados Community College, his involvement in designing desks for the students, his involvement with the Land Surveyors' Association and Engineering Association and their goodwill demonstrated through their part-time teaching. He was pleased with the adjustment of teachers from their school setting to the college (Best 1989):

> The first decade also saw growth in the popularity of work and study among all ranks of the population especially among the younger people who were eager to take advantage of the new opportunities where Barbadian society was no longer ruled by a patrician gerontocracy. It is remarkable to note how the professional bodies and associations contributed out of their vast experience, and how the general population began to applaud the institution, thus showing the natural civility of our people's disposition.

Further, he remarked (Annual Report, 1971–1972): "It [the college] has experienced noteworthy development from a modest roll of a few programmes to a rapidly growing campus with broad multi-purpose courses. . . . It seems only natural that the College should hold itself in a state of readiness to initiate new activities that will enable it to respond to the changing objectives with which education will be faced in the years ahead." The principal's own evaluation (Annual Report 1973–1974) was: "The launching of the college was met with various types of reaction, ranging from jubilation to total rejection, and the early years were filled with the task of selling the curious concept to a curious and questioning public. In the end, most of the detractors fell off and the college won many friends." He commented further: "That the BCC is now a big segment of post-secondary education, is a fact. That the College is rapidly identifying itself as a family member of educational institutions, is apparent. That great expectations are held by its adherents, is obvious."

He also noted "The programmes are organised so that individuals may harmoniously accomplish their own aspirations and at the same time accomplish the designated institutional goals. The technical students have settled well and interact positively with students of the Liberal Arts, Fine Arts and Humanities. Indeed, Barbados seems to be enjoying an enviable climate where the technical students show no complex about the aura surrounding the liberal arts mystique" (Best 1987, 34).

Conclusion

The Barbados Community College offered educational access to students who would not normally have found places in the sixth-form schools because of their limited capacity. In addition, the entrance requirements for the college were lower. Therefore, access was broadened to include a more educationally diverse student body. The college also widened access to students of all ages and offered both day and evening and full-time and part-time courses. Unlike the US community college, the Barbados Community College did not offer open access; successful completion of secondary school with a specified number of certificates was a prerequisite for entry. However, the divisions of Technology and Health Sciences offered bridging courses.

The community college was publicly funded, so no fees were charged. Students had to purchase their books, though. Unlike the sixth-form schools, students were spared the expense of school uniforms. Of course, some may argue that buying suitable clothes to wear to school was an added expense rather than a relief.

Innovation was evident in some of the courses offered to cover topics in the General Paper A-level examination, as well as in the offerings by the Division of Community Services. The flat organizational structure into divisions and the assigned labels of instructors and tutors were also original. The activities and offerings of the Community Service Division constituted a formal response to community needs and the extracurricular activities of the students – a less formal manifestation of relating to the community.

At the college's outset, the focus of the three divisions was primarily on transferring to university, hence the emphasis on science and liberal arts in A-level examinations. The Division of Commerce opened the door to vocational training, and the divisions of Fine Arts and Health Sciences continued that trend. However, adult and continuing education was not a part of the formal offerings of the college until later. Considering these changes, it can be concluded that the breadth of the college's offerings and its diversity of functions followed an evolutionary path.

The college was developed in response to an act of Parliament, funded by the government, and was part of the development plan of Barbados. Its programme development was intricately linked to the development needs of the country, and therefore funding was tied to function.

In these early days of the college's development, there was local outreach to professional bodies and government agencies and leadership both from behind and in front. Leadership was given and received through consultation with the regional University of the West Indies. The international articulation arrangement with Penn State University was a highly valued validation point.

There was progressive growth in student enrolment and divisional expansion. In these initial years, more men than women attended, especially in the evening science and technology programmes. Perhaps this was related to the secondary school output, cultural norms and the responsibilities of women in the home during the evening hours. A-level and other examination results were modest and uneven, perhaps because of the college's educational foundation and the steep learning curve for both staff and students. However, the college's confidence was boosted by the award of its first Barbados Scholarship. It enjoyed good success with the transfer of students to universities, better success with its placement in jobs and added gratification in the high-level job performance of its graduates.

In the pool of staff recruited to the college, there were experienced persons with master's and bachelor's degrees, including a few with qualifications in education. By the end of this period, during which there was ongoing academic and continuing education training, one staff member had his PhD, a few had earned master's degrees, many had earned qualifications in education and several had taken short, professional development courses. By all reports, the staff members were highly motivated and had established family-like bonds that were so strong that even the students were able to sense them.

It is noteworthy that the principal had travelled to eleven US community colleges to get new ideas for establishing a homegrown institution. New structures were being constructed to accommodate three divisions, while old buildings were being prepared to house the new divisions of Health Sciences and Fine Arts. In addition to its name and the principal's visits, the most striking evidence of north/south global flows was the early articulation arrangement with the Penn State University.

Figure 7.1. The Harbour site (west view): Home of Barbados Community College, 1969–1975. Courtesy of the Barbados Government Information Service.

Figure 7.2. The Harbour site (east view). Courtesy of the Barbados Government Information Service.

Figure 7.3. Sherbourne House: Home of Barbados Community College, 1969–1976. Courtesy of the Barbados Government Information Service.

Figure 7.4. Division of Technology – first buildings at the Eyrie site, opened 1973. Courtesy of the Barbados Government Information Service.

8.

Filling the Gap with Arthur Sealy, 1976–1978

Keith Hunte, who was appointed the second chairman of the board of management of the college in 1972, dealt with the retirement of Charlie Best in 1976 and the search for a new principal to replace him. Although the board was responsible for selecting the principal, it is common knowledge that the minister of education and the government would have to approve the appointment. As stated in the act establishing the college, at 14.1: "Principal of the College, in this schedule referred as the Principal, shall be appointed by the Board with the prior approval of the Minister." An advertisement for the job was placed in 1977, but the new principal was not hired until 1978. No doubt because of his seniority in terms of qualifications, years and level of service as senior tutor since 1969, Arthur Sealy, an easy-going gentleman, acted as principal in the interim period between 1976 and 1978.

He expressed concerns about job placement for students and advocated for the establishment of the career counsellor position. He was interested in curriculum expansion into such creative areas as music and dance and a wider range of vocational training even in such professions as haircutting, especially during the summer. He kept alive the college's original plan for agricultural training. It was during his tenure in January 1977 that the Barbados Community College signed a second international articulation arrangement with Wilberforce University in Ohio. Arthur Sealy also had the pleasure of overseeing the opening of the college's new campus at Eyrie and the admission of eager students who joined the continuing Division of Technology students at the new location. The transfer took place in January 1978 under the supervision of Otho St Hill, the project manager.

On 1 November 1977, the campus at Eyrie was officially opened by Queen Elizabeth II. The opening address was given by the minister of education, the Honourable Louis Tull. His speech was interesting because of what was included in it, but even more so because of what was *not*. He acknowledged earlier visits by the queen and thanked her for her role in the opening of the St Elizabeth School in St Joseph and her visit to the temporary site of the UWI Cave Hill campus in 1966. He also mentioned Princess Margaret's role in the opening of a secondary school in St Philip which bore her name.

He noted that the college had been established by an act of Parliament in 1968, and that its enrolment had grown tremendously from three hundred to fifteen hundred full-time students in eight years, between 1969 and 1977. He graciously acknowledged the funding of the college building via a loan of US$2.8 million from the Inter-American Development Fund. He paid tribute to the main contractors, architects, engineers and other consultants, subcontractors and workers. Finally, he thanked the Government of the United Kingdom for the gift of equipment donated to the Division of Technology, which had been operating at the Eyrie site since 1973.

It was no secret that the ruling government of Barbados had opposed the establishment of the Barbados Community College. In addition, the minister had recently expressed major concerns about the college because he had commented in the press that it was not staffed by the right people, and the situation presented a problem that desperately needed to be sorted out.

The board of management was responsible for staff appointments, but it was generally understood that the government could exert influence on that process in two ways – first through the persons whom the minister appointed to the board, and second by the requirement for ministerial approval of candidates for senior positions such as principal. The Barbados Community College staff reported that the board, chaired by Hunte, had made suggestions to the minister of education about candidates for principal, but that they were not accepted. In addition, there were rumours and opinions expressed about the possibility of the appointment of Sandiford, who was thought by many to be eminently qualified. However, there was a major political problem; he was an opposition member of Parliament.

Figure 8.1. Arthur Sealy, acting principal of the Barbados Community College, being received by Queen Elizabeth II

Figure 8.2. Eyrie House, home of the BCC Project Office (1968–1974). Photograph compliments of the Barbados Government Information Service.

Figure 8.3. A group of first BCC students, 1969. Photograph from the *New Bajan*, 1987.

Figure 8.4. Fine Arts portfolio class of 1991. Photograph compliments of Hartley Alleyne.

9.

Growth and Consolidation Years under Alvin Barnett, 1978–1988

Dr Leonard Shorey was appointed chairman of the board of management in 1977. One of the board's first duties was finding a principal, and Alvin Barnett was appointed. He had a sound reputation, earned initially from his association with the prestigious Harrison College, where he had taught physics to many Barbados scholars and others who had become outstanding citizens and leaders in both the public and private sectors. Further, he had served the Barbados Community College for eleven years as senior tutor in the Division of Science since 1969, and senior tutor in Health Science since its establishment in 1974.

He had also benefited from further training in education in England, as well as in management in Canada; so he was well respected within the college. He had presided over both academic and vocational offerings, both externally and internally examined. He was mild-mannered and even-tempered. His appointment met with the approval of almost everyone. If the Charlie Best years are characterized as the foundation years, Alvin Barnett's tenure as principal may be characterized as the growth and consolidation years, which built on that foundation and saw every sector grow and develop.

In his first annual report, Barnett emphasized the objectives of establishing desirable links with the community and promoting all aspects of the Barbados Community College as a tertiary institution. He signalled as important the offering of a number of new programmes, including general education programmes, with a focus on curriculum. He also spoke to the establishment of comprehensive regulations for students, with a focus on administrative policies; and he spoke with admiration about the training of teachers in collaboration with Erdiston Teachers Training College and the Division of Technology, an interinstitutional venture. Barnett was to serve as principal for ten extremely productive years at the college.

He was committed to the college as an instrument for nation building, human resource development and economic growth. He outlined this in his own words in a presentation to management staff (Barnett 1985): It is "my belief that education is a process through which a country makes preparation for its total development, and that education at tertiary level in a developing country such as Barbados, should be geared towards the development of that country's resources, both physical and human. In particular, I believe that education must be so geared that it makes a direct contribution to the development of the economic sectors on which a country depends." The sectors he identified were tourism, agriculture (including diversified farming) and manufacture (including handicraft and electronics).

In the late 1970s, the national strategy called for increasing productivity and efficiency. To that end, Barbados Community College attempted to improve its curricula for building relevant skills; increase its involvement in teacher training and physical education; and advance foreign language training. It sought to expand hospitality training, including the restructuring of curricula not only to meet the needs of the industry, but also to adapt its hotel management courses so that they would dovetail with those of the University of the West Indies.

Barnett addressed student organization, regulations and enrolment growth; staff organization, development and regrading; and the establishment of new divisions, new departments and new programmes. He presided over the development and delivery of the associate degree – a transformative initiative. He exploited the benefits of partnerships with local, regional and international institutions. Enabled by the Canadian International Development Agency, the twinning of the Barbados Community College and St Clair College of Applied Arts and Technology was undoubtedly extremely developmental and beneficial to both institutions.

New Developments

Principal Barnett oversaw a number of important developments, many of which were already in the pipeline. These included establishing new senior administrative posts; creating two new divisions and a centre; setting up new departments; launching new programmes; and forging or strengthening new local, regional and international partnerships.

More specifically, these included the following:

- Establishing the posts of deputy principal, registrar, college counsellor, physical education officer and college librarian
- Separating the post of registrar/bursar into two positions, registrar and bursar, in 1979
- Setting up the Counselling Department in 1979
- Establishing the Staff Association in 1979

- Establishing the Division of Hospitality Studies in 1980 and subsequently considering its feasibility for self-financing
- Launching short vocational training courses in 1980
- Establishing the Physical Education Department in 1980
- Delivering a General Education Programme in 1981 and establishing a Department of General Education in 1987 and Division of General and Continuing Studies in 1988
- Introducing the college's first summer school in 1981 and the Division of Health Science's summer day camp
- Establishing the Barbados Language Centre in September 1982, including transferring foreign languages from the Division of Liberal Arts
- Implementing joint teacher training between the Department of Fine Arts and Erdiston College in 1981, and between the Division of Technology and Samuel Jackman Prescod Polytechnic in 1985
- Launching the paralegal studies certificate in the Division of Commerce in 1981
- Introducing from 1983 the UWI Preliminary Science (N1) programmes in biology, physics, mathematics and chemistry for four years
- Establishing the Computer Department in 1984
- Launching associate degree programmes in 1987, and the first attempts at their recognition by and articulation with UWI programmes
- Launching the certificate in business studies (1987) and associate degrees in fashion design and mass communication.

In 1979, in an effort to improve the governance arrangements, Principal Barnett moved towards the establishment of advisory committees for all divisions. (The Division of Technology had had a technical committee for some time.) More broad-based advisory committees had been established in the divisions of Science, Liberal Arts and Commerce in 1979, and the newer divisions followed this pattern. These committees were chaired by the senior tutor and included the principal and professional and experienced persons in the relevant disciplines. They advised on programme development, relevance and evaluation, as well as on student attachments during training and job placement after graduation.

Barbados Community College's board of management also instituted meetings with the staff which allowed for building communication bridges and sharing information. Soon after his appointment, the principal set up a committee to plan the tenth-anniversary celebrations, which included the production of a supplement in the *Advocate News* and a documentary compiled with the assistance of the Barbados Government Information Service.

New Posts

The much-discussed posts of deputy principal, registrar, college counsellor, physical education officer, college librarian and other library staff were soon established. This was an important achievement because these positions spurred on major development. The deputy principal's position was expected to provide needed assistance with staff development, timetabling and the evening programmes.

Deputy Principal

In 1984, Norma Holder was appointed as the first deputy principal, a position which she held for four years. She was one of the college's original nineteen assistant tutors. Having taught chemistry and mathematics in the Division of Science and served as senior tutor in the Division of Health Sciences, she brought extensive knowledge and experience to the position. Her energy and insights would prove very useful at a time when the college was undergoing rapid development. Upon Barnett's retirement in 1988, Holder was appointed principal of the college, and Calvin Yard became her deputy in 1989.

Bursar

The post of registrar/bursar was first held by Ambrose H. Stoute beginning in 1969; next by Carl Lowe, seconded from government; and third by Eureka Brathwaite, also seconded from government in 1977. Brathwaite recalls that in the early years, the board chairs helped with the minutes and other records, giving her time to deal with financial matters. Although the physical environment was inadequate, the community ethos was strong, and the staff in the Accounts Department felt like valued members of a strong team, pulling together.

She recalls that moving to Eyrie lifted the morale of the college. Team members included messenger Keith Maxwell, who, under great pressure, always maintained his cool and wore a smile. The supervisor, Eric Phillips, calmly looked after the maintenance of the buildings and administration of the stores. He also supervised the work of groundsmen Wharton Goulbourne, St Clair King and Geoffrey Greenidge, who joined the college in 1970, 1971 and 1974, respectively.

Registrar

In 1978, the position of registrar/bursar was separated into two distinct jobs, allowing the registrar to focus on general policy and on serving as secretary to the board. In April 1979, Grace Pilgrim was appointed as the college's first registrar. Her prior experience included teaching at St Michael's School, Foundation School and Harrison College in Barbados, as well as at The Convent School in St Lucia. As reported in the *BCC Staff Association College Update 1994*, she came to an institution where the principal, board chairman and bursar "soon made her feel comfortable and gave her the added confidence which she needed". She recounted how she drew on the experience of the board secretaries in the schools that she had taught at previously. She also disclosed that "working with Brathwaite was an excellent experience in the benefits of close association and friendship".

Her main assignments were to set up the systems in the registry and serve as board secretary and personnel officer. The latter position allowed her to interact with all the members of the staff and become involved with all the sections of the college. Her assessment was that "in the post of Registrar you could feel a real part of the College – you could influence the entire College. It was a great feeling working with the Board that had such a clear vision!" When she left the registry to become director of the newly established Barbados Language Centre, the development of which she orchestrated, Rosemary Simmons stepped in to hold the job until Grace Thompson became the second registrar in 1982.

Thompson was an accomplished musician and an experienced former teacher at St Lucy Secondary School; she was subsequently head of the General Studies Department at the Alexandra School and president of the Barbados Secondary Teachers' Union. She set out to transform the "Registry" into the "Office of the Registrar", which she also saw as the centre for computerized students' records and a communications hub for correspondence floating among the principal's, deputy principal's, registry and bursary offices. She gave freely of her industrial relations experience and led the drafting of administrative policies for students in general, and those related to the associate degree programmes in particular.

New Departments

Bursary

The separation of posts enabled Eureka Brathwaite, the bursar, to focus on finance and accounting, including guiding the senior tutors in the preparation and administering of their divisional budgets and educating departments about the public sector's financial rules. Brathwaite became the college's first bursar in 1979, and she was impressed with the support given by the board chairs (Keith Hunte, Leonard Shorey, Colin Kirton and Trevor Hassell). She enjoyed a good and close relationship with Acting Principal Sealy, as well as Principals Barnett and Holder. Quite early in her tenure, in 1981, the college facilitated her taking two years of study leave to England, during which time her duties were covered by Norma Hall.

Counselling

The Counselling Department was established and the position of tutor filled in January 1979 by Frederick Inniss, who had served the college since 1971 as a teacher of geography. In 1974, he, along with Nigel Bradshaw and Anne Hewitt, enrolled in the first in-service diploma in education at the Cave Hill campus of the University of the West Indies. Inniss's interest in the all-round development of students led him to pursue a master's degree in counselling at the State University of New York, in Albany. It was upon his return that he was appointed to the position of tutor and head of the Counselling Department. This opened up new areas of career guidance, study skills and personal counselling for the growing student body at the college.

At first, Frederick Inniss used the proactive model by engaging students in the classroom in modules on Career Development, Human Sexuality, Peer Counselling, Assertiveness Training, Drug Awareness and Psychology of Interpersonal Development. As the student enrolment increased, and with a single tutor, the college adopted a reactive model – an approach which he did not readily identify with, but worked around. He later advocated the appointment of additional counsellors to deal with the academic challenge, many related to the change to the associate degree.

Physical Education

In 1979, the position of physical education tutor was established by the college and filled by Esther Maynard in 1980. During her interview for the job, she shared with the panel her vision to train physical education teachers. She realized much later that her vision was an exact fit with the mandate of the Ministry of Education. She loved her job passionately, and Principal Barnett (and later Principal Holder) allowed her to use her creativity and professional networks to advance the development of physical education in the college.

Prior to her appointment, the students' guild had made ad hoc arrangements for competition among themselves, and in 1979, the guild organized its first athletics meet. Beginning in 1981, Maynard took over the formal annual interdivisional athletics meet.

College Library

What are the chances that a small room in the Sherbourne Great House, the former servants' quarters with dimensions of 169 square feet, would become the library of a community college? This happened in 1969, when staff members from the English department elected to operate a library which opened only periodically. Two library assistants, David Trotman and M. Harewood, were appointed in April 1969, and they later took over the operations at that site.

When the library was constructed and opened at the Eyrie campus, a whole new world opened up. A requirement imposed by the World Bank on the college was that a professional librarian should be appointed. This led to the secondment in 1977 of a professional librarian, Monica Simmons, formerly an English teacher at the Springer Memorial School. Transferring books from Sherbourne and acquiring and setting up a new library was a big challenge, and this was exacerbated by the desire of some divisions to have their own libraries. During this transitional period, 1978–1979, acquisitions were fast paced, and it is reported that tensions were sometimes high. A few students demonstrated, showing their frustration with getting their needed books on time. In a short time, both the stock and service of the library improved.

Monica Simmons was appointed in the post of college librarian in 1979, but this post was initially aligned to that of a tutor at the college. As the library continued to expand and the responsibilities increased, the case was made for upgrading the position. However, it was not until 1980 that it was reclassified to the level of senior tutor. By the late 1980s, there was also a senior librarian, Hetty Stoute-Oni, and eight library assistants, as well as a small, specialized branch at Jemmotts Lane for the Division of Health Sciences.

New Divisions

Hospitality Studies

In 1964, before the establishment of the Barbados Community College, the Hotel School was established, with two hundred students. It was designed to provide trained personnel for the hotel industry. In 1973, the government purchased the Marine House and used the west wing of that building to accommodate the Hotel School. In 1980, the school was transferred to the Barbados Community College and became the Division of Hospitality Studies. There were plenty of problems: the classrooms were very noisy due to road traffic; the library was inadequate; kitchen and storage equipment were outdated and security questionable. To ease overcrowding at the Marine House, first- and second-year students in hotel catering and institutional management were located at Eyrie, in the Division of Science.

John Sollaway was offered an acting appointment as senior tutor in April 1980, but by the end of August, the arrangement was changed and the division reported directly to the board of management. In February 1981, Hugh Barker was assigned to act as senior tutor from his substantive post in the Division of Science. In 1982, Bernice Critchlow-Earle, formerly of Bermuda College and the United Kingdom, who had been working in the division since 1981, was appointed senior tutor.

This transfer of the Hotel School represented the first assimilation of another institution into the college. Immediately, there was much activity in the area of curriculum revision. This move, including a parallel organizational structure for the staff, was another effort by the college to create technical/vocational education on par with its academic offerings. It also made possible the academic strengthening of hospitality training through the cross utilization of resources to achieve greater efficiencies and better economies of scale.

In 1983, the twinning with St Clair College of Applied Arts and Technology was beginning, and help with curriculum development was forthcoming. A needs assessment was conducted by the senior tutor, in collaboration with Jean Breckhow and Lou-Anne Flanagan at St Clair. Bernice Critchlow spent six weeks at St Clair to redesign the curriculum based on the determined needs. In May 1983, Michelle Crovisier, followed by Jean Breckhow from St Clair, visited the college and conducted training workshops. A one-week seminar was later conducted by Brian Desbiens and Thomas McCarthy from St Clair, and Workeley Brathwaite from the University of the West Indies.

The final draft of the curriculum was handed over to the college by Richard Gates, chairman of the board of St Clair, and the curriculum was implemented in January 1984. However, funding for practical activities was a limiting factor. The Ministry of Civil Aviation and Tourism initiated funding for the division from the European Economic Community.

Language Centre

In the late 1960s, the Barbados government acknowledged that there was a need for and value in adopting Spanish as a second language. An agreement was made with the Organization of American States to assist with the improvement of the teaching of Spanish and the adoption of Spanish as a second language. Emerging from an OAS-commissioned feasibility study on the teaching of Spanish and Portuguese, conducted in 1969 by Clemens Allman of Temple University, the Barbados Language Centre was established in November 1981. The recommendations included the location of the centre at an educational institution which would provide sufficient autonomy, but network with government, business, industry, Organization of American States and the University of the West Indies, for financial and advisory support. It was decided that the centre should participate not only with Spanish- and Portuguese-speaking countries, but also French-speaking ones. The centre was officially opened in 1982 by the Honourable Billie Miller and Sarah Milner, the OAS director of Barbados. Day classes commenced in 1982 with Conversational French, Conversational Spanish, German for Hotel Workers and courses for secretarial students in the Division of Commerce.

The centre was headed by Grace Pilgrim, appointed at the level of a BCC senior tutor. She was supported by an advisory committee composed of educational, economic and commercial interests. She was also supported by an audio-visual library assistant, a translation and interpretation tutor in Spanish, Arlene Kirkpatrick, and a clerk/typist. Lauretta Hackett joined the staff as a part-time tutor in 1983.

After losing its part-time grant in 1983, the Barbados Language Centre embarked on self-financing projects, so students were charged fees. In 1984, the centre launched its first intensive, full-time programme in English as a Foreign Language (EFL), catering to students from France, Guadeloupe, South Korea, Martinique, Peru and Venezuela. The proceeds from that venture provided seed money for the development of the associate degree in business and tourism. In 1986, the Language Centre offered its first summer English as a Foreign Language Programme, mainly to students from Martinique, Guadeloupe and Venezuela. In 1987, the centre introduced the regular Test of English as a Foreign Language and the associate degree. The centre did several on-site programmes of training for industry, including for telephone operators and receptionists.

The future would see the centre becoming a host for overseas students and a foreign exchange–generating unit, offering conversational courses in French, Spanish, German, Portuguese, Italian, Japanese, Chinese and English as a Foreign Language, as well as an associate degree programme in language, business and tourism. Students would come from China, Colombia, Brazil, El Salvador, France, Guyana, Guadeloupe, South Korea, Martinique, Puerto Rico, Uruguay, Venezuela and even Namibia, as part of a special project.

New Programmes

From as early as 1979, Anne Hewitt started to introduce and coordinate general education "enrichment" courses for students. The courses, which were initially given to first-year students, were offered for two hours per week and developed in divisions or by part-time staff. Ivan Waterman from the Division of Commerce taught civics and tourism; Arlene Kirkpatrick from Liberal Arts and later the Language Centre taught conversational Spanish; Jeff Whitehead from science taught Hydroponics. Freddie Inniss from the Counselling Department taught psychology. Sociology was taught by Robert Morris and Trevor

Marshall, and Use of English by Wendy Donawa, Jeanette Springer, Anne Hewitt and Jacqueline Wiltshire-Forde. There also were part-time teachers – Richild Springer and Danny Hinds taught dance; Daphne Hackett taught drama; and Gilda O'Brien taught fashion design. Health education – which I coordinated – included contributions from Health Sciences tutors in nutrition, drug abuse, mental health, sexually transmitted diseases and first aid.

In 1980, Wendy Donawa, also from the Liberal Arts Division, began to offer short vocational training courses to students and the general public in ceramics, batik, weaving and printing. She also offered a course in puppetry. These laid the foundation for a General Education department. These courses had no prerequisites, and a small fee was charged to cover some costs.

The college's first summer school was launched in 1981, and staff from various divisions made contributions to the effort. In 1986, there were offerings from the Division of Health Sciences by Rose Atherley in medical records technology and typewriting; from the Division of Science by Gladstone Best a course in introduction to computers; and from the Language Centre an offering in conversational Spanish. These courses charged a small fee. Outreach to the public was also attempted in 1982 by the Division of Health Sciences through a free summer day camp for children, offered for children in the environs of the college and at children's homes.

From the late 1970s, media personnel in Barbados had identified the need for upgrading the standard of journalism and providing training opportunities for local practitioners and aspirants. Angelita Sandiford, who joined the college in 1986, took this opportunity and wrote a funding proposal. Her work for the community college began in 1985, when she replaced the college counsellor, Freddie Inniss, who was on a term's leave. She was a nurse and teacher who had recently returned from pursuing a double master's degree in education and psychology and was concerned about second chance educational opportunities for young women who had dropped out of school as a result of pregnancy. She helped to expand the general education courses in psychology. Having been involved in the General Education Programme as a psychology tutor, she replaced Wendy Donawa, who was on leave for a term, and also covered for Esther Maynard, who was on leave the following term. After Donowa's sudden resignation, the post became vacant, and Angelita Sandiford took up the position to coordinate the General Education Programme. She had prepared herself for this work in 1987 by pursuing training at the Institute of Management of Lifelong Education and undertook studies in lifespan clinical development psychology at Harvard University. She did an internship in continuing education at Penn State University, which later earned her credit towards her doctorate.

In 1987, sponsorship was secured from Barbados External Communications Limited, and the General Education department developed the associate degree in mass communications, one of the first associate degree programmes at Barbados Community College. This programme was coordinated by Gladstone Yearwood.

The General Education department was the unit which would deliver the core and elective courses for all students pursuing associate degrees. By 1988, the General Education department had become the Division of General Education and Continuing Studies, headed by senior tutor Angelita Sandiford.

Other New Developments

Students

In addition to the students' organization of games, they were now represented on some of the college's advisory committees. Fine Arts students were required to donate a piece of their coursework to the college. This served not only to enhance the decor of the college, but also to give exposure and prominence to the students' artwork. In 1969, there was also a review of the policy guiding the award of scholarships to students. The gender balance varied across divisions, and Technology was traditionally exclusively male. In 1983, the Division of Technology had its first female graduate, Noreen Cox.

The students were doing well. Cleopatra Branch, one of the first pharmacy students from the Class of 1974, graduated from the Division of Health Sciences in 1977. After working for two years in the private sector, she received an OAS scholarship to Oregon State University, from which she graduated with a Bachelor of Science in pharmacy in 1983. She was on the honour roll and was one of the top students at the college. She was accepted at Duquesne University to pursue her doctorate in pharmacy. She undertook a one-year residency at Mercy Hospital, Pittsburgh, where she gained experience in adult clinical pharmacy administration. On her return to Barbados in 1985, she was appointed as chief pharmacist at Queen Elizabeth Hospital in Bridgetown. In 1986, she was invited to present prizes at the college's graduation.

Staff Association

Calvin Yard was one of the original nineteen assistant tutors; he rose to the position of tutor in 1972 and senior tutor in 1979 in the Division of Liberal Arts. Both at the Sherbourne and the Harbour sites, staff would meet informally to share their concerns and make plans. As the college staff expanded in number and to other locations, the traditional close-knit bonds were becoming difficult to establish or maintain. In addition, there were growing concerns among the staff about appointments, promotions and conditions of service. They expressed their anxieties in staffroom discussions and advisory committee meetings. Yard had recently completed a master's degree in the United States, and this experience probably sensitized him to American community colleges' organizational issues and their relevance to the Barbados Community College setting.

In consultation with friends and long-standing colleagues such as Frederick Inniss and Nigel Bradshaw, Yard set about the establishment of a staff association in 1979–1980. In 1981, a seminar was convened by the association, and under his chairmanship, it produced a document entitled "Restatement of Role, Philosophy and Concept of the Community College". It included recommendations related to the role of the college in preparing students for higher education (university transfer); the role of the community college in training for employment; and the role of the community college in responding to the needs of the community.

There were also growing industrial relations undercurrents. The earliest teaching staff of the college had severed ties with the teachers' union which had led a strike in protest of their remuneration package in 1968. Many had later joined the Barbados Workers Union, which represented many newer teaching and nonteaching staff. Since then, staff had come from both the older secondary and the newer secondary schools and retained ties with their respective trade unions, Barbados Secondary Teachers Union and the Barbados Union of Teachers. Many nonteaching staff who had come from the public service were members of the National Union of Public Workers.

For this motley crew, though it was not a trade union, the Staff Association provided a unifying professional and bargaining umbrella that could consider industrial relations matters, as well as offering a unified base that could be a broker for health insurance and other collective benefits. The Staff Association produced a journal which provided information for staff at all levels.

On his appointment to the post of Staff Association president, Yard was immediately tasked with looking at the reorganization and reclassification of staff. The regrading of college posts had become urgent, in light of the earlier regrading of the civil service, which had disturbed some traditional alignment of posts between itself and the college.

In 1983, the General Purpose and Entertainment Committee, which I chaired in my capacity as the Staff Association treasurer, "spearheaded the beautification of the staffroom, successfully organised a Christmas dinner, two luncheons at which guest speakers addressed the staff, and a farewell luncheon at the end of the academic year for staff members who were terminating their services at the college" (Annual Report 1982–1983). The association also promoted social interactions among staff in the form of games evenings, cricket matches, and an annual luncheon which morphed into the principal and Staff Association's annual Christmas dinner. It also must be noted that the Staff Association initiated a group health insurance plan.

Activities by Divisions

As mentioned earlier, the Division of Commerce, in collaboration with the Bar Association of Barbados, launched the Paralegal Studies Programme in 1981 to cater to the learning needs of workers in private law offices and government and commercial legal departments. Also, the Division of Liberal Arts reluctantly released its foreign language programmes to the emerging Language Centre in 1982.

The Division of Hospitality Studies undertook a feasibility study to explore its ability to be self-financing. However, the findings were not encouraging. The planned establishment of the Computer Department experienced delays, but it was eventually established in 1984, headed by Brenda Barrow from the Division of Technology. Barclays Bank sponsored a Farm Management Programme in the Division of Science led by Jeff Whitehead and the Fine Arts Division commenced a joint programme with Erdiston Teachers' Training College in art education for secondary school teachers.

The academic year 1983 was a very active one in terms of adding new programmes. There was ongoing discussion about the transfer of the School of Nursing to the Division of Health Sciences. In addition, the first graduates completed the Library Assistants' course, delivered by the Division of Liberal Arts and the BCC Library. The Division of Science and Technology reached out to the community and offered training for laboratory technicians for schools and colleges.

The Fine Arts Department offered its first three-year diploma programme. The Division of Health Sciences ventured into advanced training programmes, including postbasic diplomas in Microbiology and Inspection of Meat and Other Foods; Community Nutrition, in collaboration with the Pan American Health Organization and Caribbean Food and Nutrition Institute; and a Health Science Tutors' and Managers' Programme, certified by the University of Guyana.

The UWI preliminary (N1) programmes were introduced in the Division of Science with offerings in biology, physics, mathematics and chemistry and these would run parallel with A-level offerings for four years. Similarly, the Liberal Arts Division continued to work on an alternative to an A-level programme. The Division of Commerce added a two-year Business Education Programme and a two-year Computer Science Programme was planned in advance of an anticipated, fully functioning Computer Studies Department.

Alvin Barnett's Final Years as Principal

In the academic year 1985–1986, the mood at the college was one of growth and optimism; the pace of development was frenetic. The A-level programme recorded its greatest successes to date – five scholarships and three exhibitions. The plan for the expansion at Morningside was approved by the government, its funding was secured and the continuing education and summer programmes were expanding.

In September 1985, the college opened the Universal Equipment Gymnasium for the use of students in fitness programmes. The Physical Education Department also offered basketball and dance. By 1988, the department collaborated with Erdiston Teachers' College in the delivery of a one-year postbasic programme for teachers. Erdiston used the BCC facilities and benefited from the services of the BCC tutor in teaching organization and administration, as well as physical education and athletics officiating. The Division of Commerce added the certificate in business studies, the Computer Department was being planned, the Division of Hospitality Studies received gifts from the European Economic Community and St Clair College of Applied Arts and Technology, and plans were in progress to relocate the division from Marine House to a hotel.

An offer of secondment had been made to nurses from the Tercentenary School of Nursing in the Ministry of Health. In April 1986, the transfer of nursing took effect, with former principal tutor Peggy Inniss as the department head. This added a three-year general nursing certificate, a one-year day-release nursing assistants' certificate and a one-year postbasic midwifery certificate to the college's offerings. Graduates were doubly certified by the college and the General Nursing Council, which provided additional licensing examinations for registration of general nursing students to practise.

In 1985–1986, the government was very interested in promoting the product design element, and Minister Bernard St John, who had initially opposed the establishment of the community college, urged the senior tutor of Fine Arts to offer design courses for industry, including Craft Design and Fashion Design. The senior tutor also envisaged a division offering music, dance and drama. Tutor Joyce Daniel made contact with fashion designer Joyce Price, who was working for the Barbados Industrial Development Corporation, and with designer Gilda Miller, who would play a pivotal role in the division. In January 1987, three programmes were launched in fashion design – a two-year associate degree in fashion design, a one-year certificate and a six-month, part-time certificate for a skills upgrade.

Staff exchanges were continuing under phase 4 of the Project of Institutional Cooperation. There was OAS-funded training for the Board of Tourism, conducted by the Division of Hospitality Studies; training in St Vincent and the Grenadines and Grenada, funded by the Canadian International Development Agency; and integration of productive work in General Education, coming out of UNESCO/CARNEID (Caribbean Area Network for Educational Innovation and Development). Economics students under tutor Ivan Waterman carried out a survey on computer education in Barbados, leading to the college's offer of Introduction to Computers as a General Education course. The history department arranged attachments at the Barbados Museum. The Division of Fine Arts was celebrating the long-awaited establishment of the post of senior tutor.

The pace of course development was rapid. New courses included a two-year certificate in computer studies; a two-year certificate in physical education; modules of the computer programme in the Division of Technology; expansion of continuing education and summer programmes, with contributions from many divisions; a one-year programme for electronic technicians in collaboration with Samuel Jackman Prescod Polytechnic and the Industrial Development Corporation; and a six-week course in Basic Workshop Theory and Practice for the Meteorological Institute.

The certificate in physical education came out of the Commonwealth Sports Development programme and was planned in collaboration with experts from US universities and UWI campuses, especially Mona and St Augustine. The college also benefited from the services of Jack Costello, a physical education specialist from St Clair College of Applied Arts and Technology. In its first offer in 1987, the programme was delivered full time, but to accommodate untrained and new teachers who could not get leave, it was delivered in subsequent years over two years, on a part-time basis.

Under the Improvement of Justice Project, in collaboration with the University of the West Indies and the US Agency for International Development, the launch of the Paralegal Programme took effect in seven OECS countries: Antigua and Barbuda, Dominica, Grenada, Montserrat, St Kitts and Nevis, St Lucia, and St Vincent and the Grenadines. This project promoted the Barbados Community College as an institution which had the capacity to provide regional leadership through the supervision of delivery, external examination and certification of the programme.

Other initiatives taken by the college included overtures to the University of the West Indies in relation to the certificate in business studies and other programmes. In response, the University of the West Indies generally recognized the associate degrees for normal matriculation, and the ordinary technician diploma, under certain conditions.

In addition, the improving computerization of administrative operations; technical assistance to other Caribbean countries; imposition of late application fees; and technical assistance from the Japanese government in the form of attachment to the Technology Division were other exciting activities.

In August 1987, the board was advised that the Ministry of Education was seeking a home for the Richard B. Moore library at Eyrie House. According to this plan, the library could be on the ground floor; the upper section could be made into an exhibition hall to show the best work of the students and the project was to be funded by the World Bank. Unfortunately, this refurbishment did not materialize.

The opportunity was used for the senior tutor to make a case for the inclusion of accommodation for the Division of Fine Arts in the World Bank Morningside Project. Senior Tutor Joyce Daniel proposed designs for lighting, including window placement in the art studio, an outlay for big machines in printing and an outlay of a small performance hall.

The Associate Degree

Perhaps the most significant academic event of Principal Barnett's tenure was the introduction of the associate degree. The proposal for the establishment of the Barbados Community College had been advanced by the Honourable Erskine Sandiford. At the college's establishment in 1968, he was minister of education, and the senior education officer, Colin Kirton, served briefly as the first principal. Amidst much opposition, Sandiford used his position to promote and enable the establishment of the college. In 1986, he was appointed again as minister of education and deputy prime minister, and Kirton was appointed the fourth chairman of the board of the Barbados Community College.

Placed again in a position of influence, Sandiford submitted to the college an eight-page document entitled "Framework for a Revised Programme of Studies for the Academic Certification of Students, and for Related Matters". The paper detailed existing certification, deficiencies, range and levels of programmes and a proposal for a revised programme of studies, academic load and certification requirements for graduation and grading system. It concluded with recommendations for all two-year programmes to become associate degrees which should include majors with in-depth study; three compulsory general education college-level courses including English and Communication, Ethics and Morals in Modern Society, and People, Politics and Society in Barbados and the Caribbean, as well as two introductory elective courses with a variety of options.

The college community reacted to all this – some with disbelief, others with scepticism and yet others with enthusiasm about an opportunity for self-determination and self-reliance. Many senior staff saw this as the college coming into adulthood and graduating from A-level status. The paper was thoroughly discussed, scrupulously critiqued and revisions made to the proposal. To ensure swift action, the minister had informed the board that he expected the associate degree to be in place by September 1987. The board informed the principal of this, and the principal laid the matter in the laps of the college's advisory committee, composed of senior tutors and special department heads.

It was like a two-way relay team, working apace, or perhaps like an acrobat, walking on a tightrope, balancing the fears of students, scepticism of the public and anxieties of many staff members, as well as the caution of those who were managing the change against the mandate for developing the associate degree. The board of management, the principal and staff of the college acted swiftly. By July 1987, the principal had submitted draft proposals to the board, which expeditiously presented to the minister of education the proposals for the award of associate degrees by the college. The proposal was accepted, and the planned programmes were given full media coverage in July 1987. By this time, the sudden death of Prime Minister Errol Barrow in June 1987 had provided the opportunity for Erskine Sandiford to assume that vacant position – one which still allowed him to continue to provide leadership for this bold step in the offer of associate degrees.

The board directed the college to proceed with the development of associate degrees in arts, sciences, applied arts and applied sciences. It set out the pending objectives as follows:

- Standardization of a grading system
- Institutionalizing of a credit system
- Coding of college courses
- Preparation of course outlines
- Organization of all programmes into associate degrees in arts, sciences and applied arts or sciences
- Preparation of advertising brochures
- Preparation of general advertisements for print, radio and television

On invitation from the Ministry of Education in 1987, and funded by a US agency, Dr Frank Schultz, director of international and intercultural activities, Dr Winston Richards and Robert Simks from Penn State University visited the Barbados Community College to renew collaborative links, established in 1975, as well as to look at recognizing the associate degree. At that time, Erskine Sandiford was also promoting the establishment at the college of the Institute for the Study of Democracy. The Penn State team was also asked to provide technical assistance and offer advice to the Barbados Community College, in establishing the proposed Institute for the Study of Democracy.

New Forms of Collaboration

Local

During the Barnett years, the Barbados Community College actively explored intrainstitutional, interinstitutional, regional and international collaboration for efficiency and programme expansion. Intrainstitutional collaboration was evident in the Library Assistants' Programme resulting from the collaboration of the Liberal Arts Division and the College Library, as well as the work of the Language Centre resulting from collaboration with the Division of Liberal Arts.

Locally, working relationships were established with the University of the West Indies, Samuel Jackman Prescod Polytechnic, Erdiston College and local businesses. With the University of the West Indies, there was the off-campus delivery of the Preliminary Sciences; with Erdiston Teachers Training College, there was joint training of industrial arts secondary school teachers; with the Polytechnic, a one-year course in air conditioning, as well as joint training of electronic technicians; and there was extensive use of college facilities by the public.

The establishment of advisory and technical committees provided a forum for the interchange of ideas with business and industry. Working together provided the opportunity to work out mutually beneficial arrangements for attachment and internships for students in most divisions.

There was a cabinet directive for the transfer of the School of Nursing from the Ministry of Health to the Ministry of Education, and specifically to the Division of Health Sciences of the Barbados Community College. There was another obstacle, though. Only one of the nine incumbent staff members in the Tercentenary School of Nursing (TSN) accepted the offer of secondment. In response, the board of management established and advertised the positions at the college. Five applications were received from TSN staff. Staff were appointed, and the Barbados Community College accepted responsibility for nursing education on 1 April 1986.

Funded by the Organization of American States, the Division of Hospitality Studies undertook training for the Board of Tourism. In addition, the division continued to explore alternative accommodation, in light of the deteriorating conditions at Marine House. A team established by the college identified Golden Rock Hotel as a good prospect for locating the operations of the division.

Regional

Barbados Community College continued to focus on its transfer function, and also on validation for its offerings which were internally developed and examined. It turned to the regional University of the West Indies. A request was submitted for recognition of the two-year certificates in business studies and computer science, and for exemption from the first year at the University of the West Indies in the relevant disciplines. Recognition of the ordinary technician diploma for matriculation into the Faculty of Engineering was also sought.

In November 1986, UWI matriculation status was granted to a number of programmes, including Paralegal Studies, Hotel Catering and Pharmacy. However, for the City and Guilds ordinary technician diploma, students without A-level mathematics should take Introduction to Math (M100). Lower-level matriculation was accorded to public health inspectors. These requests and offers would continue to be revisited.

Collaboration with the University of Guyana took the form of the Health Science Tutors' and Managers' Programme, with courses jointly delivered and certified by the university. BCC staff offered training in Grenada and St Vincent and the Grenadines, funded by the Canadian International Development Agency in 1985. Technical assistance was given to other Caribbean countries in 1986–1987. The Canadian International Development Agency also funded summer school training for secretaries from the Organisation of Eastern Caribbean States.

By 1986, the Division of Health Sciences had been in existence for twelve years. During that period, 420 students had been trained from twenty Caribbean countries and in twelve health disciplines. One-third of all students were from other countries in the region, and this had served to establish a vibrant regional professional network and create a set of agreed-on, regional, professional standards.

International

In 1983, in preparation for the transfer of Nursing Education to the college, I visited Mohawk College, Seneca College and Ryerson Polytechnic in Ontario, Canada (in my capacity as senior tutor in the Division of Health Sciences) to observe college-administered nursing programmes. Meanwhile, the Division of Hospitality Studies received gifts from the European Economic Community. The Caribbean Food and Nutrition Institute facilitated the expansion of nutrition training to the wider Caribbean. In February 1985, the Government of Venezuela sponsored the exchange of teachers with the Language Centre.

Collaboration with the Government of Argentina resulted in the attachment of two teachers (Jesus Lopez and Elena Massil) to the Language Centre. These teachers visited secondary schools, taught A-level conversational Spanish, conducted exercises in communication competence, and produced taped materials for future use under the supervision of Margot Carter-Tuach, a BCC tutor. There was a small project on productive work activities under CARNEID, which donated US$4,800 for work projects in string art, decorative lamps and horticulture.

It was declared at the outset that the Barbados Community College was not intended to be a transplant from the United States. However, in 1968–1969, as part of his orientation, the first principal of the college, Clyde Best, visited community colleges in the United States. Some fourteen years later, as part of a CIDA International Education Co-operation Project (No. 338-90/525-3-2), in collaboration with the Association of Canadian Community Colleges, there was the opportunity for the Barbados Community College to closely interact with another system, this time in Canada.

Twinning with St Clair College

That opportunity was a twinning of the Barbados Community College with St Clair College of Applied Arts and Technology in Ontario, Canada. This was a transformational collaboration. The persons who brokered the twinning of these institutions were no doubt mindful of many similarities between them, but they may not have noticed that the Barbados Community College was also established in old buildings; like St Clair had an initial cohort of three hundred students; had the start-up experience of adding new structures to an old site; and the uncanny coincidence of having sites at Eyrie in the case of Barbados Community College and Erie Street, in the case of St Clair College.

On a more serious note, St Clair College emerged from the Western Ontario Institute of Technology, which was established in 1958 in an old, east-side schoolhouse for elementary students, some ten years before the Barbados Community College was started. Their first offerings were in electronics, electrical studies, mechanics and chemistry. Two years later, three prefabricated buildings were added to the site to provide two classrooms, a thermodynamics laboratory, a common room and a chemistry department. Business courses were introduced in 1961, and the expansion of this department necessitated the lease of a building on Erie Street. Legislation was passed in 1965 to establish the St Clair College of Applied Arts and Technology, one of nineteen new provincial colleges of this kind. In 1967, the colleges' first building was completed, and three hundred students were admitted.

When the Canadian International Development Agency undertook to fund the twinning in 1983, this represented the beginning of a broad-based, multi-tiered, two-way, transformational collaboration with St Clair College. Very early,

Principal Barnett visited St Clair College and George Brown College in Ontario, Canada. Study missions to St Clair College were also arranged for deputy principal Norma Holder, senior tutors Hubert Bynoe of the Division of Commerce and Otho St Hill of the Division of Technology; and Anthony Johnson, the Health Sciences Division coordinator of medical laboratory technology.

The senior tutor in hospitality studies, Bernice Critchlow-Earle, also visited St Clair College and George Brown College. As mentioned earlier, Barbados Community College and St Clair College carried out a needs assessment of the hospitality industry in Barbados. This led to comprehensive curriculum revision and the development of three full-time, two-year programmes and a suite of shorter evening programmes for skills upgrades. These developments were done in consultation with the industry which readily absorbed the graduates of those programmes.

Twinning attachments also extended to senior administrative staff. Principal Alvin Barnett visited, at the invitation of the vice-president of academic affairs, Gaston Franklyn. The objectives of the visit were to

- Receive exposure to administrative and planning processes development
- Review the operation of certain departments, in relation to computerization
- Explore further technical assistance

A number of other exchange visits were planned, as indicated in table 9.1.

In 1984, the BCC registrar, Grace Thompson, and bursar, Eureka Brathwaite, each spent one month in Canada, studying St Clair's computerized systems. Bill Totten, registrar of St Clair, and Paul Payne, financial controller of St Clair College, were attached to the Barbados Community College for one month as well.

This collaboration also targeted not only the development of computerized systems, but also the computer studies department, which had been fully established in 1974. The college purchased some equipment as well. An additional $203,000 (in Canadian dollars) was granted to the computer studies department for the update of administrative systems. The twinning extended also to the setup of a maintenance and repair department, as well as training in electronic servicing of office equipment. Ralph Phillips of the Division of Health Sciences was identified as the local counterpart at Barbados Community College and Aylesworth at St Clair.

In 1985–1986 academic year, Ivan Waterman and Ken Archibald introduced computer awareness to all students. This had been preceded by offering Archibald's computer familiarization course to staff across divisions and a course in the BASIC programming language to land surveying students. Brenda Barrow assisted in teaching word processing to secretarial students.

Table 9.1. Other Exchange Visits between the Barbados Community College and St Clair College of Applied Arts and Technology

Name	Institution of Origin	Target Divisions	Duration of Visit
William Hockey	St Clair College of Applied Arts and Technology (St Clair)	Liberal Arts, General Education and Technology	1 term
Dave Hibbard	St Clair		1 term
Bob Sheehan	St Clair	Technology and Physical Education	1 term
Jack Costello	St Clair	Physical Education	1 term
Bernice Luqui	St Clair	Medical Laboratory Technology, Commerce and Business	2 weeks
Ken Archibald	St Clair	Computer Department	1 year
Alvin Barnett	Barbados Community College		
Norma Holder	Barbados Community College	Administration	2 weeks
Gladstone Best	Barbados Community College	Computers	1 year

Tom O'Brian, chairman of the board of governors at St Clair College, handed over computer hardware, funded by the Canadian International Development Agency. Aylesworth installed and tested the equipment and conducted orientation for registry staff. Ralph Phillips went to St Clair College to receive relevant training for one year. The visit by Deputy Principal Norma Holder led to her organizing a number of management workshops for academic and administrative staff at the college upon her return.

St Clair College also offered curriculum development assistance. In this regard, Blanche Frederick, a secretarial studies instructor, was attached to the Barbados Community College from St Clair between January and April 1987, and Hortense Elcock was asked to go from Barbados Community College. St Clair College also offered capacity-building assistance when it conducted professional development seminars for staff in July 1987. Brian Desbiens and Brook Gardner from St Clair College, and Workely Brathwaite from the University of the West Indies, conducted a seminar on evaluation and assessment for senior administrative and academic staff, including thirteen from

Barbados Community College, six from Samuel Jackman Prescod Polytechnic and one from Erdiston College. Final evaluation of the project was conducted for the Canadian International Development Agency by consultant Tom Evans, who deemed it a good investment.

In 1983, the college sought and received confirmation from Penn State University of its ongoing agreement to recognize the BCC qualifications from the Division of Technology. In 1985, Barbados Community College hosted a conference on education and training and microcomputers, jointly sponsored by York University and the University of the West Indies, co-chaired by Peter Gibbs of the University of the West Indies and Alvin Barnett of Barbados Community College. It addressed the use of microcomputers in schools, computer training, sociocultural input, promotion of software development and formation of a national task force. This reinforced the college's thrust to offer computer awareness to its staff and students.

Conclusion

Evaluation by Government

On its tenth anniversary, Barbados Community College mounted exhibitions of arts and crafts and cultural courtyard concerts, hosted two Open Days and produced a Government Information Service documentary and a mini-college prospectus. Perhaps to showcase its achievements and potential to some of its early critics, the college was pleased to welcome the Honourable Louis Tull, minister of education and culture; the Honourable Bernard St John, minister of civil aviation and tourism; the Honourable Billie Miller, minister of health; and the Honourable L.B. Brathwaite, minister of agriculture, food and consumer affairs. The party expressed "great satisfaction with the displays and the direction in which the College appeared to be heading" (Annual Report 1978–1979).

Evaluation by the Former Principal

Looking back at his own as well as Alvin Barnett's tenure in office, former principal Clyde Best wrote in the *New Bajan* (Best 1989, 18):

> On the evidence of the first twenty years (1969–1989) of growth and development of the Barbados Community College, it is safe to predict that historians of education will not only find its achievements interesting and satisfying, but will also view the college as a radiant star in the Barbados educational firmament. Over these first two decades, the BCC has demonstrated that it is neither a patch on the threadbare areas of an older system which turned out large numbers of failures, nor the fabrication of an extravagant dream.

Rather, the college has presented itself as a fresh concept in educational planning and activity, swinging in time and harmony with the pendulum of life where growth often meets prudent change in each act of the continuing drama of education for development. Through these formative years, both academic and administrative staff have drawn inspiration from the courage and integrity of this country's people, and even those persons who at first vented their irritation with the assault on the wrong targets, have since grasped the inner meaning of an institution once thought to be a modern parable. . . .

College programmes were offered by Divisions and a dedicated staff was able to breast the torrent and establish the Division of Liberal Arts, Science, Commerce, Technology and Health Sciences.

Soon society would benefit from educational training where successful students would meet the staffing needs of teaching, nursing, secretarial work, accounting, land surveying and technician jobs.

The Impact of Barbados Community College

There can be little doubt that the Barnett years were transformational and impactful. Growth was evident in student enrolment, staffing, programme expansion, course development and delivery. General and continuing education and its adult and community focus had become established at the Barbados Community College. It was now performing its full range of functions – transfer, vocational, remedial, adult and continuing education and community service.

Student performance improved. Graduates were being placed in critical positions of need. There was greater liaison with the community. Past BCC staff were serving at the highest levels of government: Erskine Sandiford as prime minister, Richard Byer as chairman of the House Committee and John Jordan as senator.

The college was providing leadership in the region to emerging community colleges, such as Sir Arthur Lewis Community College in St Lucia and Excelsior Community College in Jamaica. It was also extending its influence through the training of scores of students from the eastern Caribbean in the Division of Health Sciences and others.

It was playing a more active role in cost recovery during challenging times. The college increased its annual fee of $25 to $40 to boost its income, and charged $30 for physical education and $10 for the Students Guild. It also undertook revision of rental rates for such facilities as the Liberal Arts Auditorium and the Gymnasium. Funds were being raised from continuing education, and the government gave access to funds from the Training Levy.

At this stage of its development, the Barbados Community College experienced steering from the government; direction from the board of management;

leadership by Principal Barnett, who was working with the national development plan; and push and pull from the motivation of passionate staff who articulated clear goals and guidance from respected senior administrators.

The college had established a solid foundation, originally laid on A-level programmes. More important, a capacity was built for future programme development and assessment. The associate degree was gaining acceptance. Students were earning Barbados Scholarships and Exhibitions and community college places were in demand.

The US community college was becoming more familiar to the public and was different from the Barbados Community College (for example, in its more open entry requirements). The college did not use the nomenclature of presidents and professors, and its associate degree was different. Therefore, the institution could not be labelled as a transplant.

The public was beginning to see the college not as a school, but as a tertiary educational institution, for a number of reasons. First, many of its divisions were catering to mature students who were not wearing school uniforms and were finding good jobs upon graduation. Second, it was producing, assessing and certifying its own courses and programmes, and its teachers had a different pay scale from the secondary schools. The interface with the community and the collaboration with local organizations and other institutions were also helping to create a relevant, homegrown institution.

The student profile; small fees; flexibility in terms of day, night, day release, summer, part-time and full-time offerings; bridging courses to provide students with second chances at education; the emergence of student guild activities; use of the facilities by and participation of community members; and interface between work and school – all of these reflected community college values.

The rationale for the establishment of the divisions of Health Sciences, Commerce, Fine Arts, Hospitality Studies, Technology and the Language Centre spoke very directly to the development of human resources for employment and nation building. Fine Arts and Hospitality graduates were affecting the cultural life of the community. Although the Division of Science and Liberal Arts did not stress an immediate job placement emphasis, there was no doubt that they were also producing thinkers, teachers, middle managers and students continuing to universities. The Division of General and Continuing Education was refreshing, retooling and upskilling for jobs. Hence, the college was an integral part of the engine for the educational, cultural and socioeconomic development of the country.

The assimilation of the former Hotel School at an old site, Marine House, and its transformation into the Division of Hospitality Studies was part of the college's ongoing alchemy. The extraction of the new Barbados Language

Centre from the older Division of Liberal Arts also represented an ongoing reinvention of form. The launch of the associate degree – albeit an adapted version – suggests borrowing from the United States. The introduction of new certificates, the establishing of advisory committees and collaboration with the business sector demonstrated local partnerships to address local needs.

There were new posts, new departments, new divisions, new programmes, new staff and new student ventures. There were new global trends of north/south influences through such innovations as the associate degree and the twinning with St Clair College in Canada. Even in the latter, however, there were south/north influences, exemplified by staff exchanges. The regional links with institutions in Latin America, the University of the West Indies and the University of Guyana showed south/south interactions. In these ways, Barbados Community College continued to reinvent itself using the old, the borrowed and the new.

Figure 9.1. The Tercentenary School of Nursing Building, used by Division of Health Sciences 1975–1991. Photograph compliments of the BGIS.

Figure 9.2. Marine House, home of the Barbados Hotel School from 1973 to 1980, and the BCC Division of Hospitality Studies from 1980 to 1996. Photograph compliments of the BGIS.

Figure 9.3. Division of Health Sciences staff, 1986: (*rear, left to right*) H. Bell. H. Estwick, P. Inniss, C. Franklyn, R. Griffith; (*front, left to right*) C. Roberts, A. Johnson, L. Proverbs, V. Roberts, B. Gittens

10.

Expansion, Outreach and Reputation Building with Norma Holder, 1988–2004

Norma Holder served Barbados Community College for thirty-five years, from 1969 to 2004. She was one of the first assistant tutors who pioneered the work of the college; initially teaching A-level mathematics and chemistry in the Division of Science, as well as the World of Science Survey course across the college at Sherbourne and the Harbour site. She moved to the Eyrie campus and became a tutor. On the promotion of senior tutor Alvin Barnett to principal in 1978, she succeeded him as senior tutor in the Division of Health Sciences and worked at the Jemmotts Lane campus. Soon after the post of deputy principal was established, she was appointed to it in 1984. Assuming the position of principal in 1988 upon Barnett's retirement, she served in that post until her official retirement in 2001 and beyond that, for an additional three years.

Principal Holder was a graduate of the University of the West Indies and Oxford University, and this profile brought her academic recognition. She was regarded as an excellent teacher who had also earned a distinction in her diploma in education from the University of the West Indies. Her talents in music and sports, her height and imposing presence, her ease in relating to people and even her celebrity in the wider society endeared her to many, but estranged her from others. However, her appointments at each rung of the ladder generally were met with approval and optimism.

In the *New Bajan*, the college's first principal, Charlie Best, wrote of her (Best 1989, 19):

> A highly qualified science teacher in Chemistry, Mrs Holder moved up the ranks from Tutor to Senior Tutor, to Deputy Principal and finally to the top post as Principal. The new Principal's suitability is not measured by her strong academic background alone, but also by the freshness of her concept of education for a developing nation. She certainly does not appear to belong to the fixed and conservative brigade pushing worn-out clichés and brandishing platitudes and classic tags where students are treated as automatons. Rather, she is known for her ability to train students into freely developing their capacities into full and zestful living, and that is what the Community College is all about.

The first two phases of the college's development have been dubbed as first, the establishment of a foundation and second, growth and consolidation. This third phase can be regarded as one of expansion, outreach, maturity and reputation building. Norma Holder has the distinction of being the first and only woman to be appointed to the post of principal (up to 2019) and the longest to serve. Her fifteen-year tenure enabled her, as an astute leader, to build on the achievements of her predecessors.

From the outset, Clyde Best envisaged the Barbados Community College as a tertiary institution. However, he started with a three-division (Commerce, Liberal Arts and Science) institution that many considered to be a sixth-form school. These divisions were grounded in the Cambridge A-level syllabuses and those of other external examination boards. The fourth division, Community Services, which was earmarked to foster more curricular autonomy and community engagement, floundered. Initially, the college relied on external curriculum support and validation and did not need or have its own internal capacity for programme design, development or assessment.

The establishment of divisions of Technology and Fine Arts, though also linked to external examinations, had more potential for self-determination and linkages to the world of work. The Division of Health Sciences was intricately linked to the world of work, both locally and regionally, and was a large step that the college took towards self-determination and capacity building for curriculum development and assessment. Endorsement of the Technology Programme by Penn State University was an important and timely vote of confidence in the work of the college.

In the 1971 academic year annual report, retired principal Charlie Best shared:

> First, it was seen as urgent and necessary for new programmes to be designed – programmes which would upgrade the educational and technical skills; and secondly, since poverty for the most part means having a very low income, it was considered that the college should promote the growth and expansion of occupational education, especially at the middle manpower level. And lastly from the analysis of research, that the College must make a matrix of offerings in continuing education for the entire constituency. (Annual Report, 1970–71, 2)

As reported in chapter 9, the Barnett years saw the establishment of the division of Hospitality Studies and the Barbados Language Centre, which provided the opportunity for even greater responsibility for curriculum design, development and assessment and relevance to community needs. The Physical Education, Counselling and Computer Studies departments had no local operational template and allowed the creativity and innovativeness of the enthusiastic and skilled staff. The development in the Division of Commerce of the paralegal studies certificate, in collaboration with the Barbados Bar Association, and the certificate in fashion design by the Division of Fine Arts, in collaboration with Erdiston Teacher's Training College, as part of the delivery of a programme for teachers of art, were all reflective of a maturing college.

The introduction of the associate degree was the pinnacle of the college's excursion into staff engagement and the responsibility for determination of learning outputs, outcomes and curricular content. Simultaneously, the General Education department was evolving to support the associate degree programmes, and also to respond to adult and continuing education needs, filling and expanding beyond the gap which would have been left from the demise of the Division of Community Services in 1976. In the absence of an accreditation body, the recognition of some college certificates and of the associate degrees for normal matriculation by the University of the West Indies was a critical validating factor for the maturing community college.

This foundation presented a solid platform for the work of Principal Norma Holder, who will be remembered for the following achievements:

- Improving the public image of the college
- Completion of the infrastructural expansion at Morningside, Marine Gardens and Eyrie
- The delinking of the associate degree from A levels and the award of Barbados Scholarships based on associate degree performance
- The upgrade of the Computer Studies Department to a division
- The launch of the Curriculum Development Desk
- The introduction of bachelor's degrees in 1996
- The maturing of the visual and performing arts
- The change to semesterization
- Increasing regional and international articulation agreements
- Continued staff development
- The idea of the University College of Barbados (UCB)

National Leadership

At the graduation ceremony in January 1990 at Marine House, the Right Honourable Erskine Sandiford, prime minister and minister of economic affairs, gave the feature address. Inter alia, he outlined his vision for the country – the context in which the college was nested:

> I envision a Barbados that will have evolved into a truly educated society.
>
> I envision a society that respects environmentally the physical condition of our land, its vegetation, animal species, the waters on and round about it, and its atmosphere.

I envision a society of healthful people who through their lifestyles and efforts seek to prevent disease, and promote and protect health.

I envision a society sustained by the highest possible levels of literacy on which is based a comprehensive curriculum and body of learning experiences for living and for livelihood implemented through a continuing lifelong network of formal, non-formal and informal settings.

I envision a society that promotes the integration of drama and dance, music and art into the fabric of daily living. I envision a society sedulously practicing the processes of democracy; protecting human rights, promoting orderly, disciplined behavior, and eschewing violence, crime and all forms of lawlessness through an enlightened criminal justice system.

I envision a society in which our citizens earn a satisfying standard of living based on dedicated high quality work for which they are adequately rewarded.

I envision a society in which the young, the old, the weak, the handicapped, the sick, the disadvantaged and the underprivileged are cared for in a concerned and caressing network of social support.

I envision a society which maintains its loyalty and sovereignty to the motherland of Barbados, but which at the same time, embraces our brothers and sisters in St Vincent and the Grenadines and St Lucia, in Dominica, Antigua and Barbuda, in St Kitts, Nevis and Montserrat, in Jamaica, Guyana and Trinidad and Tobago as the natural patrimony of the new Caribbean nation and of Caribbean Peoples.

But for that new society to come into being, certain developments must take place now. The seeds for the future are already implanted in the present time. For this nation to achieve its full potential, education must be available for all and at the highest possible levels. Special emphasis must also be given to adult and continuing education so that those persons, who for whatever reason were unable to complete their education in their youth, may be able to do so at a later stage; those who wish to prepare themselves specifically for the job market or to retrain may do so; those who wish to learn more about healthy living or about functioning as good citizens may do so.

When we in Barbados have succeeded in achieving these objectives, then will we be able to say that Barbados is an educated society. . . . The progress of the college over the years has been unique in its growth and contribution to national development – a contribution unparalleled by any other educational institution in Barbados. These programmes clearly demonstrate what is meant by the theme "Training in relation to National Development". The Community College has certainly been playing a crucial role in preparing for change in this community, and has itself been adapting to required changes.

I have spoken in some detail on the outstanding achievements of the BCC and of the possibilities that exist for future expansion. This has not been without some pride and satisfaction, having been a former member of the staff, apart from other involvement. The expansion presently being undertaken is a practical indication of my government's commitment to the future role of the college in national development. (Sandiford 2011, 68)

Infrastructure Development

The college's hardcourts were in the making since 1983, when a fundraising drive for that project commenced under Tutor Esther Maynard. The courts were completed in 1989 and put to immediate use.

Up to that time, both the administrative and teaching operations of the college had expanded and the facilities were stretched as a result of the expansion in staff and student numbers. Soon after Norma Holder became principal, she presided over internal adjustments to facilitate the extension of the administration block, which took place through the building of a third floor, completed on December 1989. This provided much-needed additional offices, especially for the registry, the finance department and the deputy principal. In addition, the World Bank Second Educational Training Project funded the third floor of the technology block, completed in October 1990.

Division of Health Sciences

Buildings at Jemmotts Lane, housing the Division of Health Sciences, continued to deteriorate, and the branch library was deemed by students to have inadequate stock and be inhospitable and even unsuitable. Happily, the buildings at Morningside were completed (with help from the Chinese government) and handed over to the college in June 1991. The staff and students of the divisions of Health Sciences, Fine Arts and Computer Studies moved into the Morningside facility late that year.

Division of Hospitality Studies

In the meantime, the Division of Hospitality Studies continued to experience severe accommodation challenges. It moved into the remodelled Ballroom of the Marine House, but there was inadequate lighting and ventilation. During the 1990–1991 academic year, the senior tutor even sought permission to use facilities at the St Matthias' Girls School, but this did not pan out. While plans for new facilities were being made, from 4 to 10 March 1990, the senior tutor and the principal visited the Runaway Bay Heart Academy for Resort Skills in Jamaica to observe their operations. Around the same time, tutor Rosie Reifer visited the Hotel School of Venezuela to look at lessons which could apply to the Barbados Community College. Both of these visits were funded by the World Bank. In June 1993, an agreement for equipment for the Hospitality Institute was signed jointly by Prime Minister Sandiford and Philippe Darmuzey, the delegate to Barbados and the Eastern Caribbean for the European Union.

Plans had been approved in 1987, but it was not until October 1993 that the ground-breaking ceremony for the Hospitality Institute was held. The senior tutor played a critical role in the design of the institute and involved her staff in the process to ensure that there was blending with, yet separation of, the hotel accommodation commercial space and the training facility. The architects – Design Collaborative, under consultant Brian Begg, and Robert Neal, a BCC graduate – tried to harmonize the new structure with the old building. However, the old building soon had to be demolished.

Bernice Critchlow-Earle insisted that the mature landscape of the forefront, including the mahogany trees, should be maintained, and that the complex be organized around a spacious and welcoming courtyard, fitted with a central swimming pool and bounded by administration offices and classrooms on the western side; the public meeting and dining rooms on the eastern side; and the cafeteria on the northern side. The twenty-room Hotel PomMarine was located over the foyer on two upper floors, ventilated by a cooling cross-breeze ("Institute Designed with Care," *Sunday Sun*, 26 March 2007). The Division of Fine Arts added the finishing touch of an attractive, colourful mural. The restaurant was named Muscavado, which literally translates as "unrefined sugar" – a name suggested by Tutor Trevor Marshall of the History department.

The Hospitality Institute was handed over to the college on 29 October 1996 and was officially opened on 8 February 1997 by Barbados prime minister Owen Arthur. This attractive building was well received as a signature landmark by the community and has served as a model for similar institutions in the Caribbean. The hotel has established a reputation for service; the Muscavado restaurant has become an integral part of the local culture, and the Golden Apple cafeteria is well known for its creative use of local foods in the dishes made by the institute's students.

The impact of the change brought about by the Hospitality Institute was indicated by the meteoric increase in the number of academic, ancillary and administrative staff from 18 in 1996 to 93 in 1997, while student enrolment increased from 250 in 1996 to approximately 1,200 in 2017. In October 2001, the Hospitality Institute opened its first satellite unit in the annex of All Saints Primary School, in the northern parish of St Peter. As part of its community engagement, in collaboration with the Technical and Vocational Training Council, the Homemakers Programme was also launched to offer training for the unemployed. The Hotel PomMarine has had an active greening programme since 2004, an initiative that has won it international awards.

College Library

During the 1995–1996 academic year, the World Bank also funded the installation of the mezzanine floor in the library, which provided additional space for the expanding programmes of the college. It was closed for refurbishment for almost one year, reopening in April 1998. During the closure, limited services were available in the science auditorium. The library reopened with a boost, especially by books for the bachelor's degree programmes.

Cable and Wireless Property

In September 2003, the board approved and the Barbados government acquired the Cable and Wireless Building, the former residence of Sir Arnot Cato, across the road from the Eyrie campus. This was vested in the Ministry of Education and earmarked for the future development of Barbados Community College. The grounds provided ample parking for students.

More Recent Developments

In 1988, successful negotiations took place with the Ministry of Education for the extension of the Textbook Loan Scheme, which was available to A-level students in secondary schools with sixth forms. This enabled community college students, like their peers, to pay a small rental fee for their books with no extra charge, so long as the books were returned in good condition. This was welcomed by students and their parents, who had difficulty purchasing expensive books. It was also in keeping with the accessibility and affordability goals of the college.

To support the training of technical teachers in the two-year in-service programme, the Technical Teachers' Resource Centre was handed over to the college by the British high commissioner, Kevin Burns. The British High Commission provided books and a computer, and other equipment was donated by the British Development Division in the Caribbean.

In November 1989, the Institute for the Study of Democracy held its inauguration at Frank Collymore Hall. The feature address was given by Dr Allan Boesak of South Africa, who was visiting Barbados to celebrate the country's independence. The institute, which was located in the Division of General and Continuing Education, was set up to promote the understanding, concept and practice of democracy through training and the provision of resources for the use of individuals, as well as private- and public-sector organizations, in the wider Caribbean.

From 8 May to 2 June 1995, the Institute for the Study of Democracy mounted its second certificate course in election administration, conducted for six persons drawn from the Barbados Electoral Office in Barbados and one participant from the British Virgin Islands. Interest was also expressed by people in Mauritius, Anguilla, Guyana, Kiribati and Seychelles.

The Muscavado Awards, Communifesta and Interdisciplinary Seminar

Staff in many divisions worked with students to establish departmental or divisional integrating activities. For example, BCC Spanish students entered and won a competition with UWI Cave Hill students, funded by the Venezuelan Cultural Centre. Final-year history students took part in the Muscavado Awards, introduced by history tutor Trevor Marshall and continuing annually from 1988.

Marshall was also instrumental in working with the Students' Guild to help students develop and showcase their talents to the public through Communifesta. In 1991, three of the five entrants from Mass Communication won prizes. Some years, there were competitions for the crowning of Mr and Miss Communifesta.

In 1992, Tutor Joseph Inniss of the Division of Liberal Arts initiated the Community Expo'. This was intended to be an educational exhibition led by the Barbados Community College, but including all other educational institutions and related organizations. In 1994, the "Education for Living" exposition featured forty-four external exhibitions, twenty-five businesses, five schools and fourteen organizations, as well as the vast majority of BCC divisions.

In the Division of Health Sciences, I instituted a well-received, annual, interdisciplinary seminar in 1988, which drew on health professionals in various areas to address cross-cutting themes and issues. This was an attempt to break down disciplinary barriers and assist students to adopt a holistic team approach to addressing challenges and seeking opportunities to address national health issues as a unified team.

Portfolios

The Division of Fine Arts showcases students' work to the public at events called Portfolios. The Portfolio is also part of the in-course assessment of students' work and contributes to their final grades. Portfolios are traditionally held in a number of disciplines. In fashion design, models present the work of final-year students and the work of former students. Portfolio Fine Arts is a display of fine arts and graphic design. Performing arts students put on dramatic presentations. In 2001, for instance, the performing arts students put on "Scenes from Another Life" at the Daphne Joseph Hackett Auditorium. In 2017, there were seven Portfolio productions.

Village of Hope

In 1994, Barbados hosted the first United Nations Global Conference on Sustainable Development for Small Island Developing States at the

Sherbourne Conference Centre. That was a new structure erected at the original site of the Barbados Community College, now bearing the name of Sir Lloyd Erskine Sandiford, who was responsible for the establishment of the college.

In its facilities close to the Sherbourne Conference Centre and building on the experience of the Community Expo', the college was pleased to provide a parallel event on its grounds. It offered its facilities and the services of its Division of Fine Arts to create displays in a Village of Hope. More than 1,000 volunteers assisted in creating some 3,000 exhibits, which were open to the public over two weeks. Some of the students' displays included "Marine Fantasy", "The Garden of Eden", "Survival Garden", and "Explosion of Kites". There was also a press room, transmission room and press lounge. Some of the sustainability themes from the Village of Hope have been re-created in the Future Centre and managed by the Future Centre Trust in St Thomas as "An Interpretive Centre for Lightening the Impact on Our Environment".

Student Health Clinic

The Student Health Clinic was officially opened on 19 January 1995 at the Eyrie campus. The college registrar, Grace Thompson, was instrumental in working with the Student Guild president, Wayne Stuart, and the Department of Nursing in setting up the clinic. Betty Mayers was the nurse. Two visiting doctors, Edwin Thompson and Stephen King, volunteered their services, and H.K. Melville of Harcourt Carter offered free eye examinations to students upon presentation of a letter from the clinic. Twenty-six firms donated cash, medical and office equipment, furnishings and fixtures.

Industry Services Unit

A partnership between Barbados Community College, Barbados Industrial Development Centre, Cable and Wireless and Barbados Institute of Management and Productivity resulted in a high-level training facility at the Harbour site, the Barbados Technology Training Centre, within which the College Industry Services Unit was located. In 1997, the unit was launched to identify and offer customized training to meet the identified needs of Industry. In 1999, a partnership was established with Carnegie Technology Education, a subsidiary of Carnegie Mellon University in Pittsburgh, to offer specific high-end IT courses from that university via the Internet. Two faculty members visited the university for orientation in 2000. The agreement was to deliver ten courses in a programme in software systems development. Instructors from the Division of Computer Studies would be certified by Carnegie Technology Education to deliver the training.

The unit currently operates from the Division of General and Continuing Education at Eyrie. Ongoing courses include Corporate Governance, Cottage Industries Programme, Effective Debt Collection, Foremen and Small Contractors' Course, Industrial Relations, Math for Construction, Occupational Health and Safety, Property Management, Psychological Applications for Workplace Management, Quick Books Pro, Real Estate Sales, Taxation and Tax Management, Web Applications Programming and Design, and Passenger Transport Service Operators Training. Courses are operated on a cost-recovery basis.

Counselling

During this period, the Counselling and Placement Department was expanded and a counselling and placement director appointed. Educational advisory materials were donated by the United States Information Service and included CDs, a video library, career information and directories which were accessible to the college, as well as to the eastern Caribbean institutions.

Division of Computer Studies

In September 1993, the Department of Computer Studies was upgraded to a division, with Gladstone Best as senior tutor. The department had previously established relationships with a number of employers. Computer studies students were interning with the Ministry of Foreign Affairs, Coopers and Lybrand, Systems Caribbean, Caribbean Tourism Organization, Barbados Telephone Company, Peat Marwick, Caribbean Data Services and the National Insurance Office.

Radio GED and Newspaper

On 27 March 1995, the college's community radio station, GED 106.1 FM, was licensed; it was opened by Senator Glyne Murray, the minister with responsibility for broadcasting. It resulted from many contributions. The US Information Service donated broadcasting equipment; Solar Dynamics provided four solar panels; Samuel Jackman Prescod Polytechnic soundproofed the studios with egg boxes; No. 1 Record Shop donated items for the music library; and students conducted fundraising activities. The radio station proved useful for the training of Mass Communication students, who operated it on weekdays from 11 a.m. to 3 p.m.

The Mass Communication Department also instituted a college magazine called *College Vibes* in 1995. A newspaper comprising two tabloid sheets called *Wallpaper* replaced the magazine. The practice was established to post the *Wallpaper* on notice boards throughout the college at the beginning of each week. The division also acquired a Mac laboratory, which is used to create virtual reality (for example, settings for visual recordings).

Liberal Arts Mission Statement

Over the years, the enrolment in the Liberal Arts Division continued to decline while students gravitated to the Division of Commerce and the vocational areas. In the 1997–1998 academic year, the division reflected on its purpose and articulated a "New Liberal Arts Mission Statement". It asserted that "Liberal Arts, through the systematic study and analysis of man's attempts to make meaning of his experience and his environment, seeks to develop the creativity, knowledge [and] understanding of skills of students in order to enrich the quality of life". Coming into its own, the decision was taken in September 1997 to implement the college's programmes, untethered from both the A-level and UWI curricula. The programme was implemented in September 1998.

Internships

In 1999, through innovative internship for students of the Hospitality Institute, fifteen students were recruited to the International Hospitality/Culinary Exchange Programme at Walt Disney World in Orlando and one student to a relevant institution in Martha's Vineyard. Twelve students completed internships on board the *Dawn Princess* cruise ships, and two more interned in the Dominican Republic.

Outreach – Lecture Series

In 2000, the Division of Fine Arts Lecture Series included "The Harlem Renaissance", by American Stephen Harding; "Postmodernism in the Caribbean", by David Gill; "The Market for Contemporary Photography", by Alan Klotz, owner of the NY Photography Gallery; and "Contemporary Black Artists", by Eddie Charles, an art history critic from the United Kingdom.

New Programmes

At the outset in 1987, many associate degree programmes had been constructed, using the A-level content as majors. A few were also designed around occupational/vocational training programme competencies as majors. During this expansion phase, 1988–2004, as the college moved into other development areas, it saw the development of many new associate degrees and revision of older associate degrees in order to meet current occupational and professional demands. The associate degree in physical education was an upgrade of the certificate to meet current needs.

Some of the new or revised associate degrees included:

- Physical education (1989)
- Adaptation of the delivery of the associate degree in computer studies (1989) to evening students
- Business studies (1990); rehabilitation therapy (1990), electronics (1990)
- Marketing, offered as an evening programme over three years (1994)
- Agriculture, upgraded from the Farm Management Programme (1994)
- Performing arts (1995)
- Music as a major in associate-degree performing arts (1998) and an associate degree in architectural studies (1998)
- Psychology (1999), offered by the General Education Division
- Social work (2000), offered by the General Education Division
- General nursing (revised September 2000) to facilitate students pursuing a major in general or psychiatric nursing, with a common programme in the first eighteen months
- Culinary arts, tourism and travel, and another in hospitality studies – both replacing the former Division of Hospitality Studies associate degree in hotel reception and sales (1997)
- Office administration and management (2004)
- Sport management (2004)

There was also a diploma in health informatics, developed in collaboration with the Pan American Health Organization and funded by the Kellogg Foundation (1997). Ten students enrolled from the Caribbean region.

Certificates

Similarly, there was a proliferation of new certificates. This may relate to the college's newly developed in-house skills and confidence in curriculum design, as well as the growing need for general education and elective courses to meet the needs of the various associate degrees. The college had also come of age in its continuing education, retooling and leisure offerings. In addition, it had found a way to raise funds towards its own financing because expanded short-course development and delivery provided a growing market for the Division of General and Continuing Education.

Certificate courses came from many sources. In January 1997, a computer-assisted transcription course was offered to court reporters from the Division of Commerce. The Department of Computer Studies also mounted a twelve-week microcomputer applications course, which was offered while the second-year students were on work attachment. A summer programme was also offered for bar and restaurant students in the Division of Hospitality Studies. And it delivered a series of workshops in Microsoft Word (1991–1992).

The Division of Fine Arts delivered the certificate in interior decorating during the evening (1995), catering to a working clientele. Summer school courses were organized by the Division of General Education and Continuing Studies to enable students to take general education courses and electives to meet programme requirements, to provide courses for advanced credit, and to cater to the wider community that wanted to take credit and noncredit courses. Short courses charged a fee (1990–1991).

The courses included Interior Decorating, Dressmaking, Ceramics, Creative Basketry, Cake Icing, and Introduction to Drawing and Painting. These were open to school leavers who did not necessarily have formal qualifications, retrenched workers, professionals needing retooling and retraining and other interested persons. The response to the summer courses was modest, perhaps because of the $50 fees, albeit in a highly competitive market. In 1997, the division also offered an accelerated basic training course for prison officers.

The Division of Health Sciences offered a five-week course in alcoholism and addiction (1990–1991), as well as training for ambulance service staff, in collaboration with the Ministry of Health and Essex Ambulance Trust (2004).

The Language Centre delivered courses in conversational Portuguese, French, German and Spanish for business and tourism (1989). Subsequently, its offerings included French and Spanish with translation; French and Spanish with cultural studies; German for Receptionists; English as a Foreign Language (1990–1991); Italian General Conversation; and Spanish for EFL Students. The Language Centre became the recommended authority for official verification of government and other official documents (1991–1992).

The expanding Physical Education Programme included not only recreation, but also extramural activities in athletics, basketball, badminton, cricket, netball, lawn tennis, table tennis, volleyball and even elective courses. The intramural, interdivisional games which started in 1980 continued to expand. The college extended itself regionally to compete in the Sir Arthur Lewis Community College Games in St Lucia.

After four years, the Division of Science continued to experience challenges in offering the UWI Preliminary Sciences (the N1 equivalent to the A level) because it was proving difficult to harmonize the content and objectives of the one-year accelerated courses with the slower-paced, differently structured, two-year A-level courses. Some students also preferred to complete the two years so that the preliminary science did not appeal to that group. The senior tutor described the venture as "fifty-fifty".

Against the normal trend to meet a need, A-level Geometrical and Mechanical Drawings was introduced in 1990 by the Division of Technology. More consistent with the trend of internal development and examination was a Site Planning Programme introduced in January 1995, with the intention of offering it on demand.

The First Bachelor's Degree

In 1996, the first bachelor's degree was offered by the Barbados Community College. This was the bachelor of fine arts (BFA), with majors in fine arts and graphic design. This was a bold step by the Barbados Community College. The degree was the culmination of Joyce Daniel's initial enthusiasm for raising the profile of art and bringing art to more people in the country. She recounted that growing up in Barbados and at the Foundation Girls' School, the majority of people did not understand art; they thought that it was a vocation for only expatriates. She was glad to have the opportunity to go overseas to study and bring her experiences back to the island. She went to the United States to pursue a master's degree in art education at the University of Iowa in 1978 and was even more fired up about how art could develop the person.

When she joined the college in 1973, she was the lone tutor, but she had a big vision for art at the college. Charlie Best encouraged her efforts, after establishing the Division of Fine Arts earlier that year. The acting principal, Arthur Sealy, was extremely supportive, and he hired another full-time member of the staff, an assistant tutor named Denyse Menard-Greenidge. She was industrious and very supportive and had a wealth of knowledge and meaningful and different experiences from Canada. She acted as tutor from 1978 to 1980, while Joyce Daniel was on study leave. Appointed as senior tutor after Daniel's resignation in 1990, Menard-Greenidge played a critical role in the development of the bachelor's degree. Russell Hatcher, an expert in graphic design, also played a major role.

The department encountered many hurdles. For example, after it was established, Principal Alvin Barnett was hesitant about promoting the tutor to the position of senior tutor because of the limited number of staff, students and offerings. However, through much advocacy from various stakeholders, the promotion eventually happened in 1984. The division started with about twenty students pursuing A-level art. However, the government was pushing for the product design element of art. The senior tutor also wanted to move beyond A levels to the fundamentals of design.

Government requested some design courses for industry and work was done initially on fashion and craft design. However, Joyce Daniel's vision was a comprehensive one for fine arts, including the performing arts – music, dance and drama. She found an ally in Principal Norma Holder, who was an accomplished musician. In search of prototypes and ideas, Daniel and the principal travelled to observe the Edna Manley College for the Performing Arts in Jamaica and an institution in New York.

Daniel encountered at the Barbados Industrial Development Corporation a great fashion designer, Joyce Price, as well as designer Gilda Miller. She also met Gloria Chung, a pottery designer from Guyana. She invited all of them to join her at the Barbados Community College. Many short courses were given, and students who graduated were able to form their own companies.

An important milestone for the Fine Arts Division was the collaboration with Erdiston Teachers' Training College to train primary and secondary school teachers of art in 1984. This was important because it had a multiplier effect. Initially, trainee teachers came to the college once a week, but later they attended full time. The division trained great art teachers, and soon every school had a qualified art teacher.

As fashion design flourished, there was the first big show at Frank Collymore Hall to showcase the work of the students. Portfolio was launched and became institutionalized, continuing annually for other areas such as dance and music. In 1970–1971, many students shone, like graphic design student Ricky Redman, who opened Acute Vision on Bay Street; and Pauline Bellamy in fashion design in 1978–1980. In 1987, Joyce Daniel was fully involved when the division completed and launched two associate degree programmes in graphic/advertising art and art education; this happened at the same time as the General Education and Computer Studies departments launched their first associate degrees.

Daniel moved on to the Barbados Industrial Development Corporation in 1990, having lived her passion. Many institutions were involved in preparing for the bachelor's degree, including Nottingham Polytechnic and the Nottingham Fashion Centre in England. Funds were also available under the second Education and Training Project.

Denyse Menard-Greenidge also played a critical role in the development of the bachelor's degree. She was an artist with a master's degree who came into education by default. In Canada, she had taught at the pre-university and university levels at Concordia University and at the Universite du Quebec. On arriving in Barbados, she looked for a job at the University of the West Indies and at Erdiston Teachers' College. She found nothing in her field at the University of the West Indies and was not enthusiastic about the opportunity at Erdiston which she learned about.

Without any knowledge of a position at the Barbados Community College, she decided to apply. She found it interesting that she was asked at the interview: "Who told you about the job?" Because English is a second language for her, she is not sure if she responded appropriately, but she said that no one had told her anything about it. However, she believes that her knowledge of Latin impressed the acting principal, Arthur Sealy, who was a Latin scholar. She got the job. Over the years, she came to see education as complementary to her productivity as an artist and believes that she made a very good choice of profession.

Having worked through the development and launch of the associate degree in 1987, she saw the bachelor's degree as a natural progression. Encouraged by the principal, and in spite of doubt expressed by some colleagues, she mobilized departmental support and collaborated with colleagues at Mount Alison University in New Brunswick and Concordia University in Montreal, with which the Barbados Community College later signed memoranda of understanding in relation to recognition of the degree.

The Second Bachelor's Degree

In 1997, the Barbados Community College launched its second bachelor's degree programme, the bachelor of education for technical/vocational teachers in home economics and industrial arts. Perhaps, it was emboldened by the success of the Division of Fine Arts in the launch of the bachelor's and encouraged by local and external resource persons. In the 1980s, the college had worked with Erdiston and Samuel Jackman Prescod Polytechnic to train technical/vocational teachers for primary and secondary schools. However, in the 1990s, there was still limited training for technical/vocational teachers to meet increasing demand in schools, or even at the college itself. Thought was given to a suite of programmes spanning a certificate, diploma, associate degree, bachelor's and post-bachelor's diploma. However, the decision was taken to concentrate on the bachelor's and post-bachelor's levels.

Two short-term consultants from Seneca College in Canada assisted with the development of the curriculum using a Canadian framework. The programme started under the umbrella of the Computer Studies Division because of the heavy technology component. However, the senior tutor of the division became the deputy principal, and the programme soon migrated to being under that office. Antonia Coward continues to be the overall coordinator of this programme, with responsibility for the home economics option. Initially, Hamilton Jemmott was a coordinator, but he went on study leave in 1999 and on completion, moved to another institution. Peter Powlett was seconded from Deighton Griffith School as resource officer in the Resource Centre.

The development of the programme was supported by the HR Project, which provided the Resource Centre with relevant equipment and journals. All BCC teachers have access to the centre, especially for technology updates. Many of the technical courses are taught by SJPP staff; Erdiston College delivers two diploma in education courses at Barbados Community College, while Antonia Coward of Barbados Community College teaches technical/vocational courses at Erdiston.

Initially, the programme was offered full time, but later it was delivered part time to accommodate teachers who were not able to get study leave. The University of the West Indies recognized the qualification. Feedback on students who have gone on to get the master's degree has been positive. By 2017, about ten or twelve students had gone on to do the master's, and a few more to do doctorates.

Staff Development

From its inception, the college enabled staff development. Initially, this took the form of ongoing academic or professional education. Some staff went to other institutions but also were able to take courses at Barbados Community College as the range of offerings increased. Over time, the staff had developed their own knowledge and reputations and were able to offer training and technical assistance to other institutions and lead their own professional associations. To facilitate advanced study without paid leave, the board of management agreed to pay 50 per cent of the cost of Distance Education Programmes up front, with the remaining 50 per cent paid upon successful completion. During this maturity phase of the college, Lesia Proverbs attended a Pan American Conference in Miami (1990), and Pauline Sarjeant went on study visits to St Clair College and Cambrian College in Canada, as well as Pace University and Colombia University in New York, sponsored by the World Bank through the British Council (1990–1991).

Under the 1991–92 HR component of the second Education and Training Project component, Peggy Rickinson from the Nursing department went to Harvard University, and Kay Skeete, curriculum development specialist, to the University of Connecticut, where she looked at innovations in curriculum development and implementation. Dianne Grant-Medford, assistant registrar, spent two weeks at the Santa Fe Community College. For seven weeks, Randolph Brice from the Hospitality Institute was at Eastern Michigan University to look at the development of hotel administration IT applications to the hotel and tourism sector.

Representation on Boards/Consultancies, Training and Technical Assistance

Division of Health Sciences staff served the public as leaders and members of the Pharmacy Council, school boards, Barbados Registered Nursing Association, and the Barbados Basketball Association. Members of the Division of

Fine Arts gave their expertise as judges in exhibitions. As part of the twinning arrangement in 1991, St Clair College of Applied Arts and Technology was expected to carry out the second half of an IT consultancy. The situation was that the system donated by St Clair was unable to generate the statistical information in the required format for academic reports and financials at the college. As a maturing institution, the Barbados Community College had been successfully building capacity and was able to convert this into a local consultancy, undertaken by Dianne Medford and Gladstone Best. They repaired the design specifications and developed the required software for the college's student management information system.

Technical assistance on the design and delivery of associate degrees was given to Grenada National College by myself and Neville Badenock. The Division of Hospitality Studies was greatly involved in external training, contracted by the Canadian Training Awards Programme to conduct workshops for the Tourism/Hospitality sector in Antigua and Barbuda, St Lucia, Montserrat and St Kitts and Nevis. The Caribbean Development Bank also funded technical assistance to Antigua, Grenada, Guyana, Jamaica, Nevis and Aruba, through the Caribbean Hotel Training Initiative. The Language Centre offered training at a number of hotels, including Sandy Lane and Paradise Beach.

Staff Association

The Staff Association was formed in the 1980s, but its constitution was adopted on 1 April 1991. Its newsletter of 2001 made a case from a tertiary institution which had come of age, and which had little semblance of an A-level secondary school. It called for reforms and rewards to match responsibilities. In this regard, it envisaged a new administrative structure for the changing organization and a restructure of the staff, based on the growth in the number of students, staff and programmes at the college.

It saw the need for new promotional opportunities based on criteria such as qualifications, length of service and workloads. It appealed for a new framework of relationships with the civil service and school system and new conditions of work and remuneration across the college. It also sought to have a new financial arrangement with government, the private sector and individuals, as well as greater consideration given to academic freedom.

The 1998–1999 proposals by the college administration and the Staff Association to the board of management called for upgrade and restructuring. It posited that

> development of the college into an institution of high standing not only nationally but also regionally and internationally, its expansion of offerings to include Bachelor's degree programmes, its importance in providing education and training for

health, tourism, informatics and other sectors, and its mandate to continue the development of applied Bachelor's degrees can only continue, if regrading of staff is addressed. Already the College is losing staff to the public sector and it is becoming increasingly difficult to recruit and retain suitable staff especially in the informatics and Tourism Hospitality sector.

Articulation and Internationalization

During Principal Barnett's tenure, relationships with the University of the West Indies were brokered, presumably for validation of the college's programmes. No doubt the university's willingness to divest its Preliminary Science programme to the college was influenced by the reputation of the senior tutor of the Division of Science, Alvin Barnett, who was himself involved in that UWI programme. By 1986, the University of the West Indies had been invited to assess and had made a determination that the certificates in pharmacy and business studies would be accepted, like A-level qualifications, for normal matriculation to the university; that is, students would be able to complete the respective bachelor's degree in three years. In 1987, the paralegal certificate was similarly accepted for entry to the bachelor of law programme. However, the certificate in public health inspection was accepted for lower-level matriculation (that is, entry to a four-year bachelor's degree).

During Principal Holder's tenure, articulation arrangements continued to be brokered with the University of the West Indies, but they also were extended to international institutions. At the University of the West Indies in 1989, the medical record technology certificate had only lower-level matriculation status, but all the college's associate degrees were accepted for normal matriculation on the condition that students had a minimum cumulative grade point average (GPA) of 2.5. Normal matriculation status was accorded in 1992 to the diploma in land surveying, and in 1994 to the associate degree in computer studies.

In 1996, the two institutions agreed on a framework for articulation. By this time, enlightened by experience and aided by a Curriculum Development Desk at the college in 1998, and the university's own experience (residing in me – a former BCC senior tutor) and then UWI progamme officer in the Tertiary-Level Institutions Unit, which was established in 1996, there was greater transparency and better understanding of the articulation process. As a result of these developments, a number of programmes were assessed and gained advanced placement. These included associate degrees in mass communications, business studies and agriculture in 1999, as well as associate degrees in pharmacy in 2002, and in psychology and sociology in 2002 and 2003, respectively.

An Articulation Agreement was also worked out with the University of Miami, which agreed to accept associate degree graduates with a minimum GPA of 2.5 for entry into the third year of the four-year degree programmes, with a possible transfer of 30 credits. An agreement was also signed with Monroe College in New York City in 2001.

Many students applied to universities all over the world, and some got recognition of their qualifications and credit transfers. Some cases that were reported by the college include associate degrees in:

- Science at the University of Massachusetts, Amherst (Science); University of Florida, Gainesville (72 credits to Bachelor of Science in Pre-Veterinary Science)
- Applied Science, Building and Civil Engineering at Florida A&M University (44 credits towards Building and Civil for Architecture)
- Physical Education at Southeast Mission State University (all 71 credits towards the Bachelor of Science in Physical Education)
- Mass Communication – 30 credits to Howard University in Washington, DC, and exemption from Year 1 at UWI CARIMAC (Caribbean Institute of Media and Communication)

As the Division of Hospitality Studies evolved into the Hospitality Institute in 1997, it gained confidence and reached out to many international institutions to form partnerships. An articulation arrangement was formed with Johnson and Wales University in 1998.

The Department of Nursing's international partnerships began with an agreement of cooperation with the University of Texas Medical Branch at Galveston in December 1992. Following that, links were made with Georgia Health Sciences University and Bowie State University in Maryland, as well as with universities in the wider Caribbean. Nursing students visited from Guadeloupe; BCC Public Health Inspection students visited Trinidad and Tobago; BCC Cytotechnology students and the tutor attended a symposium in St Lucia; and Spanish students at Barbados Community College and the University of the West Indies took part in a competition funded by the Venezuelan Cultural Centre. Fine arts students won national competitions.

The position of Principal Holder as the president of the Caribbean Association of Tertiary Institutions also provided a platform for showcasing the work of the college, also fostering greater understanding and acceptance of the BCC programmes across the region. The internationalization thrust of the college was also evident in such arrangements as the Small Business Management Programme, funded by the Canadian International Development Agency and initiated by Mohawk College in Hamilton, Ontario. This attracted fifteen students, nine of whom completed it.

The college was obviously feeling the impact of the IT global trend. It had established the Computer Studies Division and expanded its offerings, continuing to computerize not only students' records but also the library stock, the latter funded by the World Bank. It also committed to a York University Microcomputer Development Network Project.

In 1996, there was evidence that overseas institutions had recognized the quality of the work of the college, not only in establishing articulation agreements, but also offering scholarships to students, exemplified by scholarship offers by Wilberforce and Syracuse universities to Mass Communication graduates; Florida Institute of Technology to Nicholas Gittens from the Division of Science; and from the Government of Brazil to Dianne Browne and Kerrie Marie. Fine Arts graduate Pauline Bellamy was awarded a scholarship to study design in England. In addition, the number of students registered at Barbados Community College from other countries in the region continued to increase, especially in (but not limited to) the Hospitality Institute and the Division of Health Sciences.

As part of its community outreach, the college allowed widespread use of the Liberal Arts Auditorium, facilities in the Division of Technology, its staff room and the Gymnasium.

Student Performance

Students distinguished themselves, earning national scholarships and exhibitions, as well as awards of excellence. They achieved a record performance in 2002 – ten scholarships, eleven exhibitions and three awards of excellence that year. In 1990, a liberal arts student, Quinton Hunte, became the first BCC student to win a Barbados Scholarship in the area of history, accounts and economics. In 2000, Stefan King gained a Physical Education football scholarship; Tonya Joseph from Commerce gained a volleyball scholarship to the United States; Glenn Watson, a graduate of the Music Programme, was awarded a National Development scholarship to pursue music at Acadia University in Canada; and Kellyann Patrick earned a Berklee College of Music, Boston, summer scholarship. Private secretary's diploma (PSD) students earned the World Silver Award in Business Practice for achieving the second-highest mark in the PSD examination.

In 1990–1991, Fine Arts students excelled. Graphic Design students designed signs and models for companies such as FB Armstrong, Bajan Queen, Mount Gay, Bodyline, the National Conservation Commission, Caribbean Tourism

Organization and McCann-Erickson. In the highly rated Portfolio Fashion Show sponsored by Abed and Co. Limited, twelve students participated at Queens Park Gallery; John Springer was awarded an advertising promotion by Bajan Queen and was hired by Mount Gay to conceive designs for the Royal Pavilion Hotel. Mark Hall won the ACTI logo competition and was awarded a scholarship by the Design Centre, Barbados Export Promotion Corporation, to study furniture design at Leicester Polytechnic. In addition, Mass Communication students had successful internships at the island's radio stations and television station.

The 1997, the bachelor of education programmes graduated sixteen students in industrial arts and twelve in home economics. The first BFA graduates (1998) included eleven students in fine arts and nine in graphic design, and of the 475 associate degree graduates, there were ten distinctions and thirty-nine credits. Graphic design students designed a logo for the UWI Tertiary-Level Institutions Unit. Fine Arts students started a weekly column called "BJ Art" in the *Nation* newspaper; Graphic arts students developed webpages for Life of Barbados, the Central Bank of Barbados and the Barbados Manufacturers Association.

Several physical education students won international football trophies in 1998. In addition, they collaborated with UWI Cave Hill to stage the Caribbean University Sports Association Men's and Women's Basketball competition; participated in a triangular men's and women's volleyball tournament involving Barbados Community College, the University of the West Indies and the University of the Virgin Islands. Barbados Community College also participated in the annual TLI Athletics meet, hosted by Sir Arthur Lewis Community College.

Agriculture students spent a week at Sir Arthur Lewis Community College with their tutor, Marcia Marville. The Division of Health Sciences hosted nursing students from the College of North Atlantic in Newfoundland and Labrador, Canada; George Mason University in Virginia; Addenbrookes Hospital in Cambridge, United Kingdom, and BCC students visited Suriname. Barbados Language Centre hosted students from Martinique and Guadeloupe.

Policies

The Barbados Community College had come into its adulthood, turning twenty-one years old in 1990. It had launched its computerized administration systems and graduated its first senior citizen (that is, someone over sixty years old). It was practised in the development of its own programmes for a diverse population, driven by workplace and community needs. This was reflected in the wide range of topics and in the passion inherent in articles written by the staff in the college's twenty-first anniversary celebration magazine. It was also reflected in the nature of the policies that were being instituted.

In 1968, the BCC Act made the following provision:

> 3.(2) The aim of the College shall be to provide a place of education offering instruction in all or any of the following fields of education, that is to say:
>
> (a) Agriculture
> (b) Commerce
> (c) Fine Arts
> (d) Liberal Arts
> (e) Science
> (f) Technology
>
> and in such other fields of education as the Minister may, from time to time, determine.

By 1990, the Barbados Community College was offering programmes in the following divisions: Liberal Arts, Science and Commerce (1969); Technology (1973); Fine Arts and Health Sciences (1974); Hospitality Studies (1980); Computer Studies (1988); Barbados Language Centre (1981); and General and Continuing Education (1987). In 1987, the college added the associate degree to its pool of certificate and diploma offerings and was contemplating offering the bachelor's degree.

The step was taken to make the language in the act more explicit. In November 1990, the BCC Act was changed at section 3A as follows: "(a) to enable the granting of certificates, diplomas, associate degrees, degrees and other awards to persons who have successfully completed a course of study approved by the Board; and at (b) to enable the conferral of honorary degrees and other awards upon persons who have rendered distinguished public service in Barbados and elsewhere". It also enabled at 3B, "the association or affiliation with universities, colleges or other institutions of learning as the College may consider necessary or appropriate, under the direction of the Minister and in accordance with the rules of the Board".

The college was beginning to provide access to students with various disabilities, and it sought in 1995 to formulate a policy to deal with that special category of students with dyslexia and schizophrenia.

By 1995, the associate degree had been available for eight years and had gained acceptance locally and internationally not only for entry to university, but also for transferring credits. The feedback from employers on graduate performance was positive. Performance in external examinations had also improved, and students were winning national scholarships, exhibitions and other awards. With this newfound external validation and reputation, the decision was taken internally to separate the associate degree from the British A level. This not only allowed wider freedom in programme design, but also provided the scope to achieve better relevance and greater functionality.

Enabled by the BCC Act, the confidence of the institution, the validation of other institutions and endorsement by stakeholders, the college moved forward in 1996 to offer its first bachelor's degree. However, with this new mandate, there was an acknowledgement of greater accountability. Therefore, 1997 was a period of strategic planning, upgrading of student information systems and refinement of academic policies and procedures as part of the college's quality assurance system.

Strategic Plan

In May 1997, the first BCC strategic plan (1997–2005) was funded by the World Bank Project and undertaken by Gaston Franklyn of Hickling Corporation and Gladstone Best of the Barbados Community College. Six broad challenges were identified: programme excellence; recognition as a tertiary-level institution; range of relevant programmes based upon future employment needs; organizational autonomy; improved access to qualified applicants, and flexibility and responsiveness to the lifelong learning needs of employed workers.

The plan acknowledged the reality that the college was a tertiary institution, created to provide education and training to as wide a cross section of the post-secondary and adult population as its facilities permitted. Some of its strengths were the diversity of its programme offerings; its highly qualified and motivated staff; public respect for its contribution to the economic and cultural life of the country; its high-quality programmes, valued by employers; the reasonable transfer function to universities; and increasing demand for the college's offerings by qualified applicants. But there were also identified weaknesses, including inadequate resources; low staff morale influenced by heavy workloads; limited financial resources; deteriorating physical infrastructure and a discrepancy between the reality and ideal of Barbados Community College as a tertiary institution; the span of control of the principal; uncoordinated (and therefore inefficient) continuing education initiatives; individualistic departments; uncoordinated planning; inadequate marketing and research; its image as a secondary school; the limits of its physical and programmatic capacity; and its limited institutional autonomy, sustained by too much government control.

The plan proposed revision of the act to improve the autonomy of the board; recognition of the institution as the University College of Barbados; changes in staff conditions of service; ongoing staff development; expansion of applied degrees; development of applied research capacity; formal accreditation; enhanced organizational structure; entrepreneurial activity for cost recovery; wise use of technology; revitalized infrastructure with the assistance of the private sector; identifiable quality assurance indicators; future-driven training for employment; enhanced systems for student transfer; flexibility and responsiveness to learning opportunities; and a strategic thinking culture.

Curriculum Development Desk

In line with the college's strategic direction, in 1998, a refinement of policies and procedures was undertaken and a policy document produced as part of a quality assurance drive. Disciplinary and grievance procedures, the study leave policy and performance appraisal policies were updated. A Curriculum Development Desk was also established in 1998. A new post was created in line with the institutional strengthening initiative of phase 2 of the World Bank project through Hickling Corporation, and a staff member of the college was appointed.

Kay Skeete had been a student at the Barbados Community College and returned as a tutor II (formerly designated as assistant tutor) in the General Education Programme between 1986 and 1998. During this time, she worked on associate degrees across the college and gained invaluable experience in curriculum development. She had had the opportunity to work across the divisions, and according to her accounts, the senior tutors were very positive and helpful. She had a rich experience at the Division of Health Sciences, where she also worked with the Pan American Health Organization, leading the development of a policy and curriculum on national food safety. She worked with the Environmental Division and trained government officers to become trainers of the trainers. She produced a manual for the Vector Control Unit and also worked on an assessment plan which was used for training persons involved in putting on the Cricket World Cup in 2007.

With Norma Holder as BCC principal, Skeete was appointed as the curriculum development officer at the level of tutor I (formerly designated as tutor) and served from 1998 to 2011. In collaboration with the Office of the Deputy Principal, the curriculum development officer contributed to the internal quality assurance of the college in areas such as curriculum management and staff development.

She proposed initiatives for prior learning assessment, portfolio building and computer-assisted learning. She conducted needs assessment across the college and consulted with all divisional and departmental managers and staff. She reinforced ideas of external moderation, promoted professional development seminars for staff, sought out potential curriculum linkages and identified resource requirements of the curriculum development desk. For her own professional development, she completed a fellowship attachment in 2003 at Humber College, Ontario where she received commendation.

Joint Degree with the University of the West Indies

As part of the move towards institutional maturity, in 1998, negotiations took place with the University of the West Indies towards the implementation of a joint bachelor's degree in hospitality and tourism management. Under this arrangement, associate degree graduates with a minimum GPA of 2.75 could earn the UWI three-year management studies bachelor's degree in two additional years. It could be conceived of as a two-plus-two arrangement. Students successfully completed the programmes. However, from 2000 on, the idea of joint certification proved legally difficult, and the degree was in fact a UWI degree – an arrangement which could be defined as joint delivery, but not joint certification. This was a disappointing outcome for Barbados Community College.

Thirtieth Anniversary

In 1999, the college marked its thirtieth year of existence with a number of events. On 30 June, it held thirtieth anniversary celebrations and an awards ceremony. The thirtieth anniversary theme was "Building Our Community, Learning for Life". Recognition was given to a number of individuals for their long service. Of the nineteen initial staff members appointed in 1968, only two remained – Principal Norma Holder and Keith Maxwell, a messenger/driver. Heather Hood, the retired senior executive officer for three principals; and David Trotman, a retired library assistant, had completed twenty-nine years. Science Tutor Mohamad Muhajari, Library Assistant Ronald (Gene) Philips and Groundsman Goulbourne Wharton also were recognized for twenty-eight years of service apiece.

The thirtieth-anniversary edition of the English department's magazine, *Words*, was edited by Jeanette Springer, head of the department. The Language Centre held annual language competitions jointly with the Venezuelan Institute of Culture and Cooperation and presented situational dramatizations by Spanish students from the fourth and fifth forms of secondary schools. It also organized "A la Vista", a poster competition in Spanish for associate degree students; and "Encuentro", a speech competition in Spanish, for A-level and second-year UWI students. All competitions were gradually reproduced in French. A plan for a Founder's Day celebration was approved but later stopped by the board of management.

Separation of the Associate Degree from A Levels

The year 2000 was very significant in BCC history. In June 2000, the board of management agreed to separate the A level from the associate degree, effective September 2000. The cabinet passed Education Act Cap. 41, to grant Barbados Scholarships, exhibitions and awards of excellence to students based on their associate degree results (July 2001). The criteria which were spelled out required students under twenty-one years to gain a minimum GPA of 3.8 as well as A grades in the two courses: English and Communication and Caribbean Politics and Society to qualify for scholarships; and earn a GPA of between 3.66 and 3.79 as well as A grades in English and Communication and Caribbean Politics and Society to qualify for national exhibitions.

The Idea of the University College of Barbados

In the Caribbean, the tertiary institutions of the 1960s and 1970s were maturing and in search of advancement. The university college presented itself as an option for advancement. Many institutions had established franchise and articulation links with the regional university, the University of the West Indies, which had set up a Tertiary-Level Institutions Unit in 1996 to explore more mutually beneficial interinstitutional arrangements. The community was mindful of traditional "Colleges of a University", as at Oxford and Cambridge, where the college was a member of a university community. The University of the West Indies was conscious of its own evolution from the University College of the West Indies, a college of London University, from 1948 until 1962. During this time, it was guided by the policies and practices of the parent institution, and its governance, funding pattern and award of degrees were under the control and direction of the parent institution. The experience of former colonies did not predispose the potential candidates to repeat such dependent arrangements.

What seemed to have emerged in 1996 was a desire for institutional independence and looking towards another type of university college – an independent, autonomous institution, a hybrid of the university and community college. The outlined British Colombian model appeared to be appealing: "They attempt to incorporate two fundamentally different cultures, the comprehensive community college and the conventional university, and strive to preserve a climate in which values such as 'parity of esteem', status equity, and internal cohesion prevail" (Dennison 1992, 121). It is interesting to note that the Community College of the Cayman Islands, which had been established as a part-time institution in 1975, had evolved into the University College of the Cayman Islands in 1985, the first of its kind in the English-speaking

Caribbean. In 1986, the University College of Belize evolved from the Belize College of Arts, Science and Technology, founded in 1979. However, this closed after fourteen years.

A point of view expressed is that the demise of the Belizean university college was "fueled by powerful competing external and internal forces, ranging from desperate educational need and outright political ambition to basic economic survival". There also was resistance generated by competing forces of nationalism which sustained the Belize College of Arts, Science and Technology versus colonial conservativism and drove the government-sponsored alliance with Ferris State College of Michigan to offer joint degrees with the University College of Belize (Perriot 2000).

In its strategic plan of 1995, the Barbados Community College signalled its intention to explore a new institutional development type – the university college. Interest by other institutions, such as the Bermuda College, led to the convening of an international conference in 2000, with the theme "New Approaches in Higher Education: The University College". At that conference, many local and international thinkers advanced views of the university college.

Two Canadian contributors, Jacquelyn Thayer-Scott and John Dennison, added to the dialogue as follows:

> The University College is more than a content and service provider. . . . It is a broker, mentor, facilitator and catalyst for its learners and communities in which the institution or its learners is grounded. (Thayer-Scott 2000, 16)

> The university college, as a new participant in the galaxy of post-secondary education, faces a formidable challenge to develop credibility in the minds of students, the community and its educational peers. Credibility will not be attained by simply adopting uncritically the practices and protocols of universities and community colleges. The reputation of a university college will ultimately rest upon its ability to interpret its unique mandate to government, to the education sector, and to the wider community, and to demonstrate that the mandate is being realised while maintaining a commitment to quality in all aspects of its operations. (Dennison 2000, 114)

A view from Malta was expressed as follows:

> The key characteristics of a UC in a small territory is to promote vibrant, healthy and regular interchange between education and work, between local and foreign staff and students, between students and workers, between youths and adults, between liberal and vocational education. Multi-functionality should dovetail nicely with the universality expected from a full fledged, tertiary education institution. (Baldacchino 2002, 28).

Keva Bethel (2000, 33), former president of the College of the Bahamas, expressed the view that

> university colleges are expected to provide educational programmes of varying levels and of relevance and quality, to retain their community service orientations and to be responsive to their many constituencies. In such contexts, there are inevitably broad-ranging demands from a wide spectrum of stakeholders, whose sometimes competing interests and priorities pose significant challenges to those who must plan and lead such institutions, usually in a reality of limited resources.

The conclusion for the host country was that "Bermuda needs a national strategic plan for tertiary education, that plan should consider whether or not a change from Bermuda College to Bermuda University College is the best answer to the national need for broader and more advanced tertiary education opportunities for Bermudians" (Berquist, Hammerston and Holder 2000, 104). The university college choice was not made.

The principal of the Barbados Community College (Holder 2000) seemed committed to the university college idea and suggested in her presentation at the conference that the university college, "an entity which has evolved as a result of changing education and training demands, needs faculty and other staff with certain characteristics to ensure that it fulfils its mission". She recommended a newer staff development focus consistent with "the rapid growth in knowledge over the past few decades; the growth in demand for tertiary education; the diversity in students entering tertiary educational institutions; the need to prepare graduates not only for further/higher study or for the world of work but also for life; the need for faculty to be equipped to position the institution to offer research and consultancy services to business and industry, and the need for staff, academic and administrative, to be able to use educational technology".

The BCC board of management agreed to this strategic direction and retained Oraco Consulting in 2001 to prepare a master plan for redevelopment of the aging infrastructure of the college. It appears that at the same time, the Ministry of Education was giving consideration to reorganizing the entire tertiary education system in Barbados and the creation of a new institution, the University College of Barbados, resulting from the amalgamation of Barbados Community College, Erdiston Teachers College and Samuel Jackman Prescod Polytechnic. The scope of the Oraco consultancy was broadened by the ministry to include this projected consolidation. The intention was to have the master plan completed for evaluation in January 2002, with prospects for its financing, building and management as a private/public-sector partnership.

In July 2001, the cabinet approved the establishment of the University College of Barbados and a planning committee was established to develop the parameters. Oraco submitted a comprehensive final report on 31 December 2001, presenting the venture as a once-in-a-lifetime opportunity. The master plan was drawn up in consultation with many stakeholders, including the Barbados Ministry of Education, Youth Affairs and Sports; UCB Planning Advisory Committee and Governance Sub-Committee; UCB Infrastructure Committee; boards of management of the three target institutions, and the administration and staff of the three institutions.

Phase 1 would include, at Eyrie, the Ring Development and UCB Administration, parallel with the EU-funded Language Centre, along with the start of work on the Technology Park at the SJPP campus. Phase 2 would include the Technology Centre at SJPP and Health Science Centre at Erdiston, along with renovations to several buildings at Eyrie. Phase 3 would include renovation work at Erdiston Teachers Training College, SJPP and Eyrie, as well as implementation of the Marine Gardens Plan.

Shortly after the minister of education announced the intention to establish the University College of Barbados in 2000, BCC staff went on strike. The discontent was not so much about the aspiration and status of the new institution, which included the word *university* in its name, but more about the consequences for staff. There were apprehensions about graduation of the institution to a higher level without commensurate improvement in the conditions of service for staff, particularly in relation to increase in remuneration for teaching at a higher level.

The occasion was seen as a long-awaited restructuring opportunity. The college's community ethos deteriorated into distrust. The Staff Association put on a well-supported two-day strike, organized by the Barbados Workers' Union arm of the college, to protest plans to "arbitrarily impose University College Status without consultation". The staff believed that the strike would galvanize the group, strengthen their case and put pressure on the government to set up committees and discuss projected conditions of service.

The Project Office was created in September 2002, and its work assigned to Patrick Rowe, who was substantively the Barbados Community College's assistant registrar in student affairs and who was appointed to that position at the college in November 2000, having completed postgraduate studies in Ohio.

To prepare for the project implementation, senior members of staff, including Gladstone Best, Patrick Rowe, Lindsay Waterman, Hartley Alleyne and Patrick Welch, went on a study tour to Halifax, Nova Scotia, to view educational institutions operating in public/private-sector partnerships. There was also a UCB Planning Committee co-chaired by Joseph Goddard and Robert Morris, and with Bevis Peters as deputy. The Infrastructure and Information Committee was chaired by Senator John Williams; Governance, Administration and Public Relations Committees by Lolita Applewaite; Finance by John Goddard; Human Resources by Robert Morris; Student Support Services by Anne Hewitt; and Programming and Curriculum Development by Bevis Peters.

In December 2002, an economic impact assessment of Oraco's recommendations was carried out by L.H. Consulting. This assessment was generally favourable. L.H. Consulting commented that although greater efficiency would be had by the expansion of capacity under an integrated institution, the establishment of the University College of Barbados was not necessarily the least cost-effective alternative. However, the consultant advanced the view that the project had the potential to generate significant externalities for the entire society, and that the projected increase in activities had the potential to increase productivity and contribute to overall development. The financial findings were that the total estimated costs of the UCB under a public/private-sector partnership arrangement would be $253.34 million, and not the $255.14 million estimated by Oraco. Under a government direct build arrangement, the total estimated project costs would be $254.78 million.

In 2003, a business plan was undertaken, and possible programmes were examined. For programme development, the growth areas identified by Roberts (2003c) were information and communication technology, hospitality and tourism, medicine and applied health, community services and entertainment. A range of forty-three new certificate, diploma and bachelor's degree programmes was identified for delivery by the University College of Barbados, either independently or in collaboration with other institutions.

Oraco did a presentation to the cabinet outlining the approximately $300 million project which would support the achievement of the UCB vision for a world-class institution, having renewed programme excellence, expanded capacity of ten thousand and a driver of economic development. It unveiled a once-in-a-lifetime opportunity for information and communication technology and communications; performance, media and entertainment arts, languages and commerce and enterprise at the Eyrie campus. It showcased the possibilities at the SJPP campus for trade technologies, advanced industrial technologies, environmental engineering and resource management.

The potential for the advancement of the college in education, health sciences and professional development was reflected in the plan for the Erdiston campus, and the possibilities of the Marine Gardens campus were captured in the plans for hospitality and tourism, international business development and commercial services. The Pine Basin Initiative unfolded possibilities for physical education, agro-sciences and technology, horticulture and landscaping. Importantly, the proposal also provided a seven-year plan for a phased development, with Phase 1 costing (in Barbados dollars) $85 million; phase 2 costing $95 million; phase 3 costing $80 million; and phase 4 costing $40 million. The cabinet deemed the costs to be prohibitive and turned to Inter-American Development Bank and the Caribbean Development Bank for infrastructure funding assistance. The attempts proved unsuccessful.

Change to the Semester System

In 2002, the college embraced a change from having three terms to two semesters. The change to the semester system was embraced as another sign of transitioning from the secondary to the tertiary system. This initiative was led by Deputy Principal Gladstone Best and senior tutor Neville Badenock, who conducted a number of workshops and seminars for staff and students.

This policy was expected to establish greater compatibility with regional and international academic calendars; enable greater flexibility in course scheduling; provide increased opportunities to rationalize the credit system and facilitate credit transfer; offer a longer teaching period of seventeen weeks; and create space for international summer programmes. For students, it would afford fewer start-ups, more recovery time, more time for internships and attachments and economic advantages such as reduction in time spent on registration. For staff, there were assurances that there would be no increase in teaching load and there would be appropriate revision of the curriculum. The change took place in August 2003.

Community Service/Awards

The maturing Barbados Community College celebrated the excellence of its staff, who earned a number of accolades: Esther Maynard, head of the Physical Education department, was awarded the 1999 International Olympic Committee Award, for the Barbadian who had made a significant contribution to the development of education and sport. In 2004, the director of the Hospitality Institute, Bernice Crichlow-Earle, received the Ministry of Education's

Inaugural Lifetime Achievement award for her contribution to tourism in Barbados.

Sir Lloyd Erskine Sandiford had incubated and supported the idea and reality of the Barbados Community College for more than thirty-five years. Some months before Principal Holder's resignation from office in January 2004, the decision was taken to confer the college's first honorary doctorate (Doctor of Laws) on Sandiford, in recognition of his contribution to education in Barbados.

The Hospitality Institute was awarded the World Quality Award (Diamond Category) from the company Business Initiatives Direction in Paris, based on seven quality principles. In July 2004, the Hospitality Institute was given the Gold Award for Quality and Commercial Prestige from the Otherways International company in Paris and, having achieved Green Globe status, was allowed to use the logo that went with it.

Thirty-five years earlier, as one of the college's first teachers, Principal Holder had no doubt encountered all three hundred students, including Ronald Williams. He had learned well and had progressed in life to become the president of Prince George Community College in Maryland. Closing the chapter, the principal must have smiled in agreement and with pride as she listened to the past student's Thirty-fifth Anniversary Lecture, "Challenge and Promise: Developing 21st Century Education in Barbados". In addition, she must have been heartened by a newspaper article which made a positive public assessment of her and the college, entitled "Holder Heads Success Story" (*Weekend Nation*, 31 January 1999).

Conclusion

Hitherto, the Barbados Community College has benefited from transformational leadership at all levels. To the Honourable Erskine Sandiford, as educator, minister of education, and later as the country's prime minister, the college owed its very existence; its ongoing maturation was supported by the awarding of its own associate degrees – a policy which he had also introduced. The idea of the University College of Barbados came from the college itself, but it was amplified and broadened by the then minister of education, the Honourable Mia Mottley.

Through the enabling environment created by successive boards of management, the college became an incubator for new ideas, policies and procedures. Because the principals believed in their staff and encouraged their creativity and innovation, scores of new programmes were churned out annually by enthusiastic teachers and committed administrators, in their attempts to meet emerging needs. The words of one senior tutor reflect the leadership from the middle which came from senior tutors and heads of departments. Her words were: "I loved what I did; I had a vision and this was not hampered by the principals."

While starting as a two-year college, with the highest level of its offerings being the same as that of the sixth-form schools, Barbados Community College soon evolved into a multipurpose institution which offered a wide range of associate degrees for university transfer as well as technical and vocational qualifications, with many programmes pitched at the middle management or professional level. To achieve the desired competencies, many of its programmes became three-year, full-time diplomas or associate degrees, pitched at a level considered by some to be at or close to the bachelor's degree. After twenty-seven years, the college was able to graduate from the confines of two-plus-two transfer arrangements with universities to conferring its own bachelor's degrees.

Initially, it distinguished itself from a secondary school by the diversity of the age of its students and the part- and full-time offerings, night and day. It was also different in the freedom it offered its students in its attendance requirements, choice of courses and course combinations and dress code. Unlike the US community college, it has never practised open access. Perhaps to protect its legitimacy and enable transfer of its students to universities, it has carefully guarded its stipulated entry requirements.

At the outset, the governance of the Barbados Community College by a board of management might have resembled that of the grammar schools. However, in the 1980s and 1990s, successive boards appeared to grow in autonomy from the Ministry of Education, and in greater sensitivity and responsiveness to the needs of the college. In the case of the twenty-first-century boards, the staff perceive closer oversight, a greater business focus and an increasing sense of divergence in vision between the college and the board.

The flat organizational structure and the limited opportunities for personal advancement outside the small numbers of established senior positions at the college may relate to the civil service links. In describing her plight, one college official explained the consequences of having a single principal, a single deputy principal and a single senior tutor for each division. In an institution of over five hundred full-time staff or a division of over thirty, she struggles with the only possibilities for upward progression as being the death or retirement of one of these senior colleagues.

The labels of principal, not president; senior tutor, not dean; tutor, not lecturer or professor; instructor, not teacher; part-time, not associate; and staff, not faculty are some of the homegrown, non-American and less popular features of the Barbados Community College. The span of control of the principal and the limited power of the academic board are other areas of concern. These are some of the homegrown features that have contributed to the lack of understanding of the nature and status of the college by outsiders, and even by insiders. These are some of the issues that were identified by the first strategic plan, and many have remained unresolved.

The Barbados Community College has remained accessible, limited only by the human, financial and physical resources to support its students and programmes, as well as by the students meeting the entry requirements to regular or bridging programmes. Fees have been kept low for affordability; application fees were nominal, and for several years, no other fees were charged to Barbadian students. Later on, a small registration fee and accident fees were applied to nationals, while non-nationals would pay registration, medical insurance and visa fees, as well as tuition. Many are funded through scholarships.

From 2007, non-nationals paid registration, medical insurance and visa fees, totalling just under Bds$9,000 per year. Part-time students pay fees ranging from $300 to $750 per semester. All students pay tuition and administrative fees for the bachelor's degrees. For locals, these range from just over $2,000 to just over $3,000 per year; for non-nationals, the fees range from just over $12,000 to $20,000.

During the Holder years, the college continued to demonstrate flexibility and responsiveness and used its advisory committees to keep in touch with the public. Needs assessments were common tools for programme development. There was a symbiotic relationship with the community. College staff served as members, leaders and advisors in the wider community and brought their experience to bear on programme planning and policies. Innovation has been evident not only in new programmes, but also in adaptation to in-service, day release and part-time, off-campus programmes, internships and attachments, as well as on the expanding pool of electives.

During Principal Holder's tenure, the college reached the age and stage of maturity. It successfully became a baccalaureate institution with the offer of its first two bachelor's degrees and the cabinet had revised the BCC Act to explicitly support this venture. The college had outgrown the validation provided by the British external examinations and asserted its ability to design, deliver, evaluate and certify its own offerings. The Government of Barbados legitimized this through legislation to offer national scholarships and exhibitions, based on student performance in associate degree programmes. Many BCC students had achieved the standard set.

Internal collaborative arrangements had grown; local collaboration among Erdiston Teachers College and the Samuel Jackman Prescod Polytechnic increased. The partnership with local businesses was strong. The influence of the college in the region was amplified through the sustained presidency of the Association of Caribbean Tertiary Institutions by Principal Holder. The quality of BCC programmes was validated by the respect accorded to it by the regional and international universities, evidenced by the plethora of articulation arrangements.

Students won prizes in sport, language competitions, and academic performance. Many of them were recognized for their contribution to society. Several showed off their talents in the Portfolio programmes of the Fine Arts Division, their culinary skills in the Hospitality Institute and their cultural talents in Communifesta.

Further, the staff won international and local recognition for their own achievements and brought credit to their divisions and their college. A public lecture commemorating the thirtieth anniversary of the college was given by an outstanding woman, Lolita Applewaite, who, while bringing prevailing gender issues to the fore, had to acknowledge the achievements of the college's female principal and other stalwarts.

It is clear that many opportunities had been embraced and the college was doing well. However, many were still preoccupied with its probable evolution to a university college, as well as with the implications for the restructure of its staff.

This period saw the borrowing of the semester system, the addition of new infrastructure, the introduction of the first bachelor's degrees and new legislative recognition of associate degrees for the award of Barbados Scholarships. New bachelor's degrees were introduced into what had been a two-year college. There was the new objective of reinventing itself to become a university college and the related new push for advanced and terminal degrees. There was widening of its global reach through an extensive array of new articulation arrangements with institutions in Canada, the United States, the United Kingdom and within the region.

Figure 10.1. Hospitality Institute, opened in 1997. Photograph compliments of Barry Tudor.

Figure 10.2. The Barbados Language Centre, officially opened in 2008. Photograph compliments of Barry Tudor.

Figure 10.3. Sir Lloyd Erskine Sandiford, prime minister of Barbados, 1987–1994. Photograph compliments of the BGIS.

Figure 10.4. Sandiford receiving an honorary doctorate in 2004

11.

A Phase of Uncertainty for Gladstone Best, 2004–2014

By September 2004, the Barbados Community College had grown up to the extent that one of its offspring was assuming the position of principal. The college had transitioned from infancy under Charlie Best, through adolescence with Alvin Barnett, and then into adulthood with Norma Holder. The adult years were replete with activity, busyness, growth, development, publicity, student success and even frustration.

When it reached thirty-five years old, the college seemed to be moving into a midlife crisis. It was searching for a new identity – an opportunity to reinvent itself and recover its self-confidence. Overcoming the apprehensions about the technical issues of Y2K (the coming of the year 2000) and the initial disquiet surrounding the announcement of the University College of Barbados in 2000, the college settled down under Principal Holder, becoming excited about a reincarnation. She presided over her last graduation in February 2004.

It was Gladstone Best who changed the month of the annual graduation ceremony to November. At his first graduation as principal in November 2004, the mood was still one of confidence and optimism about the institution. During this landmark event, the founder of the college, Erskine Sandiford, was awarded the college's first honorary doctorate, and the future seemed bright. The baton was being passed to Gladstone Best.

He had made an interesting journey through the college, starting as an evening student at the Harbour site in 1972, when he studied A-level chemistry and biology. Like his last two predecessors, he had a science background and his career at the college began in the Division of Science, where he taught chemistry and mathematics, part-time in 1979 and full-time from 1980 when he became an assistant tutor.

In 1984, he responded to an advertisement for someone to work in computer studies, an area into which the college was venturing. Facilitated by a twinning arrangement with St Clair College of Applied Arts and Technology in Canada, he spent a year (1984–1985) at that institution studying computer science. On his return, he worked with Brenda Barrow from the Division of Technology and Ken Archibald from St Clair College of Applied Arts and Technology, who had both started the unit. Archibald left, followed by Barrow soon afterwards, and Gladstone Best became the tutor in charge of the department of Computer Studies in 1987.

The BCC Registry established the post of assistant registrar, to focus on computerizing its systems in collaboration with St Clair College. Gladstone Best was invited to act in that post, while also serving as tutor in the Computer Studies department for the 1988 academic year. He took time off to pursue a master's degree in educational administration in 1989–1990 and then returned to the Computer Studies department. He became the senior tutor in 1993, when the department was upgraded to a division, and he completed his PhD in 1996.

The deputy principal, Nigel Bradshaw, retired in 1998, and Gladstone Best filled the vacancy. After four years of serving as deputy principal, a temporary position opened up at the University of the West Indies from 2002 to 2004, and he assumed the role of programme officer in the Tertiary-Level Institutions Unit. During this period while he was away from the college, Angelita Sandiford, senior tutor of the Division of General and Continuing Education, acted as deputy principal until her retirement in December 2004.

On Holder's retirement as principal in May 2004, Gladstone Best returned to the college to take up a two-year contract from 2004 to 2006 and was granted yearly contracts subsequently until 2015, when he retired. Lauretta Hackett acted as deputy principal from 2005 until her retirement in 2011, after which there were a number of appointments as acting principal and deputy principal.

There are three points worth noting. First, Gladstone Best had a long and varied career, as well as many types of experiences, as he moved through the divisions of Science and Computer Science, the office of the registry, as well as during his service as deputy principal, UWI programme officer and then BCC acting principal. Second, from the outset, the soft-spoken and unassuming persona of Gladstone Best was eclipsed by the personality of his powerful, well-known and influential predecessor. Third, unlike the principals who served before him, he was given a series of contractual appointments.

Under the circumstances, perhaps due to his ties to his substantive post of deputy principal during his contractual appointments as principal in his last eleven years at the college, there was a domino effect, generating a series of acting appointments at different levels of the organization. No doubt this had a deleterious effect on the institution in general, as well as specific negative consequences for the senior leadership, including the principal, the deputy principal and several senior tutors.

Initially, the staff associated the contractual and pervasive acting appointments with the uncertainties linked to the pending establishment of the University College of Barbados. However, when confirmed appointments were made at the other two potential partner institutions, Erdiston Teachers College and Samuel Jackman Prescod Polytechnic, the unease at the college intensified and speculation was rife.

It is well-established industrial relations practice that insecurity of tenure fosters lower staff engagement, less innovation and reduced risk-taking. This situation achieves more significant proportions if it represents an uncharacteristic and unexplained change from the established norms. The ongoing development of any community college, especially a mature one, requires a spirit of openness, enterprise and innovation. It is for these reasons that this phase of the college, 2011–2014, may be regarded as a period of constraint, uncertainty or even a midlife crisis.

In spite of these constraints, Gladstone Best's tenure achieved

- Infrastructure development
- Programme development
- Staff professional development
- Articulation arrangements
- Ongoing student success

At the end of his stint, there were many lessons to be learned about institutional development as it related to the University College of Barbados proposal, political legacy and institutional governance.

In his own words, Best observed (Graduation Report 2008, 11), "The College is in the process of reviewing its operations to effect improvements in all areas. We have submitted our registration with the BAC (Barbados Accreditation Council) and we look forward to institutional and programme accreditation with that agency. We recognise that this requires much self-examination and we are already in that mode." He also asserted:

> BCC will intensify professional development for all categories of staff and will enhance structures and systems that support student learning at the institution. We will partner with other institutions as well as public and private sector agencies to ensure that we have the resources to create the right type of environment that would permit students to maximise learning. The physical plant is an integral part of an appropriate learning environment and we will aggressively seek to enhance our plant.
>
> After 34 years at the Eyrie campus without an adequate maintenance programme, we are seeing evidence of deterioration. This will be given immediate attention so that we will have a beautiful mix of new and old buildings which are functional and aesthetically pleasing.

He even pleaded for resources, reminding his audience (Graduation Report 2013, 6):

> Given that the BCC produces graduates in critical sectors of the economy (such as health, tourism and the cultural industries), it is essential that the institution be given the requisite resources to deliver its programmes within an environment that can optimise learning. In our curriculum development and operational planning, we focus on quality assurance to ensure that graduates can compete in the global arena. Inadequate funding produces quality issues that may constrain the college's efforts in improvement. My simple plea is for adequate funding for the BCC. We need a substantial injection of funds to ensure that we can maintain a competitive learning environment and continue to fulfil our role of educating high-quality workers for the vocations. In an environment of rising costs and global competition from borderless institutions, local institutions cannot do more with less.

It is true that the principal indicated that he would give priority to quality, specifically registration of the college; professional development of staff; and brokering partnerships and maintenance of property, albeit conditional on funding. And he did.

New Developments

The Idea of Registration and Accreditation

To the outsider, it may seem quite strange that a college established in 1968 should be discussing plans for registration and accreditation in 2008. Some explanation is warranted for this. As former colonies of Britain, universities were established under Royal Charter, and they derived their legitimacy from their elitism, internal self-regulation, clearly understood standards within the university community and reputation. The University of the West Indies was initially a College of the University of London. When it became a full-fledged university in 1962, older institutions such as teachers' colleges sought and obtained affiliations and associations which served to validate their operations. As newer institutions such as community colleges emerged, many also sought associations, articulations or affiliations with and/or external examinations by the University of the West Indies and other universities in order to enhance their legitimacy.

In the region, the University Council of Jamaica was the first accreditation body established in 1987, some time after the first community college was begun in Jamaica in 1974, and the first community college in the region in Barbados opened in 1968. It was not until 2004 that the Barbados Accreditation Council was established and given the responsibility to regulate the tertiary education environment through the legal requirement for registration of all tertiary institutions. It is in that context that the Barbados Community College set out to prepare itself for registration and assigned this task to the deputy principal, Lauretta Hackett.

The college had a history of demonstrating its quality through the success of its students when they took British external examinations. It had established a number of articulation arrangements and memoranda of understanding with colleges and universities in the United States and Canada, and in 1987, it had recognition of its own associate degrees, including transfer agreements, with the regional University of the West Indies. Since 1996, discussions were in progress about an upgrade of the Barbados Community College to a university college.

In this context, it can be seen that many staff members questioned the necessity for and resisted the training which the deputy principal was attempting to organize, in order to introduce a new approach to quality assurance. However, Hackett had been academically prepared for this undertaking through her exposure in Canada; at the Leadership Foundation for Higher Education in London; at a Management of Lifelong Education seminar at Harvard University in Cambridge, Massachusetts; and in 2005, at the Center for Leadership at the University of Ohio in Athens. With the assistance of the curriculum development officer, she managed to gradually improve staff awareness about quality assurance and move slowly towards the documentation of policies and the collection of evidence for self-study – a requirement for registration. As indicated earlier, they prepared documents including "Procedures and Regulations for Academic Evaluation (Revised)"; "Disciplinary and Grievance Procedures for Staff"; "Study/Training Leave Policy" and "Performance Appraisal Instruments".

The school's fortieth anniversary was celebrated by a Barbados Government Information Service documentary, shown on 27 October 2008. The fortieth anniversary gala took place in February 2009. In 2011, the Counselling and Placement Centre co-facilitated the inaugural, weeklong Healthy Lifestyle Exposition. It also conducted graduate seminars and predeparture orientation sessions for students planning to study in Canada. In addition, the centre hosted meetings between college recruiters from Canada, the United Kingdom and the United States and local secondary school students. It also conducted workshops on study skills, computer studies and preparation for the world of work, and assisted nongovernmental organizations with community outreach.

The library conducted training and assisted students in creative projects, using new technologies including smartphones and tablets. It also initiated resource sharing with the Samuel Jackman Prescod Polytechnic and Erdiston Teachers Training College.

In 2011, the new board of management proceeded along a path of creating a more business-oriented institution, evidenced by the creation of senior administrative positions and offering them on short-term contracts. The first, in 2011, was that of manager of human resources and labour relations. The board also instituted changes in its operations, including discontinuation of the use of the registrar as its secretary. In 2012, it appointed an administrative assistant to serve as the board's secretary, in an independent office. In that same year, the board appointed a business development officer and a manager of management information systems.

The Idea of the Strategic Plan

In 1997, the college's first strategic plan (1997–2005) was developed with the assistance of Gladstone Best. Some of its goals had been realized, but many others were still outstanding. The faculty agreed that a new plan should be undertaken, this time using a deliberate, bottom-up, data-driven and strategic planning approach. The curriculum development officer, Kay Skeete, was one of the leaders of this venture. Staff members were assigned different roles; some went to the schools, while others interviewed staff. Halfway through the process, the staff were informed that the board was commissioning its own strategic plan for the college. The college halted its planning. The board hired CXC assistant registrar Guy Hewitt to develop what the college saw as a top-down plan. However, this plan was never presented to the college community.

Infrastructure and Maintenance

The deterioration and inadequacy of the BCC plant were not a secret. They were among the drivers of the proposal for its renewal through the UCB project. Students protested from time to time. The staff commented that the Liberal Arts and Commerce building was deteriorating badly: bathrooms in need of repair, offices prone to flooding, and stairways with missing steps. The principal's graduation reports of 2008, 2012 and 2013 highlighted his concern and frustration about the lack of maintenance.

However, during Best's tenure, modest progress was made in specific divisions. During academic year 2011–2012, the old General Education building was refurbished, allowing the relocation of the Industry Services Unit from the Harbour site and provision of enhanced studies for mass communication. The electrical system in the Administration and Commerce/Liberal Arts blocks was upgraded and cables installed for the collegewide cable network. In subsequent years, the tenor of the principal's graduation address was still gloomy: "The upgrading that was done on the aging plant was minimal, compared to what is needed to be done to have the optimal physical environment to provide the quality education that the college wishes to deliver" (Best 2013, 6). The inadequacy of the space shared by dance, music and theatre arts forced the Division of Fine Arts to rent off-campus space, at a relatively high cost.

The ground-breaking ceremony for the new Language Centre was held on 7 June 2006. Completion was expected in 2007, but it was delayed. The Language Centre keys were handed over to the college in March 2008, and relocation took place in May. The Language Centre building was officially opened in September 2009. Funding was provided by the European Union and the Government of Barbados. The mandate of the new centre was extended to offer lifelong learning for law enforcement, medicine and sports tourism. That was also the first Caribbean centre to offer an Internet-based Test of English as a Foreign Language. The former director and deputy principal at that time, Lauretta Hackett, recounts the relief she experienced at the opening of the centre in this new location, far from the noise of the traffic at the former venue in the Liberal Arts Division.

The college also undertook the refurbishment of the physics laboratory, including the conversion of the stock room into an air-conditioned dark room for optics, laser experiments and atomic physics demonstrations. The Hospitality Institute also saw a major upgrade during the summer breaks of 2008 and 2009, including installation of a new pool surface, upgrade of the fire alarm system, restoration of guest rooms' furniture and painting of the buildings' exterior. The most significant infrastructural work was the addition of the third floor for science, and the second floor above the liberal arts auditorium to accommodate nursing students, as well as the erection of the second floor above the Students' Centre to accommodate general education students.

Programme Development

Over this period, four new associate degrees were introduced:

- Office Administration and Management, 2004 (Division of Commerce)
- Sport Management, 2005 (Department of Physical Education)
- Paralegal Studies, 2006, open to former graduates of the Certificate Programme who needed thirty-six credits for the AD (Division of Commerce)
- Procurement, 2014 (Division of Commerce)

A diploma in gerontology was also created, with sixteen students in the Division of Health Sciences.

In addition, two new bachelor's degrees were launched:

- Pharmacy, 2014
- Nursing, 2014

The bachelor of pharmacy degree was a long time coming. In many countries of the region, the decision had been taken to require by law that the entry qualification for the practice of pharmacy be a bachelor's degree. In Barbados, however, the council continued to accept the Barbados Community College's three-year associate degree and internship for registration. Some time earlier, UWI St Augustine had assessed the BCC qualifications and offered the option to BCC Pharmacy associate degree graduates to upgrade to a bachelor's degree via distance learning.

At the same time, BCC Pharmacy coordinator Lesia Proverbs worked with Nova Southeastern University in the United States, Canadian universities and the Paramedical Council to upgrade the college's associate degree to meet international standards for a bachelor's. Associate degree graduates were allowed the option of upgrading by way of a two-year, part-time offering. New full-time students could complete their bachelor's degree in four years.

Similarly, the Regional Nursing Council and some national nursing bodies in the region had accepted the ideal of a bachelor's degree as the minimum qualifications for entry to practice. Many BCC graduates seized various opportunities to upgrade their associate degrees to bachelor's degrees through distance arrangements with the UWI Mona and St Augustine campuses, as well as US universities. With assistance from the Pan American Health Organization and approval from the General Nursing Council, the Barbados Community College was able to revise and upgrade the curriculum to a bachelor's degree, offering the options for upgrade as well as direct entry.

During Gladstone Best's tenure, short courses were also developed and delivered, including a Practical Math Elective in the General Education Division (2005); Hospitality Institute's fourteen new part-time programmes (2006); Experiential Learning (2007); and two three-credit, one-semester courses in creative writing, Short Fiction I and II, in the Liberal Arts Division (2007). The Division of Health Sciences also coordinated training for ambulance service staff in collaboration with the Ministry of Health and Essex Ambulance Trust. The Division of Computer Studies conducted the BCC Mobile Application Design and Development Programme during 2013–2014 to link ideas with entrepreneurship. Students in the associate degree programme in agriculture participated in a staff exchange with Essex County College in Newark, New Jersey, where they got training in hydroponic farming.

The pool of ongoing offerings included certificates in creative writing, paralegal studies, information technology, interior design, fashion design, dental assistance, nursing assistance, general catering and private secretary's diploma; associate degrees in arts, science and applied science; bachelor's degrees in education and fine arts; post-associate degree diplomas in community health nursing, community mental health nursing, inspection of meat and other foods, midwifery and public health administration; and Barbados Language Centre courses, customized to local and international students. The Hospitality Institute introduced its pillars: "proactive leadership, 'CAN-DO' attitudes, feedback indicators, spotlight on the customer, consistent performance, opportunities for earning and contribution". Its motto was: "Clients First. . . . We deliver more than we promise."

Changes were made in the Physical Education Department to reorganize the college into "eight teams, ten sports, one brotherhood". The eight teams combined some divisions as follows: General Education with Technology; Liberal Arts, Fine Arts with Language Centre; Health Sciences; Hospitality Institute; Science; Computer Studies; and Commerce with Physical Education. The teams competed intramurally in ten sports, culminating in an athletics competition. Futsal (indoor football) had become the most popular sport at the college and was in the national spotlight. Students from the University of the West Indies, Samuel Jackman Prescod Polytechnic and the Barbados Community College competed in that sport.

Since 2004, invitations were extended to Sir Arthur Lewis Community College, St Lucia, and the T.A. Marryshow Community College, Grenada, through the twelve-member Caribbean University Sports Association. Competitions were held in Jamaica and Trinidad and Tobago. Events in Barbados took place at the Tennis Centre, UWI Cave Hill and Barbados Community College. The local committee of the association morphed into the Tertiary Institutions Sports Association of Barbados (TSAP), which became a part of the International University Sports Federation (FISU). Senior Tutor June Caddle served as TSAP president and a council member of the Pan American Sports Association (FISU America), and her goal was to revive the Caribbean University Sports Association.

Students

Student Activities

The Students' Guild was actively involved in fundraising, self-help projects related to beautification and making contributions to charities. The Barbados Language Centre students continued with language competitions in collaboration with the Venezuelan Institute for Culture and Cooperation, instituted in 1992.

Student Performance in Examinations

The decision to award Barbados Scholarships and Exhibitions on associate degree performance resulted in many successes for the Barbados Community College. For instance, as shown in table 11.1, in 2002, there were seven scholarships and ten exhibitions; and in 2003, there were ten scholarships and fourteen exhibitions. Over the period 2004–2014, students performed reasonably well, gaining Barbados Scholarships in six of these years: seven each in 2005 and 2007 and a number of exhibitions every year, with as many as eighteen in 2006, but fewer in subsequent years.

Table 11.1. Barbados Scholarships and Exhibitions, 2001–2014

Year	Scholarships	Exhibitions
2001	2	2
2002	7	10
2003	10	14
2004	5	17
2005	7	11
2006	6	18
2007	7	15
2008	2	3
2009	0	8
2010	2	17
2011	2	8
2012	0	3
2013	0	3
2014	0	1

Public protests (that had been going on since 2001) about the ease with which BCC students seemed to get these awards led to a revision of the scholarship requirements in 2012. Achieving that revised standard (all A grades and a 4.0 GPA) proved challenging. The change in regulations in 2012 may be associated with a sustained reduction in the number of awards. After 2011, there were no scholarships in this period. In 2014, a visually impaired student, Janeil Odle, won the only exhibition. Students also won awards of excellence.

The John Wickham Scholarship was established and continued annually. There were ongoing awards for outstanding performance in the Certified General Accountant programme and private secretary's diploma. US sports scholarships in the areas of football and volleyball were awarded. BCC students gained access to scholarships to Cuban universities, awarded by the Cuban government. A few universities, including Berklee College of Music in Boston, offered scholarships to outstanding music students. From 2008 on, the Canadian government, through the Emerging Leaders in the Americas Programme (ELAP), began to offer scholarships, and several were awarded.

It became normal practice not only for students to go on overseas tours and study visits, but also for the college to host students from other countries. Agriculture students visited Guyana; music students toured and performed in Grenada; geography students went to Jamaica; language students went to Martinique and Guadeloupe; and students took part in the model OAS Assembly in the Dominican Republic. The college hosted nursing students from Duke University in Durham, North Carolina; students from University of Kentucky; two students from Canada for a semester; and a student exchange took place between Jefferson Community and Technical College in 2008. BCC nursing students also attended overseas conferences in Baltimore, Maryland.

Students competed in sports and games internally, as well as with other institutions and against national teams. In the interdivisional games, students competed in athletics, badminton, basketball, cricket, futsal, netball, road tennis (a Barbadian game), table tennis, tennis and volleyball. They won awards in the Caribbean University Sports Association football and table tennis tournaments at UWI St Augustine, and in the second Caribbean University Sports Association Games at UWI Mona, winning trophies in basketball and volleyball. They competed against Sir Arthur Lewis Community College in St Lucia, and students from the community colleges in St Lucia and St Vincent also participated in BCC Athletics meets. BCC students won intercollegiate cricket, and the volleyball and basketball teams won Premier League competitions locally. Also, students were selected to national sports teams.

Consistent with the trends of environmental conservation and entrepreneurship, science students created and showcased recycling and cosmetic projects. Students from the divisions of Fine Arts, Technology, Commerce, General and Continuing Education and the Barbados Language Centre participated in the Barbados Manufacturers Association Exhibition. As a result of their displays, some students got invited for attachments with industry. Science students won the "Best Overall Exhibit" awards in 2010 at the Sci-Tech Expo staged by the National Council of Science and Technology.

In 2014, Barbados Community College went mobile in National Heroes Square in the city of Bridgetown to advertise their offerings. Projects were submitted for funding, including an Animation Design and Development programme and a Computer Music Laboratory project from the Division of Fine Arts. The latter received funding for equipment from the European Union.

Fashion design and music students participated successfully in national competitions and exhibitions. The Division of Fine Arts continued to have successful annual Portfolio seasons at the Frank Collymore Hall, the Grande Salle, the Lloyd Erskine Sandiford Centre and at its base at Morningside. Theatre Arts students presented plays directed by their tutor, Yvonne Weekes. In collaboration with the Venezuelan Institute for Culture and Cooperation, the Barbados Language Centre continued to stage annual competitions for BCC and UWI students.

A team of one chef and Hospitality Institute students represented the Caribbean against competitors from United States, Canada, Scotland and Mexico at an international meet in Grand Rapids, Michigan, where they won a gold medal for the national dish. In addition, in 2014, out of a total of nine student entries in the Caribbean Advertising Federation Awards (formerly the American Advertising Awards), BFA students won five awards, including two gold medals.

Professional Development of Staff and Staff Awards

Perhaps in anticipation of the University College of Barbados, staff development continued apace. During this period, staff members earned five PhDs; thirty-two master's degrees; five bachelor's degrees and twenty postgraduate diplomas. Several staff members participated in or led seminars and workshops. Many were publishing books, book chapters or articles. They continued to serve on national and regional professional bodies. Many were involved with the Caribbean Examinations Council as chief or junior examiners. Several were trainers for the public and private sectors and served as judges in national cultural competitions. In addition, there were some who were part-time teachers at universities and other tertiary institutions. A staff member directed the Barbados Season of Dance, resurrected after an eight-year break. Staff served as leaders and members of such organizations as the Regional Nursing Body, the World Anti-Doping Agency and the *BIM Literary Magazine*. Antonia Coward was invited by the Ministry of Education to offer training to home economics teachers in Antigua and Barbuda.

In the Division of Fine Arts, music tutors including Roger Gittens and Andre Woodvine continued to perform nationally and internationally, and James Lovell launched a music CD. Yvonne Weekes, Nancii Yearwood and Nathan Gibbs served nationally as resource persons in the arts. In 2012, the short film on HIV scripted by chemistry tutor Annette Alleyne won a NIFCA gold award.

In the Division of Liberal Arts, staff members won national literary awards, including an award-winning book called *Blue Latitudes: Stories from Caribbean*

Women at Home and Abroad. Tutors Natalie Walthrust-Jones and Trevor Marshall of Barbados Community College coauthored a book chapter, and others produced academic papers at conferences. Allison Thompson was the coeditor for a new book, *Curating in the Caribbean*. The Hospitality Institute stood as a shining beacon. Its stellar achievements included winning the Green Globe 21 Benchmark Award; the BHTA President's Award for Hotel of the Year in the A Class category; the Ministry of the Environment Award for Youth Involvement in Sustainable Development; and the World Quality Commitment Award (Diamond Category).

An instructor won the Prime Minister's Hospitality NIFCA award. The Hospitality Institute won recognition by Initiatives Directions in Paris and achieved Green Globe Status. The Hotel PomMarine met the requirements to be recognized as an EarthCheck Benchmarked Accommodation–Vacation Hotel. The Hospitality Institute was again awarded the Gold Award for Quality and Commercial Prestige from Otherways International in Paris.

Individuals in other divisions also won awards, including Hartley Alleyne, the Fine Arts senior tutor, whose painting, *The 11+*, was chosen to represent Barbados at the sixtieth anniversary of the Exhibition of Contemporary Art in Geneva, Switzerland. The Health Sciences Division won the Outstanding Service Award by CASMET in recognition of its student support in the period 1991–2007. The library won the Award for Innovation offered by the Caribbean Tertiary-Level Personnel Association. Esther Phillips won a number of literary awards, was honoured to have her book on the reading list of the English department and was later named poet laureate of Barbados.

The Fate of the UCB Project

In 2005–2006, the UCB Project produced a detailed plan for operationalizing the University College of Barbados. The wheels of change were turning slowly. General elections were held in Barbados, leading to a change in government in 2008. The new government provided the opportunity for the UCB Project team to make a presentation to persons who were tasked with looking for a way forward. Both listened to the presentation, discussed, considered the situation, and in the end, ruled that the project would not be implemented.

The public came to its own conclusions about the nonimplementation of the project. The economic challenge was evident. The argument about the true meaning of the term *university college* and its relationship with a counterproposal of a *comuniversity* (community university) was never fully discussed and remained unresolved. Some argued that although the total costs were prohibitive, components of the project could have been undertaken; while others concluded that the whole idea was conceptually flawed, riddled with challenges inherent in merging institutions which function at different levels, in spite of the fact that there were precedents for that in Barbados itself and other Caribbean countries. Yet others saw in this idea a threat to the UWI Cave Hill campus. A few persons pointed to the question of politics and legacy because the Barbados Community College was established by the Democratic Labour Party government and the University College of Barbados was being advanced by the Barbados Labour Party government.

Under these circumstances, the UCB Project office morphed into the Higher Education Development Unit created in 2008, and continued to be headed by Patrick Rowe. The terms of reference were expanded to provide developmental advocacy on behalf of Barbados Community College, Erdiston Teachers College and Samuel Jackman Prescod Polytechnic. The aim was to bring about their alignment with international best practices, giving oversight and ensuring realization of the Ministry's objectives, facilitating access, programme growth, expansion of ICT capability and collaboration with other institutions for development.

Fortuitously, a neighbouring property formerly owned by Sir Arnot Cato and later acquired by Cable and Wireless was advertised for sale in 2005. Patrick Rowe brought this to the attention of the principal, Gladstone Best, who convinced the board and the government to buy the property. This was done and the property was vested in the Ministry of Education, but for future development of the college. In the interim, this facility currently houses the Higher Education Development Unit.

Although the UCB infrastructure project was not implemented, the Higher Education Development Unit has continued to work with the three institutions in different ways: infrastructure development at Erdiston and rationalization of programmes and professional development of staff of all institutions, such as through the two-yearly higher education conferences. The unit has also played a role in facilitating the accreditation of the institutions. Needless to say, the heavy investment in planning for the University College of Barbados has left a rich and useful foundation that can be used as a take-off point for the inevitable future institutional development of the Barbados Community College, Erdiston and Samuel Jackman Prescod Polytechnic.

Partnerships and Articulation

The college established an arrangement with Mount Allison University in 2005. In addition, over the period, the Hospitality Institute stood out in the number of partnerships which it brokered. These included partnerships with

Birmingham College of Food, Tourism and Creative Arts to conduct the Hospitality Institute's first summer school in 2006. It also established memoranda of understanding with that institution (2006); Florida Culinary Institute, West Palm Beach (2007); the Tompkins Cortland Community College in Dryden, New York; Disney Theme Parks and Resort College (2007); and Florida Institute of Technology, Miami (2008). It established an innovative internship arrangement at Walt Disney World, Nantucket Island Resorts and Janus Hospitality International in Ohio and Virginia. In 2008, it signed a memorandum of understanding with Okanagan College in Kelowna, British Columbia, Canada.

The institute held its annual international summer school for students from the Caribbean and Europe under the theme "World of Flavours", offering an advanced culinary certificate as well as certificates for hospitality departmental trainers, basic food and beverage, and events planning and management (2008). Regionally, it facilitated the delivery of programmes in Anguilla and St Vincent. Locally, the Hospitality Institute also partnered with Banks Holdings Communication on their calendar project.

In September 2007, there was an exchange programme with Jefferson Community and Technical College when two of its students came to Barbados and two BCC students went to that college for one semester. There was also a faculty exchange between Audrey Sloat of Lambton College in Sarnia, Ontario, Canada, and Joyann Taitt-Taylor from the BCC Hospitality Institute in 2012 for one semester. They engaged in teaching and curriculum development.

The college was also involved in a 2006 food safety initiative, but this time through the curriculum development officer, Kay Skeete. This initiative, coordinated by the Ministry of Health with assistance from the Barbados Community College, was intended to create and certify a pool of persons trained in safe food handling practice. This was intended to reduce the incidence of foodborne illness. Sponsored by the Pan American Health Organization, the first phase took place as early as 2001 and involved the training of environmental officers. The second phase, training the trainers, led to the certification of four thousand food handlers to meet the needs of the Cricket World Cup in 2007.

Another interesting partnership involved the Division of Health Sciences, which embarked on a joint research project with the University of Saskatchewan to study the impact of HIV/AIDS in some Caribbean countries, the migration of nurses and health sector reform. This was funded by International Development Research Centre. Cheryl Weekes and Donna Bynoe-Arthur were the BCC counterparts. The Division of Commerce was also involved in a regional partnership when it offered its associate degree in Office Administration and Management on a franchise basis to the Clarence Fitzroy Bryant College in St Kitts and Nevis.

Conclusion

Coming after a period of excitement, maturity and optimism, this phase of the college's development has been labelled as one of constraint and uncertainty, and even as a midlife crisis. Characteristic of this crisis was an apparent loss of excitement, a growing desire for change, the lingering need for adventure and anxiety about strategic realignment. In addition, concerns about governance and political legacy may have played a restraining role.

During the early years of Gladstone Best's tenure as BCC principal, he seemed to have envisaged a vibrant Industry Services Unit; imminent registration, if not accreditation of the college with the Barbados Accreditation Council; an inspirational strategic plan; additional bachelor's degree programmes from the Division of Health Sciences and the Hospitality Institute; the naming of buildings in honour of past principals, and progress towards the establishment of the University College of Barbados.

The Industry Services Unit had started with a bang under Norma Holder's tenure as principal, and its first programmes were on the cutting edge in the field of information and communications technology. Much was expected from collaboration with Carnegie Mellon University and the BCC's local counterparts. However, this momentum was not sustained, and many of the local partnerships floundered due to closure of offshore companies. Fortunately, though, this link between industry and the college has been maintained. Perhaps in response to identified needs and available resources, the offerings of the institute have expanded into other areas which may not be considered to be on the cutting edge.

The uncertainties created by governance arrangement and policy changes, the pervasive acting appointments, the initial uncertain fate of the UCB proposal and the difference in the style and personality of the new principal undoubtedly dampened staff engagement at the college. Hence, many of the activities planned proceeded at a slower pace than expected, but they still would have laid the groundwork for continuation nonetheless. For example, although the quality assurance initiatives taken by acting deputy principal Lauretta Hackett and curriculum development officer Kay Skeete did not lead to registration by the Barbados Accreditation Council, they provided useful foundational materials and an initial, irreversible sensitization of staff to facilitate later attempts. Similarly, notwithstanding the reality that the bottom-up strategic planning effort of this period was aborted, staff had started to articulate and crystallize the perceived strengths and weaknesses of the institution and their own frustrations and aspirations which would have been useful for future planning ventures.

Prior to 1980, the style of successive boards of management has been described as a "light touch". During that period from 1979, the principal was the chief advisor and the registrar was the secretary to the board. Board members met annually with senior staff to establish direct communication. After 2008, there has been the perception by some of the emergence of a parallel management system and an erosion of direct board-to-college communication. These developments may have contributed to a breakdown in the earlier established communication channels, lack of clarity about policy changes and erosion of trust.

For instance, it is not unusual for institutions such as colleges and universities to name buildings in honour of the pioneers of their institutional development. Using the appropriate channels, Principal Best is said to have sought permission from the Ministry of Education and secured cabinet approval for naming the library, the science block and the Administration building in honour of former principals Clyde Best, Alvin Barnett and Norma Holder, respectively. All the arrangements were made, including invitations extended to Holder and to the families of the deceased principals. The late halting of this event by the board of management was a disappointment for the past principals and their families, an embarrassment for the college administration and a mixed message about the importance of the history and legacy of the institution.

Above all else, however, the Barbados Community College has been a gateway of opportunity for its students and staff, and there is hardly a better example of this than Gladstone Best. He acknowledges his most positive experience from the college as the opportunity for his academic and professional development. His forty-two-year journey was that of a student progressing from O- to A-level studies; a teacher moving up from a bachelor's degree to a diploma in education, to a master's degree and a PhD; and a career spanning an appointment from an assistant tutor to principal (on contract) for eleven years.

This period showed some infrastructure development, a fair amount of programme development, continued staff professional development, some new articulation arrangements and noteworthy student success. There were new bachelor's degrees in areas of local development needs and new articulation arrangements with the global community.

Gladstone Best left the college in 2015. The next years, 2015–2018, were the last four years leading up to the fiftieth anniversary of the college's establishment – a period which can be aptly labelled "The Golden Age of Opportunities", or perhaps a period of reincarnation.

Figure 11.1. Clyde "Charlie" Best, principal, 1969–1975

Figure 11.2. Alvin Barnett, principal, 1978–1988

Figure 11.3. Norma Holder, principal, 1988–2004

Figure 11.4. Gladstone Best, principal, 2004–2015

Figure 11.5. Ian Austin, principal, 2016–2017

Figure 11.6. Annette Alleyne, principal, 2019–present

Figure 11.7. Eureka Brathwaite, registrar/bursar, 1977–1979; and first bursar, 1979–2000

Figure 11.8. Sydney Arthur, registrar, 1995–2015

Figure 11.9. *Front row, left to right*: Monica Simmons, first college librarian, 1979–2004; Angelita Sandiford, deputy principal (ag), 2002–2004; Grace Pilgrim, first registrar, 1979–1981; Nigel Bradshaw, deputy principal, 1993–1998; *back row, left to right*: Gladstone Best, deputy principal, 1998–2015; Lauretta Hackett, deputy principal (ag), 2005–2011; Lindsay Waterman, deputy principal (ag), 2013–2015, and principal (ag), 2015–2016; *insets, left to right*: Grace Thompson, registrar: 1982–1995; Calvin Yard, deputy principal, 1989–1993

Figure 11.10. Hetty Stoute-Oni, librarian, 2004–2016

Figure 11.11. *Front row, left to right*: Joyce Daniel, fine arts, 1975–1990; McFarland Howell, computer studies, 1998–2002 and general education, 2002–2007; Yvonne Weekes, science, 2012–2015; Cheryl Weekes, health sciences, 2003–2016; *back row, left to right*: Bernice Critchlow-Earle, hospitality studies, 1982–2016; Hartley Alleyne, fine arts, 1998–2009; Vivienne Roberts, health sciences, 1985–1991; Edgar Manifold, science, 1994–1997; Denyse Menard-Greenidge, fine arts, 1990–1998; Kay Skeete-Thompson, commerce, 2011–2013; Esther Phillips, liberal arts, 2004–2011

Figure 11.12. Arthur Sealy, senior tutor, liberal arts, 1969–1976; and principal (acting), 1976–1978

Figure 11.13. Arthur Fingall, senior tutor, technology, 1979–1980 and 1985–1992

Figure 11.14. Hubert Bynoe, senior tutor, commerce, 1979–1993

Figure 11.15. Vivienne Roberts, senior tutor, science, senior tutor 1985–1991, on leave 1991–1996

Figure 11.16. Lucene Bishop, senior tutor, liberal arts, 1989–

Figure 11.17. Barbara Babb-Cadogan, senior tutor, commerce, 1993–2011; deputy principal (acting), 2011–2012

Figure 11.18. Neville Badenock, senior tutor, liberal arts, 1994–2004

Figure 11.19. David Hallsworth, senior tutor, science, 1997–2011

Figure 11.20. Vincent Sisnett, senior tutor, health sciences, 1996–1998 (acting), and 1998–2008

Figure 11.21. Allison Thompson, senior tutor, fine arts (acting), 2009–2017

Figure 11.22. Frederick (Freddie) Inniss, the first BCC college counsellor

Figure 11.23. Esther Maynard, physical education head, 1980–2004

12.

The Golden Age of Opportunities for Ian Austin and Others, 2015–2018

Principal Gladstone Best had retired in June 2015, and Acting Deputy Principal Lindsay Waterman took the position for the next six months. The response from a roll call of senior tutors in Fine Arts; combined General and Continuing Education with Physical Education; combined Liberal Arts with Commerce; Science; and combined Technology with Language Centre would have been a whimpering: "present and acting". The senior tutor Samuel Rouse, appointed to the Division of Computer Studies, acted as deputy principal for the six months when Waterman acted as principal, and he also had a brief tenure as principal after Waterman's retirement in January 2016. The post of principal had been previously advertised, but not filled. A seconded principal was brought on and was, de facto, also acting. Barbados Community College had gone Hollywood.

Ian Austin, a Barbadian educator, had been employed by the University of the West Indies for several years as resident tutor, first in the British Virgin Islands, later in Antigua, and more recently as head of the Open Campus Country Site in the Pine in Barbados. After receiving his PhD, he became assistant director of the Open Campus Country Sites in the UWI open campus. He was seconded to the community college as principal and remained there from February 2016 to July 2017.

In October 2016, Cheryl Weekes, who had recently earned her doctorate and was the former senior tutor in the Division of Health Sciences for several years, was appointed to the position of deputy principal and called upon to act as principal on a month-to-month basis from August 2017. She joined the college in 1990 as a successor to Anthony Johnson, coordinator of the medical technology programme in the Health Sciences Division. In 2003, she succeeded Vincent Sisnett after his retirement from the post of senior tutor.

This phase of the college's development could be viewed through opposite lenses; on the one hand as one of instability, but on the other as one replete with opportunities and possibilities.

Programme Development

During Dr Austin's tenure, four new bachelor's programmes were launched:

- Bachelor of Science in Clinical Laboratory Science (Division of Health Sciences, 2016)
- Bachelor of Arts in Media and Journalism (Division of General and Continuing Education, 2017)
- Bachelor of Arts, Major in Arts and Entertainment (Division of Fine Arts, 2017)
- Bachelor of Education in Physical Education (Physical Education Department, 2017)

The addition of these four bachelor's degrees to the pool of already-established bachelor's degrees in fine arts (with majors in fine arts and graphic design), technical education, nursing and pharmacy brought the complement to eight. The first set of pharmacists and the first set of nurses were admitted to the bachelor's degree programmes in 2015 and graduated in 2017.

In anticipation of the establishment of the University College of Barbados and an increase in bachelor's degree offerings, the staff had been upgrading their qualifications collegewide. The intention of the physical education department was to build on the existing associate degree and develop a bachelor's degree in kinesiology to meet the combined needs of a small market. However, the decision was taken to develop instead the bachelor of education, mainly for teachers, coaches and Defence Force personnel. Inputs were received from a broad-based advisory committee, and reference was made to bachelor's degree programmes from colleges in the United States, Australia and New Zealand. Twenty-five students registered in the first programme.

For the bachelor of arts in media and journalism, there was much input from industry. The Advisory Committee had representation from all media houses, as well as from both the public and private sectors. Susan Harewood, a former BCC tutor, offered advice. The direct entry option was launched initially. To accommodate holders of the associate degree, work continued to establish equivalencies between courses in the associate and new bachelor's degrees, in order to create an option for seamless upgrade to the bachelor's.

In 2014, two associate degree Literatures in English courses were restructured: Critical Writing – Prose Fiction and Drama and Poetry. Presentations Using Productivity Tools for the Digital Age was a new course introduced in the certificate in information technology. Current Trends in Health Information Management and Technology was a new course for the associate degree in health information management. Portfolio Theatre and Introduction to Dance were two new courses in the associate degree programme in theatre arts.

New Developments

Strategic Plan

In addition to the launch of these new programmes and courses, this period saw the development of an anticipated strategic plan (2016–2021). In Barbados, it had become a legal requirement for tertiary institutions to be registered with the Barbados Accreditation Council. In seeking registration, a current strategic plan is one of the evidentiary documents that must be presented. In 2014, the Barbados Community College had submitted its building plans and its health, food and fire certificates to the council, as well as various policy documents. Three years of audited financial statements, the strategic plan and the institutional self-study were outstanding.

A draft strategic plan was apparently prepared and submitted to the board by Guy Hewitt in 2014, but it was not released to the staff or the Barbados Accreditation Council. The new strategic plan (2016–2021) was completed during Dr Austin's tenure by a consultant and submitted to the board of management. It was a very clearly laid out, comprehensive plan. However, some observers had concerns about the prominence of the business approach, the nonspecificity about the centrality of students, an apparent human resources emphasis, and the silence on the trajectory of institutional development and advancement.

Self-Study

With regard to self-study, five UWI graduate students were employed in 2014 to assist in conducting interviews and collecting relevant information from the staff in the areas of administration, academic divisions/departments, the registry, student affairs, maintenance, security, the college library and the student guild. The committees were reactivated in 2015. The self-study for registration was completed and submitted to the Barbados Accreditation Council in 2016. The assessment visit was conducted expeditiously, and the college received registration conditional on the establishment of a post and appointment to it of a quality assurance officer, and the setup of a quality assurance committee by 31 December 2017.

Photovoltaic Project

The Barbados Community College was the lead institution in the management and coordination of a photovoltaic project, under the Competency-Based Training Fund sponsored by the Government of Barbados and funded by a loan from the Inter-American Development Bank. The partners in the project were Samuel Jackman Prescod Polytechnic, Williams Solar Inc. from the private sector and Arizona State University. Barbados Community College purchased for use in the project different types of roof structures typically used in Barbados and paid the university for training kits and services, and the university trained a number of people, including three BCC staff members, one each from the divisions of technology, health sciences and science. They would serve subsequently as trainers.

Other Developments

Barbados Community College went mobile again, this time at Sky Mall and Sheraton Centre Mall to promote its programmes. Staff and students from the fine arts, language centre, human resources, management information systems and curriculum development offices also showcased the college's offerings at the annual Barbados Manufacturers Exhibition.

The Division of Commerce formed a partnership with the Delaware County Community College to develop online courses, starting with business and marketing. The college was also used as an examination centre for the University of Technology, Jamaica; Heriot Watt University, Edinburgh; College of Estate Management in Reading, United Kingdom; Northumbria University in Newcastle upon Tyne, United Kingdom; and York University, Toronto; and served as a proctoring centre for numerous educational institutions.

The Physical Education department continued to offer service to the community by allowing use of its gymnasium and outdoor facilities to the national associations for athletics, basketball, cricket, badminton, football, karate, kickboxing and volleyball, and to the neighbouring schools Springer Memorial Secondary and Charles F. Brome Primary. It also made its facilities available to the University of the West Indies, the Senior Games Committee, the National Paralympic and Goalball associations, the Israel Lovell Foundation, boxing affiliates, church groups and the National Sports Council. Fitness testing, health and fitness education and fitness programmes were delivered to community groups and assistance given to national teams as requested.

In 2017, the floor of the gymnasium was replaced. This transformed the gymnasium and offered the opportunity to further develop futsal programmes and to host international competitions. It also presented further opportunities for gymnastics.

The Liberal Arts auditorium was used by churches, private-sector and government agencies; the Science auditorium for dance classes; the classrooms for clinics, school graduations, music classes and even private lessons, examinations, workshops and summer camps. The performing hall was also used for summer day camp.

The Counselling and Placement department facilitated mandatory counselling services for students under eighteen years and introduced a new four-seminar series:

- "Get an 'A'"
- "Who Am I?" (Based on Myers Briggs)
- "It's College, Then What?"
- "Expressing My Sexuality and Staying Safe"

The LIME Academic Enhancement Centre, established in 2010, continued to function as an adjunct to the Counselling and Placement Department. Students visited on their own initiative or through referrals for remediation or performance enhancement.

The Language Centre continued to offer French, German, Italian and Spanish, as well as English as a Foreign Language both during the academic year and the summer. The director saw opportunities for the expansion of programmes, but this was contingent on a multilanguage website to market programmes, installation of a digital language laboratory, the opening of a computer laboratory for self-study by students, and the expansion of paid language programmes – English as a foreign language, general conversation and corporate language training. There were also opportunities to promote and market the centre's training room locally and regionally, once it had ongoing maintenance.

Student Activities

Law students from the Commerce department took part in a drama competition organized by the Labour Department's Occupational Health and Safety section on the topic "HIV in the Workplace". The play was written by tutor Laticia Bourne, and the performing students earned a Judge's Prize.

Also in Commerce, Samantha ("Sammy G") Greaves won the Scotiabank Junior Calypso Monarch title in 2014 and was invited to the Junior Calypso Monarch Show in Trinidad and Tobago. Five accounting, marketing and business students participated in the Walt Disney internship.

Rudolph Alleyne, a physical education graduate, went to Temple University, and after completion of his PhD, he became the coordinator of the bachelor's degree in sports medicine at the UWI Cave Hill campus. Another graduate of BCC Physical Education, Alwyn Babb, served as the coach for Ryan Brathwaite, Olympian and world champion in the 110-metres hurdles.

In November 2017, D'Sean Miller and Kiara Bailey from the Hospitality Institute brought home four gold medals, three silver and two Best of Show prizes from the biennial Nations' Cup Culinary Competition, hosted by the Grand Rapids Community College's Secchia Institute of Culinary Education in Michigan. They competed against teams from the United States, Scotland, Canada, Italy and Mexico. They won prizes for their fish, shellfish and national dishes.

In 2017, a Mass Communication student with a unique voice was selected to do commentary for futsal at the college and to prepare a YouTube video. He used this video as a part of his application to the Volunteer Leaders' Academy in Kazan, Russia. He was accepted to participate in the first Worldwide Sport Volunteer Leaders Academy.

Division of Fine Arts students partnered with the Public Broadcasting Service in the United States for students in the public screening of the documentary series *Arts in the 21st Century*. Sheri Nichols won the Prime Minister's NIFCA Scholarship Award, and eighteen students travelled to New York City on the BFA student art trip. Alumna Sheena Rose received a Fulbright Scholarship to complete her master of fine arts degree and had the distinction of exhibiting at the Museum of Contemporary African Diaspora Art in New York City, as well as in the 2014 Jamaica Biennial Art Exhibition.

Versa Harris exhibited at the Fourth Moscow International Biennial for young artists and was selected for an artists' residency at Casa Tomada in Sao Paulo, Brazil. Simone Padmore participated in artists' residencies in Trinidad and Tobago as well as in Aruba. Simbah Pile curated an exhibition at the Art and Frame Company. The exhibition included the work of BCC alumni Versia Harris, Alicia Alleyne, Kraig Yearwood, Cherise Ward and Ronald Williams.

The BCC Jazz Choir performed at the Holder's Season and raised funds for the college. Tutors (Andre Daniel and Kirk Layne), graduates (Matthew Squires and Kweku Jelani) and one student (Davidson Eversley) comprised Arturo Tappin's band, which performed in the Tobago Jazz Festival; and with the addition of graduate Kristen Walker, they performed in the St Lucia Jazz Festival. Rene Blackman started his own dance company, The Barefoot Project, and entered his Portfolio Dance in the National Independence Festival for Creative Arts, earning a silver medal.

Students in the graduating class of 2014 continued their studies at various institutions: Jai Clarke at the Edna Manley School for the Performing Arts in Kingston, Jamaica; Amaris Clarke and Danielle Alleng at universities in the United States; and Chante McDonald at the London Contemporary School of Music.

A number of 2015 associate degree graduates received partial scholarships to study overseas at the following institutions:

- Danielle Pierce to the Cardiff School of Art and Design
- Aerin Prescod and Giselle Walker to the Ringling College of Art and Design in Sarasota, Florida
- Nicholas Cozier to the Falmouth College of Art and Design in the United Kingdom
- Nicola Bernard to Portsmouth University in Portsmouth, United Kingdom
- Cherise Ward (tutor), completing her master's degree at the Falmouth College of Art and Design, United Kingdom
- Taisha Carrington (Associate in Arts graduate), completing her bachelor of fine arts, at Pratt Institute of Art and Design, United States, and winning awards of excellence

The links between education and industry were evidenced by the divisions of Computer Science and Fine Arts working with businesses to develop websites for nongovernmental organizations. The Portfolio '16 Graphic Design Showcase at the Grande Salle, entitled "Life on Mars – Design Is Oxygen", was pitched at social media and information highway enthusiasts. It explored concepts and media, using a variety of visual styles. Items included posters, packaging, web graphics, animation, television commercials, branding and packaging. The internationalization of the college continued to be seen, for example, through continued study-abroad programmes in Canada for the semester and internships at Walt Disney World, United States.

The Department of Agriculture celebrated its twenty-one years in existence by hosting a Careers Day showcase for secondary schools and the public. They showcased to the invited guests the wide range of career opportunities in this field, including the application of hydroponics.

The chemistry department went beyond academic studies to interact with the business sector and reach out to the community. They entered a number of final-year students' projects in a competition. The group Aris Qua de Treille won, and that gave them the confidence to start a company. Science students also took part in an event organized by the Corporate Affairs and Intellectual Property Office for small businesses. It was intended to showcase Barbadian culture, innovation and creativity. In May 2016, "Empower Youth International" showcased a line of personal care products from the Chemistry department. These were also displayed at the college and on national television during the CBC *Morning Barbados* programme. The Astronomy Society's Technology Expo displayed the biology department's Ecology Upcycling Project, which produced useful items from repurposed scrap wood.

Acting Principal Cheryl Weekes indicated in her graduation 2017 address that of the 1,019 graduates, 86 (a record 8 per cent) graduated with a bachelor's degree.

A future Division of Fine Arts student, Wesley Morris, brought home a violin from school when he was seven years old. His parents were puzzled and sceptical about his choice of instrument until he got a distinction in his first examination. Up until fifth form, he played mainly for fun. However, when he passed his Grade 8 Royal School of Music examinations, he applied to the Barbados Community College and was accepted. The classes were intense. He had to learn to read and write music and practise ear training and improvisation. At the outset, he was a jazz musician, but he switched to the classical genre in his second year. He joined the youth orchestra and played gigs with his friends in a band. He graduated from the college and, in spite of distractions, tried to keep focused on music.

Morris went on a number of overseas tours with one of his former teachers, who told him about a scholarship at Berklee College of Music in Boston, about which he was not too interested. Like his friend, he wanted to go to Humber College in Toronto, which was less costly. However, he was persuaded to record two video jazz pieces and he submitted them with his essay to Berklee. He was chosen for a summer internship – over his best friend. The classes were challenging, but his life was enriched by the Boston experience which his tutor facilitated.

During the summer internship, he auditioned for the bachelor's degree. That night, he waited somewhat impatiently for the announcement of the scholarship awards and had just given up hope. Morris was on his way to the bathroom when the final winner was announced – himself. He took a few moments to celebrate before figuring out where the balance of funds for those three years in Boston would come from.

He must have found them; because in 2017 Morris was off to Berklee, "hoping to see superstars Rihanna and Beyonce or Bruno Mars walk into his college and pick him to be a part of their band". He said, "That would be so cool. . . . But ultimately, I want to come home and teach what I have learned (and) show how a little boy from Barbados with big dreams with a violin can make something of himself" (Smith 2017).

Staff Professional Development and Community Service

In the Fine Arts Division in 2015, Winston Kellman completed his master's. In 2016, from the Division of Health Sciences, Adrian Hinds upgraded his qualifications to a master's and Cheryl Weekes, to the doctorate and three others earned diplomas in education. Ewan Atkinson was featured in international exhibitions in Germany, Australia and Cuba. He was a featured speaker at Yale

University at the Caribbean Queer Visualities Symposium and published in *Small Axe,* a Caribbean scholarly journal. Allison Thompson made presentations at the Victoria and Albert Museum, London, and at the MEWO Kunsthalie in Memingen, Germany. Russell Watson presented in Italy.

Khristen Corbin studied for her bachelor's degree in dance education via distance learning from the Royal Academy of Dance, London, while Shama Harding was a candidate in the postgraduate diploma in the Heritage for Cultural and Human Resource Development Joint Programme between the University of the West Indies and the University of Florence.

Allison Thompson, Division of Fine Arts senior tutor, participated in a three-month curatorial residency at the Delfina Foundation in London. She also conducted research on Caribbean artists who migrated to the United Kingdom. Roger Gittens conducted workshops for teachers at a UWI symposium and was a resource person at a CAPE workshop. Michelle Cox was a production coordinator at Carifesta in Haiti, the artistic director and scriptwriter for a cultural presentation for the CARICOM Heads of Governments meeting in 2015 and a workshop facilitator with the Pinelands Creative Workshop. Debbie Best of the Computer Division attended Durham College on the Barbados Leadership Development Programme. Cox, Gittens and Natalie Walthrust-Jones presented academic papers or published articles. Many other tutors participated in conferences as well.

Another opportunity identified by staff was the upgrading of the Performing Hall with adequate technical facilities (lighting, sound, stage and so on) in order to meet training requirements. This would not only also raise revenue through rentals, but also allow the college to offer the certificate in technical theatre to the public.

In 2018, there was a change of government, and associated changes were made to the board of management of the college as well. The new chairman is Professor Velma Newton, educator, lawyer and former senator. Also of note is the fact that the former government had a number of BCC graduates as senators and parliamentarians. However, in the present pool of twenty senators and thirty parliamentarians, there is currently a higher ratio of BCC graduates. This can be used as an indicator of the impact of the community college on the leadership of the country.

Recurring Themes – Strengths, Weaknesses and Opportunities

As indicated earlier, the college's first strategic plan (1997–2005) acknowledged its strengths in its diverse programme offerings; highly qualified and motivated staff; public respect for its contribution to the economic and cultural life of the country; appreciation of its high-quality and valued programmes by employers; a reasonable track record of student transfer to universities, and increasing demand for places by qualified applicants.

Some identified weaknesses included inadequate resources; low staff morale, influenced by heavy workload; limited financial resources; deteriorating physical infrastructure; a discrepancy between the reality and ideal of Barbados Community College as a tertiary institution; the span of control of the principal; uncoordinated and therefore inefficient continuing education initiatives; individualistic departments; uncoordinated planning; inadequate marketing and research; image of the institution as a secondary school; reaching the limits of its physical and programmatic capacity; and limited institutional autonomy, sustained by too much government control.

The plan proposed revision of the BCC Act to improve the autonomy of the board; recognize the institution as the University College of Barbados; make changes in staff conditions of service; encourage ongoing staff development; expand applied degrees; develop applied research capacity; establish formal accreditation; enhance the organizational structure; foster entrepreneurial activity for cost recovery; use technology wisely; revitalize infrastructure with the assistance of the private sector; create identifiable quality assurance indicators; have future-driven training for employment; enhance systems for student transfer; establish flexibility and responsiveness to learning opportunities and a strategic thinking culture.

In 1998–1999, the College Administration and Staff Association submitted proposals to the board of management for upgrade and restructuring. They considered this to be necessary due to the maturity of the institution, inclusive of the offer of its own bachelor's degree programmes, and also because of its importance in providing education and training for the critical health, tourism, informatics and other sectors.

In addition, the *Staff Association Newsletter* of 2001 identified with those findings and envisaged a new administrative structure for the changing organization and a restructure of the staff, based on the growth of the college in students, staff and programmes. It saw the need for new promotional opportunities based on criteria such as qualifications, length of service and workload. It appealed for a new framework of relationships with the civil service and school systems and new conditions of work and remunerations across the college. It also sought to make a new financial arrangement with government, the private sector and individuals, and advocated that greater consideration be given to their academic freedom.

It is evident that, over time, some of these concerns have been addressed. For example, the establishment of the Division of General and Continuing Education and the Curriculum Development Desk led to the consolidation of

Continuing Education. Increasingly, the college has been able to demonstrate its tertiary education status in a number of ways, including the scope and level of its programme offerings, its recognition by reputable educational institutions, the profile of its staff and their interfacing with the community, and approval of its graduates by employers.

Notwithstanding this, a look at the strategic plan (2016–2021) suggests that many of the earlier challenges have persisted. The college's identified weaknesses are related to resources – human, infrastructural and financial, including heavy reliance on government funding. The plan listed concerns about organizational structure, including career paths, leadership, governance, policies and procedures. It highlighted quality assurance issues relating to the need for data to drive decision-making, customer service and organizational policies and procedures. It also spoke to concerns about the structure and standardization of programmes.

Recent higher education global trends indicate a growing shift from full government funding; greater acceptance of cost-sharing by students; an emerging emphasis on performance funding; greater involvement in private/public-sector partnerships and matching funds in philanthropic giving. The Barbados Community College has also had to deal with these realities.

Not surprisingly, therefore, the most recent plan pointed to opportunities for the following:

- Multimodal and two-plus-two programme arrangements with other community colleges
- Partnerships with industry and the private sector
- Outreach to international markets for students, all undergirded by a focus on quality assurance

Opportunities Seized

BCC students have found and created new jobs. In the allied health professions, there are community college graduates in every pharmacy, some of which they own. There are community college graduates in every medical laboratory, some of whom have become partners. The vast majority of nurses and environmental officers in senior and middle-level positions have been trained by the college. Many fine arts graduates in fashion and design have made a mark in the community and created jobs for themselves. Mass Communication students have lifted the level of reporting and public relations. The music industry is replete with BCC graduate artists, and graduates of the Hospitality Institute are leading chefs and managers in the hotel industry.

BCC students have distinguished themselves in public life as well. For example, Rawle Eastmond and Kerrie Simmons have served as members of

Parliament; graduates Chris Sinckler and Donville Inniss served as ministers of government; Irene-Sandiford as a senator and Kerry-Ann Ifill, who is visually impaired, as president of the senate. In the current government, several senators and ministers of government are BCC graduates.

Past students with special needs have excelled at the college, including Barbados exhibitioner Joneil Odle, who graduated from the UWI Cave Hill Faculty of Law in 2017 with first-class honours.

The college has provided opportunities for further education through articulation arrangements and myriad memoranda of understanding; through the brokering of joint degrees and two-plus-two arrangements; and through its guidance and counselling services to its students. Thousands of students went on to study at universities both in the Caribbean and abroad, facilitated by articulation arrangements. However, many students, on their own initiative and belief in their institution, managed to use their associate degrees for advanced placement. For example, using the associate in science at the University of Massachusetts, Amherst, towards a degree in science; and at the University of Florida, Gainesville, earning seventy-two credits towards a bachelor of science in the pre-veterinary science programme; the associate degree in applied science, building and civil engineering at Florida A&M University, gaining forty-four credits towards architecture; the associate in physical education at the Southeast Mission State University, earning all seventy-one credits towards a bachelor of science in physical education; and the associate degree in mass communication at Howard University, earning thirty credits.

For its staff, the college provided study leave, long leave and opportunities for part-time study and in-house conferences; and allowed overseas study tours and attachments. Many staff members have advanced from bachelor's to master's to doctorates, including former principal Gladstone Best; former curriculum development officer Kay Skeete, former deputy principal Lauretta Hackett, former deputy principal Angelita Sandiford and current deputy principal Cheryl Weekes.

The Barbados Community College has used its opportunities for creating a stronger tertiary education system through partnerships with external local institutions such as Samuel Jackman Prescod Polytechnic and Erdiston Teachers College, regional institutions such as the University of the West Indies and the University of Technology, Jamaica, and international institutions such as St Clair College of Applied Arts and Technology. It has provided opportunities for ongoing staff development and for curriculum innovation to influence, follow and lead regional and national development. It has expanded its qualification pool to include certificates, diplomas and degrees, while catering to liberal education, providing bridging opportunities and responding to students with special needs. It has creatively addressed many of its infrastructural challenges by adapting old buildings, sharing facilities and even renting off-campus sites.

The offer of its first bachelor's degree in fine arts in 1996 was a significant achievement for many reasons. The fine arts department had humble beginnings, with one tutor. The Fine Arts Division, established in 1973, did not get a senior tutor until 1984. It never found a purpose-built home until 1991. However, it was one of the forerunners, in 1987, in the offer of the homegrown associate degree and, in 1996, the pioneer in the offer of the bachelor's degree.

Future Opportunities

The future opportunities for community colleges can be conveniently looked at from the perspective of different stakeholders. Taking a broad perspective, the Barbados Community College is part of a Caribbean community where the Heads of Governments (CARICOM 2014) described the "Ideal Caribbean Person" as someone who, among other things:

- Is imbued with a respect for human life because it is the foundation on which all the other desired values rest
- Is emotionally secure, with a high level of self-confidence and self-esteem
- Sees ethnic, religious and other types of diversity as sources of strength and richness
- Is aware of the importance of living in harmony with the environment
- Has a strong appreciation of family and kinship values, community cohesion, and moral issues, including responsibility for and accountability to self and community
- Has an informed respect for the cultural heritage
- Demonstrates multiple literacies in independent and critical thinking, questions the beliefs and practices of past and present and brings them to bear on the innovative application of science and technology and to problem-solving
- Demonstrates a positive work ethic
- Values and displays the creative imagination in its various manifestations and nurtures its development in the economic and entrepreneurial spheres and in all other areas of life
- Has developed the capacity to create and take advantage of opportunities to control, improve, maintain and promote physical, mental, economic, social and spiritual well-being and to contribute to the health and welfare of the community and country

- Nourishes in himself or herself, and in others, the fullest development of each person's potential without gender stereotyping, and embraces the differences and similarities between women and men as sources of mutual strength

As participants in this regional vision, community colleges in the region ought to see myriad opportunities for the development in their graduates of appropriate knowledge, skills, attitudes and, most importantly, values for creating sustainable societies.

The Government of Barbados shared its overall goal and proposed strategies for the community college, indicating that it would

> partner with the Barbados Community College and the Samuel Jackman Prescod Polytechnic to explore the development of programmes to assist the country in providing adequate training in the areas of energy efficiency, green energy and alternative energy solutions to ensure that the human capacity with the requisite skills and knowledge are available to service the emergence of new jobs in this area.
>
> ... support the development of courses for entrepreneurs and business persons to take advantage of the incentives which the government has pledged in this area.
>
> ... continue to pursue the institutionalization of articulation agreements between UWI and other tertiary institutions with the primary aim of ensuring that all Barbadian students, especially fully matriculated students, complete their programmes within the stipulated period. (Barbados Medium-Term Growth and Development Strategy 2013–2020)

There are further opportunities inherent in the stated mission of the college itself, as it strives to be "a dynamic centre of learning which exists to meet the changing education, training and development needs of the societies that it serves, by providing a range of courses and programmes of study in a learning environment conducive to the intellectual, physical and social development of students and staff, so that they can make a meaningful contribution to their country, region and the wider world community".

Additionally, the college's core values point to wide-ranging opportunities for the development of students, staff and institution as it strives for excellence in teaching, learning and research; innovation and creativity; commitment to quality; commitment to serving students and staff; professionalism and integrity; relevance and responsiveness.

Conclusion

As mentioned earlier in this book, in its first decades, the Barbados Community College gained its legitimacy from its Ministry of Education umbrella; via external validation provided by external examinations offered, inter alia, by Cambridge University; and through the earning of Barbados Scholarships and Exhibitions, based on student performance in these examinations. After the introduction of the associate degree, the college continued to gain external validation by the recognition and acceptance of these qualifications in the workplace, by their endorsement for university transfer and the development of articulation agreements not only with the University of the West Indies but also with US, British, Canadian and regional universities.

In addition, the government enacted legislation to recognize excellence through the award of national scholarships and exhibitions, based on student performance in college-designed and -administered associate degrees. This also served as an instrument for building the Barbados Community College's credibility. The outstanding performance of students in gaining awards, success in the workplace and the growing reputation of transfer students also built a sound reputation for the college.

During the period under review, with the establishment of the Barbados National Accreditation Council and the requirement for compulsory registration and voluntary accreditation, quality assurance took on new features – the conduct of self-studies, peer review and periodic accreditation. Quality assurance at the Barbados Community College had acquired a new internal orientation and added responsibilities, and the college has successfully taken the first step in that new process.

In addition, new global patterns were emerging not only with local students studying abroad and regional and international students studying at the college, but also with local students engaging in international competitions, global exhibitions and international study tours. Staff continued to do advanced study abroad, but also increasingly served as overseas consultants, single and joint authors with colleagues in the north and resources for technical assistance not only for partners in the south, but also to institutions in the north. Hence, globalization was taking place at all levels and in many directions, and a new global profile of students, staff and their institutions was emerging.

Figure 12.1. The Planning and Advisory Committee at the Barbados Community College (2017) *Front row, left to right*: June Caddle, senior tutor (ag), general and continuing education; Jean Butcher-Lashley, senior tutor (temp), liberal arts; Cheryl Weekes, principal (ag); Judith Newsam, finance officer; Cheryl Licorish, director (ag), Counselling and Placement; Terri Ward-Gaskin, director (ag), Language Centre; *second row, left to right*: Roger Worrell, registrar; Joseph Inniss, tutor I, curriculum; Francis Sutherland, senior tutor (ag), science; Samuel Rouse, senior tutor, computer studies; Peterkin Brome, building and property manager; Captain Debra Marshall-Stuart, curriculum development specialist; Karen Worrell, senior tutor (ag), health science; Sherrol Gaskin, secretary, Principal's Office; *third row, left to right*: Peter Peter, senior tutor (ag), technology; Kobie Broome, Student Guild president; Patricia Gall, senior tutor (ag), commerce; O'Neal Small, chief of security; Letitia Bourne, president, Staff Association; Celia Blenman, college librarian; Michael Slocombe, manager, Information Systems; Gomell Elcock, business development officer; Zann Ward, senior tutor (ag), fine arts

Figure 12.2. Oraco's vision of the University College of Barbados – Eyrie Campus. Photograph compliments of the Higher Education Development Unit.

Figure 12.3. The Muscavado Mural in the Hotel PomMarine, Hospitality Institute

Conclusion

Over the past five decades, the Barbados Community College has not only held onto some of its traditions, but also borrowed new ideas and managed to create a unique institution, a global community college counterpart. This final chapter looks back at the college's history, highlighting some lessons which can be learned and areas for future research or action.

The book concludes by addressing the questions raised in the introduction about the following: the past leadership of the college; its evolutionary journey; the nature of the institution – a hybrid, transplant or home-ground creature; the extent of its manifestation of accessibility, affordability, flexibility, community engagement and innovation; its responsiveness to national educational, cultural, societal and economic needs; its local, regional and international impact and the impact that globalization and educational borrowing have had on it.

Lessons Learned and Areas for Future Research

In this history of the Barbados Community College, many lessons can be learned in relation to institutional planning and policy, governance, management, curriculum reform, information and communication technology, organizational reform, partnerships, student-centredness, infrastructure development, research and centres of excellence.

Planning and Policymaking

Over the years, the Government of Barbados has enacted policies which led to the establishment, expansion, legitimization and acceptance of the Barbados Community College as a tertiary institution. Initially, the BCC Act prescribed the range and levels of the college's offerings. The government steered the development of the associate degree and legislated, on behalf of the holders of the qualification, the acceptance of the qualification for appointment and promotion within the public service. The college introduced the associate degree in 1987 and the bachelor's degree in 1996. In 2000, the associate degree was delinked from the British A level and the Education Act was amended to offer Barbados Scholarships and Exhibitions based on students' performance in the associate degrees. It recalibrated the requirements when it deemed it necessary to do so. The government also supported the award of bachelor's degrees. Through the use of the Barbados Accreditation Council, it has made an ongoing provision for quality assurance. All those actions legitimized the institution.

At the outset in 1968, there were arguments for and against the Barbados Community College having a monopoly in A-level education. For decades, the Barbados Community College coexisted with four sixth-form schools and enjoyed enabling government legislation and policies. The college progressed from a perceived inferior institution to one which offered competitive advantage in its range of offerings, its costs, the flexibility of its subject combinations and the chances of gaining awards and finding places for employment and further study.

Over time, a number of developments have introduced competition into the potential market for the Barbados Community College. Over the period 1974–2009, several community colleges were established in the region. In 1998, the Caribbean Examinations Council introduced the Caribbean Advanced Proficiency Examination for the region, as well as the associate degree in 2005. In 2013, the Government of Barbados began a wave of expansion of sixth-form education to the Springer Memorial School, and subsequently to Alexandra School, St Leonard's Boys School, St Michael School, Christ Church Foundation and Alleyne and Ellerslie Secondary Schools.

While the new sixth-form schools in Barbados laud the establishment of sixth forms as a positive intervention, and even though the Caribbean Examinations Council itself would welcome their establishment as an opportunity for the offer of its associate degrees and Caribbean Advanced Proficiency Examinations, some divisions in the community college suggest that this policy has resulted in declining enrolment. Many observers inside and outside the college assert that the policy undermines its mandate, diminishes efficiencies in the national educational system and runs counter to the achievement of economies of scale. Others also argue that the resources of the secondary schools may be better directed to the large number of underachievers in those schools, while allowing the community college to optimize its resources to handle higher achievers from the schools. Under the present arrangement, both institutions compete for the latter, but the needs of the former are not fully addressed by either.

Specific research is needed to confirm these assertions. However, in light of these realities, there are also possibilities for more efficient division of labour and demonstration of competitive advantage among the different groups. Beyond the potential for competition with the sixth-form schools, there are win-win possibilities that can emerge from Barbados Community College partnering with the sixth-form schools to accept their graduates into BCC bachelor's degree programmes. In addition, they can continue on the path of addressing unmet curriculum needs.

In addition, recent government policy requires the payment of tuition fees by Barbadian students at the University of the West Indies, while maintaining the policy of paying lower or zero fees by students at the Barbados Community College. This establishes a platform for the two institutions to work out new two-plus-two bachelor's degree arrangements. There are also possibilities for further collaboration with UWI Cave Hill campus through the transfer of more BCC graduates into bachelor's and master's degree programmes or the offering of joint degrees.

For the community college, the challenge remains to confirm assertions through research and to carve out an optimal operational niche to achieve its mission. It also needs to confirm, through research, and publicize the ongoing quality of its programmes and performance of its graduates.

Governance

Across the region, college boards of management and directors have a critical role to play in the policymaking and financing of institutions. Principals and presidents serve not only as advisors to the boards, but also as mediators between the boards and the college staff to facilitate communication, bring about understanding and build trust. Staff members seem to work best with boards which have a "light touch" from governments and which themselves exert a "light touch" on day-to-day operations, leaving the senior administration to manage and the staff to educate. Therein lies the opportunity to optimize governance arrangements.

The Barbados Community College is administered by a nine-member board of management, appointed by the minister of education. The board meets monthly to (BCC website):

- Manage, conduct and supervise the activities of the college
- Perform general supervision of the buildings, premises and grounds of the college
- Enquire into and adjudicate upon disciplinary charges against students or members of the college staff.

In general, and in other settings, boards of directors or trustees focus mainly on legal and fiduciary decisions, approval of the institution's mission, strategic goals and objectives, establishing policies for student admission, approving the annual budget and fees and working closely with the president, who is responsible for managing the organization and advising the board.

In the past, the BCC registrar served as secretary to the board, and the principal as the advisor. Periodically, the board met with senior staff to build bridges. This had emerged as a best practice. Over recent years, the board has appointed its own administrative officer, and there has been a series of unexplained acting staff appointments and perceived closer managerial supervision.

Research is needed to inform decisions on the merits of having a board of directors instead of a board of management. In addition, research could establish the underlying causes of governance issues. It can also identify what are the most effective practices to adopt in such an environment.

Management and Leadership

The Barbados Community College has gone through the usual organizational development phases of establishment, consolidation, expansion and reputation building and uncertainty. Viewed through an alternative lens, it has progressed through childhood, adolescence and adulthood and into a midlife crisis. It can be argued that the college is currently living in an age of golden opportunities to leverage the possibilities for strategic realignment, which would take it into a new era of reinvention or reincarnation. Sound leadership, effective resource management and skilful change management are critical for a successful transition.

Over much of the life of the college, there was evidence of transformative leadership, alignment of governance and management practices, leadership from the middle and engagement of staff and enthusiastic students. To this leadership has been attributed greater creativity, including the emergence of and support for good ideas, emanating from any level. However, the span of control of the principal was identified as an issue in the college's first strategic plan. Subsequently, the establishment of senior administrative staff in human resources, business development and information management, as well as the growing authority of a strong academic board, may have addressed some of those concerns.

The principal is seen by many as the chief executive officer and academic leader of the college. However, short contractual appointments appear to have slowed the momentum of the position. This is not surprising because there is general agreement that insecurity of tenure, evident in pervasive acting appointments, can be a damper on productivity. In an atmosphere of so many opportunities, it is envisaged that a search for and appointment of an appropriate principal can take the college into another reincarnation. In order to sustain or improve the momentum of a dynamic institution in the future, this points to the need for ongoing and deliberate succession planning, talent recognition and the promotion and timely filling of necessary vacant posts.

Curriculum Reform

Curriculum development and reform have been ongoing. The launch of a varied pool of associate degrees, a widening pool of bachelor's degrees and the establishment of the post of curriculum development officer reflect the centrality of curriculum development and change to the college.

Traditionally, the Caribbean has practised relatively early specialization in secondary school education. The associate degree was an attempt to broaden and diversify the educational experience. However, both in its content and delivery, it has retained a significant focus on specialist skills and major disciplines.

Nationally, the goal for a caring and productive society has been made clear by the government. At the same time, there are notable changes in the society in relation to crime, violence and materialism. As society changes, it has become clear that a greater focus on values is required to create sustainable societies. This points to a new approach to programming: increasing the relative importance of the General Education core and on the development and fostering of positive attitude and values.

This overarching objective presents a beckoning opportunity to give students the chance to get a better understanding of themselves and the society, a better appreciation for the value of life, greater facility in working with others, growing inclination to service and better understanding of the environment and the need for its sustainability. This points to the need to look into achieving the appropriate balance between the economic and social objectives of the curriculum through additional research.

In addition, governments and institutions embrace the current importance of science, technology, engineering and mathematics. However, we cannot neglect the arts and the opportunity which they provide for the development of soft skills. This addition of the arts creates a STEAM (science, technology, engineering, arts and mathematics) engine to propel personal and national development. Graduates can then seize the possibilities of service learning, volunteerism, civic responsibility, job creation, self-employment and sustainable living. This assertion also invites further research.

Information and Communication Technology

The Barbados Community College has evolved from a low-tech institution to one which has a Division of Computer Studies, information and communication technology applications across all divisions and administrative offices and access to the Internet at its various campuses. It now has a greater opportunity to maximize local, regional and international partnerships for growth and development through collaboration with other institutions. Using the network of the Association of Caribbean Tertiary Institutions, regional institutions can share and exchange resources for staff development and student education. Real or virtual student exchange and study-abroad experiences should become increasingly commonplace.

Information and communication technology coupled with international travel have enhanced global awareness. Articulation links and study-abroad programmes have established international networks. The college can exploit further the possibilities for living and working in global communities. It can continue to specialize in areas of excellence, recruiting and supplying international experts to serve in special areas of need and enable more international students to study abroad in student exchange programmes. There is scope for global cooperation in curriculum design and delivery.

Organizational Reform

Organizations evolve and missions change. Community organizations are especially dynamic, constantly adapting to the needs of the communities which they serve. Community colleges all over the world are protean institutions, adapting to change. Many have experienced so-called mission creep or mission growth in response to changing mandates. In the United States, community colleges which offer the baccalaureate are allowed or encouraged to change their designation. In the Caribbean, some institutions have undergone marked changes in name and nature. The Barbados Community College has undergone a change in nature from a two-year A-level college with occasional vocational offerings to a multidisciplinary, multilevel institution, so it needs to revisit the question of whether a change in name is appropriate.

The Cayman Islands Community College has become the University College of the Cayman Islands; the College of the Bahamas has become the University of the Bahamas; the College of Arts, Science and Technology in Jamaica has become the University of Technology, and in Trinidad and Tobago, a number of institutions have merged to create the University of Trinidad and Tobago.

Some years ago, Barbados entertained the idea of the creation of the University College of Barbados from the merger of three institutions. However, this initiative was aborted. Were the challenges conceptual, financial, or political, or a combination? Is the idea worth revisiting?

On its own merits, however, there is no doubt that there has been advancement in the Barbados Community College's development as a tertiary institution. It has an impressive slate of associate and bachelor's degree offerings. Its staff show an improving academic and professional profile. The college reflects a strengthening regional and international image and growing aspirations for connecting and collaborating with other higher education institutions on the same plane. Therefore, is there a possibility for an elevation of the institution to become the National College of Barbados, Barbados National College, Barbados Community University, University of Barbados or even the Technological University of Barbados? Does the label even matter?

Whatever the name of the institution, the opportunity exists for putting students at the centre and unleashing their potential and creativity. In Barbados, the opportunities in the cultural industries and emergence of so-called green jobs are clear. The divisions of Fine Arts, Computer Studies, Commerce, Technology, Science, Liberal Arts, Language Centre, Health Sciences and Hospitality Institute are rife with possibilities that call for decision-making with sensitivity to the trends and opportunities in job markets – locally, regionally and globally – in the near and longer term. This requires also working more closely with the Guild of Students, facilitating cocurricular activities, having student representation on decision-making bodies and providing avenues for their recommendations and input.

Many BCC academic staff have been uncomfortable with their designations as instructors, assistant tutors and senior tutors. This can be attributed to the fact that in the wider community, tutors are considered to be private teachers or teachers of small groups. It is unlikely that an outsider would consider a senior tutor to be a director or head of a section or division. Other staff have reservations about the classification into divisions, not faculties. Some have expressed a preference for the chief executive to be called a president, a title that is so prevalent in other Caribbean and North American community colleges. On the administrative side, there is a preference for the title "finance officer" over "bursar" and "administrative assistant" over "clerk/typist". What's in a name? There may be opportunities for amendment of these misnomers, with positive effect on performance at little cost.

The college's short career paths and appointment of senior staff at points and not scales could affect staff engagement, particularly in the case of relatively young appointees. Perhaps there should be the opportunity to progress on merit to a senior position, outside of the limited opportunities presented only by a senior's retirement or death.

The Barbados Community College operates within a Caribbean context and a worldwide movement. Research of best practices internationally and regionally may make the wholesale reinvention of the wheel unnecessary.

Partnerships

The community college has a history of partnering with other institutions for validation, quality assurance, programme development and advancing student transfers. Working with advisory committees has maintained relevance and enabled targeted planning and student placement.

The days of full financing by governments are over. New models of financing and increasing entrepreneurial activities are on the cards. The opportunities inherent in private/public partnerships, partnerships with alumni and philanthropic giving must be invoked. Realistic increases in tuition fees for nationals and nonnationals also have to be continued. Supplementing funds from consultancies, contract training and technical services also offer possibilities.

There are new possibilities for partnerships with the private sector. The story of the private sector's involvement with the College of the Bahamas (now University of the Bahamas) is instructive. Attempts were also made to conceptualize the University College of Barbados as a private/public venture. With a deteriorating and inadequate physical plant at the college and emerging growth areas which the Division of Fine Arts, Physical Education department and others would specifically like to address, there are many business opportunities begging for private/public partnerships.

Student-Centredness

There are possibilities emerging from the aspirations and ambitions of students who are venturing into new areas of knowledge and new enterprises in such areas as hydroponics, performing arts, hospitality, gerontology, applied science, cosmetic lines, software, music and fashion, and who are creating projects which they are already showing at exhibitions and expositions. The possibilities in the cultural industries need to be exploited, and the talent of all students should be nurtured. Students are excelling in physical education and must be supported in that direction as well.

Infrastructure Development

The college had its beginnings in an old building, the Sherbourne House, and its Hospitality Division was accommodated initially in the historic Marine House. Both have been demolished. The Division of Health Science started in the Tercentenary School of Nursing Building, which is now dilapidated and abandoned. The project office for the Eyrie campus and the Fine Arts Division were located in the Eyrie House, which is in ruins and may be deemed to be beyond repair. The record of restoration or maintenance of historic buildings has been poor. The UCB Project had tried to salvage the Eyrie House and upgrade the current Eyrie structures around it through a private/public-sector partnership. Over the years, the infrastructural development practice has been evolutionary rather than revolutionary. At this juncture, in terms of infrastructure, there are opportunities and possibilities for both. Policies and strategies need to be developed for the sustainable maintenance of infrastructure.

Research

Institutions require data for decision-making, to preserve institutional memory, to test hypotheses and prepare cases for change. The impact of the recent establishment of sixth forms in secondary schools, the role and functions of a college board of management, the effectiveness of amalgamation of multilevel institutions and the impact and fit of institutional labels and titles are research areas which have emerged over the fifty-year life of the college. Findings would be instructive not only to policymakers, but also enlightening to students, educators and administrators who undertake the research.

In educational leadership and administration, there are several opportunities for promoting and using the findings of applied and action research, as well as rewarding staff who conduct this research. At fifty years old, the Barbados Community College is well placed to evaluate the extent to which it is fulfilling its mission. In preparation for accreditation, it has the chance to examine and improve its processes, policies, structures and services. It also has the opportunity to be assessed by its stakeholders and the possibility to blossom into the type of institution which it aspires to be.

Centres of Excellence

The current phase of the college's existence has been called "the golden age of opportunities" or "the age of reincarnation". Among the retired staff who were interviewed for this book, many see a lull and feel a chill in the college's recent development trajectory. Barbados Community College has not appointed a permanent principal since Norma Holder left in 2004. A few incumbents feel discouraged, some perceive that the institution has been forgotten, while others are excited about their students, their institution and the future: sharing their dreams of creating a world-class institution and looking beyond opportunities and towards the possibilities.

To illustrate this latter point are the dreams of the Department of Physical Education and the Division of Fine Arts. The Physical Education department envisages creating a Faculty of Human Performance, equipped with purpose-built, dedicated classrooms and performance laboratories no longer shared with other disciplines. They also have a vision of maximizing the use of other facilities, such as the Gymnasium Activity Path for Fitness for Living, the Aquatic Centre for water sports training and the UWI indoor cricket facility. And they dream of maximizing the opportunities for dance and gymnastics.

On 14 August 2017, in the presence of the acting senior tutor Alison Thompson, Michelle Cox, head of department Roger Gittens, acting principal Cheryl Weekes and registrar Roger Worrell, a presentation of a grand piano was made to the college by Michael Gibbons, the pianoman. This was the culmination of years of effort by Gittens, who had started the department some twenty years earlier as the only full-time staff member, working with scores of part-time tutors.

It was reported that in 2015, at the college's instigation, Gibbons who had been brought into a partnership, located an appropriate grand piano in Grenada and sought to acquire and restore it. This was eventually done with funding from individuals and foundations, especially the Barbados Community Foundation. At the handover ceremony, a recital was given by outstanding past and present BCC music students, including Rhea Drakes, Abigail Sandiford, Stefan Brathwaite, Andre Daniel and Aaron Layne.

It was nothing less than heartwarming to hear the senior tutor and the department head speak passionately of the vision of the division becoming the Barbados Community College Centre for the Visual and Performing Arts, as well as the realization of a flagship department. They envisaged the department becoming an international centre of excellence, training persons beyond the associate degree and helping them transfer to universities in Canada, the United States and the United Kingdom. Beyond that, it would also provide more advanced and diversified training and serve as a hub for student musicians from all over the Caribbean, and indeed all over the world.

On the face of it, this may seem unlikely to the sceptic against the background of a shrinking public budget. However, resilience, optimism and enthusiasm had kept alive similar aspirations by the Division of Hospitality Studies, which blossomed into the viable Hospitality Institute, including the Hotel PomMarine and the well-equipped Language Centre. Perhaps, the dream can be kept alive by a focus on earlier possibilities conceived and opportunities seized over the fifty years of the college.

Final Analysis

In conclusion, the success of the Barbados Community College over its fifty-year existence can be assessed against the backdrop of its historical context, leadership, evolutionary path, nature, as well as its local, regional and international footprint.

Manifestation of Accessibility, Affordability, Flexibility, Community Engagement and Innovation

In the United States and in other countries, the community college has played an outstanding role in providing opportunities for the advancement of local people by virtue of its commitment to accessibility, affordability, responsiveness and community development. Internationally, the community college global counterparts have been uniquely suited to promote the personal development of the disadvantaged and contribute to national development. The Barbados Community College has touched the lives of students from every village and walk of life and contributed to meeting the aspirations of a developing nation.

It has provided opportunities for student access to affordable tertiary education, catering to every age, stage, gender and educational background. It has fostered the holistic development of its students, helping them become their best selves. It has instilled the desire for learning and created an environment that encourages excellence, opening up the opportunity for people to compete, excel and earn scholarships and recognition. It has provided opportunities for developing leadership, further study or job placement.

Responsiveness to National Educational, Cultural, Societal and Economic Needs

The community college has embraced opportunities for advancing economic development through human resource development; addressing market demands; providing new and upgraded programmes for technical vocational education; seeking the guidance of experts and advisory committees; organizing and supervising internships; and using its networks to assist with job placements. It has enriched, broadened and deepened the cultural life and cultural industries of the country and broadened the pool of nationals who participate in higher education in Barbados and beyond.

Its Evolutionary Journey – The Nature of the Institution

The Barbados Community College has distinguished itself as a pioneer in community college educational leadership in the Caribbean in its evolution from A-level college to an engaged, progressive, comprehensive community institution and a partner on the world stage with international colleges and universities. It is poised to continue to create history. With a focused development thrust and visionary leadership, like true Barbadians, its empowered staff and engaged students will continue to "punch above their weight", so to speak.

The Barbados Community College was not an implant of the US community college, but it obviously came under its influence. Unlike the majority of the community colleges in the region, it did not emerge from expansion of a pre-existing specialist institution or a merger of antecedent institutions. It was created as a new entity which eventually expanded its scope and reflected many of the values of the US community college. It was the first community college in the region.

Like a few of its sister institutions, it expanded its breadth of offerings and diversity of its student body by the assimilation of other institutions such as the Hotel School and the School of Nursing. It is not the largest college in the English-speaking Caribbean. However, it appears to have developed the broadest scope of programmes in the widest range of disciplines and at multiple levels: certificate, diploma, associate and bachelor's degrees, as well as at post–associate degree and postgraduate levels.

The college has been on a quest for quality assurance, initially through external validation including examinations, later through articulation with regional and international universities, and continuing through to registration and planned accreditation by the Barbados Accreditation Council. It has been propelled by strong leadership from the top, the middle and from the trenches. Senior tutors of all divisions, heads of departments and even single individuals loudly articulated their vision and fought to realize their dreams for their units, departments and divisions, kept alive by the hearty support and the passionate advocacy of enabling principals and the efforts of empathetic boards of management.

Leadership of the College: Local, Regional and International

The development of the Barbados Community College has reached this juncture not by accident or sloth, but through the vision of leaders and educators and the sweat, tears and sacrifice of workers at every level.

The college is among the first institutions in the Caribbean to have franchised a UWI programme, the Preliminary Sciences, in 1983. It was also the first to have its own technical/vocational certificate qualifications formally recognized by a reputable US university (Penn State University in 1975), and the first to develop its own associate degrees in 1987 and obtain UWI recognition, at the outset for normal matriculation in 1988. Following the College of the Bahamas, it was the second to launch its own bachelor's degree programme, in 1996.

It provided early mentorship to Excelsior Community College in Jamaica and Sir Arthur Lewis Community College in St Lucia, and offered advice to the Turks and Caicos Community College. Its paralegal certificate programme was offered to all the OECS colleges for several years. Technical assistance was offered to the Grenada National College as it transitioned to the T.A.

Marryshow Community College. Currently, there is a franchise to the Clarence Fitzroy Bryant College in St Kitts and Nevis.

The Hospitality Institute has been a flagship institution in the Caribbean, earning several local and international awards. Working with the Caribbean Tourism Organization, it has had an impact on hospitality and tourism education across the Caribbean and even beyond. It had input into the governance and programme development at the Anguilla Community College. The Division of Fine Arts has affected the cultural life of Barbados, and its graduates are making their presence felt regionally and internationally. The leaders of the Physical Education department have influenced sport in the region, through the Caribbean University Sports Association, and internationally through the Olympic Association.

BCC principal Norma Holder, in her capacity as vice-president of the Association of Caribbean Tertiary Institutions from 1990 to 1995 and president from 1996 to 2002, and Gladstone Best as the group's vice-president between 2013 and 2015, offered leadership and influenced policy and the direction of tertiary education in the region. The Association of Caribbean Tertiary Institutions must be credited with promulgating some common standards for the associate degree in the Caribbean. Similarly, registrar Sydney Arthur, as a leader in the Association of Caribbean Higher Education Administrators, shared lessons from the Barbados Community College as the college in turn benefited from the professional development opportunities of the association.

Composed of fifteen members and five associate members and a population of close to six million, the CARICOM Caribbean region is small in a global context. Covering 166 square miles (431 square kilometres), with a population of close to 286,000, Barbados is a very small country. Gaining independence from Britain in 1966, it is also young. An educational institution established in 1968, and with a current staff complement of fewer than six hundred and a full-time student count of about four thousand, is both small and young. However, in the Caribbean, we know that small entities can have big dreams and young entities can make a significant impact. We know that excellence is neither a function of size or age.

We have seen this small region produce a world-class Caribbean Development Bank and our regional university produce Nobel prize winners in 1997 and a UWI Cardiac Surgery Simulator in 2012. Jamaica has taken centre stage in world athletics; Trinidad and Tobago has created the mind-boggling steel pan; St Lucia has produced two Nobel laureates; the tiny British Virgin Islands has distinguished itself in world-class boatmaking; and Barbados is the home of not only "The Three W's" (Worrell, Weekes and Walcott) and Sir Garfield Sobers in cricket, but also the amazing Rihanna.

As indicated earlier, from its inception, the BCC experience has been a story of contested missions – academic, vocational, adult and continuing education, as well as community service. In the beginning, its mandate was little embraced or understood by leaders, educators or laypeople. However, as time progressed, the veil gradually lifted, and its potential was revealed. Its interests have been championed on both sides of the political divide, in a largely two-party state. The college was a creature of the Democratic Labour Party government, supported by both parties to maturity, arguably at different periods and with uneven enthusiasm. While its candidacy to university college status was championed by the Barbados Labour Party, the Democratic Labour Party must bear some responsibility for its failure to reach consummation.

The Barbados Community College has been fortified through the power of partnerships, notably in the Division of Health Sciences with the Pan American Health Organization, Project HOPE and the Ministry of Health; and across the entire college in its twinning with St Clair College of Applied Arts and Technology for several years. It was strengthened through bonding with the private sector by way of advisory committees and even via such special arrangements as the Industry Services Unit. Its regional impact was enhanced through collaboration with regional and international tertiary institutions, and particularly through its varied articulation and other agreements negotiated with the University of the West Indies.

The BCC story is one of patience and persistence, long waits on pending staff appointments to promised positions and delayed refurbishments of deteriorating buildings. It has been a lesson in creatively moving with ideas ahead of resources: "riding a cow, in the absence of a horse". It has been an adventure in finding niches in between the cracks and opening up opportunities for the underserved, especially in vocational and adult and continuing education, ahead of the curve. Introduced before its time, it has been an experiment of providing educational opportunities for thousands of Barbadian school leavers and adults who otherwise would not have stood a chance at getting a tertiary education. No doubt this story represents a worthy exemplar for other colleges in the Caribbean.

Something Old, Something Borrowed, Something New

From its inception, and during each phase over the past fifty years, the Barbados Community College has developed around the concept of "something old, something borrowed, something new". It is acknowledged that educational borrowing occurred, mainly from several sources from North America and at several points along the journey. There is evidence also of alchemy, blending the old and the borrowed and recreating something fit for its own purpose, but also of value to others.

In 1968, when the community college was established, its very name suggests the borrowing of an idea and construct from the United States. Nevertheless, during the 1968–1975 phase, the divisions of Liberal Arts, Science, Commerce and Fine Arts were essentially transplants from Britain (the old). The Division of Technology had elements of the old in the form of externally driven British curricula and examinations. However, the mentoring provided and the endorsement of its programme by Penn State University signalled influences from other sources.

The Division of Health Sciences inherited the goals, objectives and practices of apprenticeship, Allied Health programmes which had been fashioned in the old British way, albeit modified by the Caribbean colonial experience. The division borrowed from and exchanged ideas with the training institutions in seventeen Caribbean countries involved with the UNICEF/UNDP-funded, PAHO-implemented Development Project, of which the college was a beneficiary. Programme development was also influenced by collaboration with the regional University of the West Indies, University of Guyana, the College of Arts, Science and Technology and the West Indies School of Public Health in Jamaica.

During 1978–1988, curriculum development and programme delivery in the Division of Health Sciences were under the direct influence of American volunteers, drawn from colleges, universities and other institutions – an arrangement with the Project HOPE Foundation. The establishment of a department, and then a division, of General and Continuing Education was borrowed from the United States but built on the earlier provision of enrichment courses for the old British A-level programmes.

The development of new joint certificates with the Teachers' College and the Polytechnic Institute was a new venture, as was the launch of a homegrown paralegal programme and certificate in business studies, nurtured by local professionals and approved by the University of the West Indies. The delivery of the UWI Preliminary Science programme reflected the university's local influence on the college. Perhaps the most significant transplant from the US community college was the idea of the associate degree, launched in 1987. However, the desire to facilitate transfer to the University of the West Indies constrained full transplantation, inspired new local adaptation and ignited institutional innovation and creativity.

The idea of open access was a feature of the community college that also may have been borrowed from the United States, but the Barbados Community

College reinterpreted it in light of local sociopolitical realities. One may assume that in the US context, *open access* means opportunity, unimpeded by barriers of cost, ethnicity, gender, disabilities, beliefs or educational achievement. Philosophically, this was embraced locally; but historically, equity of access had a different interpretation. Elitism and pragmatism had been accommodated. Traditionally, in an environment of insufficiency of money, space and other resources, filters had been put in place to select only the numbers that could be accommodated. While the public had grown to accept that there were some factors, such as economic circumstance, ethnicity, gender, disabilities, geography and even beliefs, over which prospective learners had no control, many felt that educational achievement is a variable which individuals could control and was also a predictor of success. This led to the setting and acceptance of strict standards for admission to various levels of education, based on national examination results.

The regulations for admission to the community college were slightly lower (four O-level subjects at one sitting and five at two sittings, including some specifics) than those for sixth forms or university (five ordinary-level passes, including specific courses or A-level and CAPE passes, respectively). These were strictly observed and could be varied only through the achievement of approved, equivalent qualifications. This practice was adopted and defended as a quality assurance measure which made a statement not only about the quality of the student, but also the quality of the institution.

Of course, there was no deliberate discrimination in relation to age, gender, ethnicity, religion or disability, and education was free at the point of delivery. In addition, there were day and evening programmes, as well as summer offerings. Viewed as a whole, the Barbados Community College was providing more open access than other institutions.

Commencing in 1983, the extended twinning of the Barbados Community College with St Clair College of Applied Arts and Technology reflected borrowing from Canada, aided by exchanges of staff in teaching and administrative sections of the college. This resulted specifically in new curricula for the newly established Division of Hospitality Studies, computerized administrative services and the Division of Computer Studies.

In 1981, the old Division of Liberal Arts was transformed as it gave birth to a new, related entity, the Barbados Language Centre, which grew out of the local national aspiration of having Spanish as a second language in Barbados. This centre was developed through the assistance of the Organization of American States and provided an interface with the world – it had students from China, Colombia, Brazil, El Salvador, France, Guyana, Guadeloupe, South Korea,

Martinique, Puerto Rico, Uruguay, Venezuela and Namibia; and teachers from Venezuela and Argentina.

It is reported that the Barbados Community College was able to lend advice and assistance at the time of the establishment of Excelsior Community College in Jamaica (1974), Sir Arthur Lewis Community College in St Lucia (1984) and Grenada National College (1988). In addition, the Division of Health Science was a training hub in Allied Health Sciences for students from the Eastern Caribbean and lent development assistance in this way – a form of south/south global flows.

The period of 1988–2000 saw many transformations in the college as well. Assisted by the work of the Association of Caribbean Tertiary Institutions and the emerging scholarship in defining the Caribbean associate degree construct, member countries were more boldly introducing this qualification by borrowing or creating. The qualification was gaining credibility and currency. At the Barbados Community College, the delinking of the old A-level programmes from the new associate degree programmes and the new policy of awarding national scholarships based on the latter were major developments. The establishment of the Curriculum Development Desk was a new idea to support this venture.

The idea of semesterization was also borrowed from the United States, but it was reshaped and fine-tuned to meet the local needs of students. By the end of this phase, new formal articulation arrangements had been established with six US universities, as well as many with the University of the West Indies. Students were beginning to earn credits and advanced placement at universities in the United Kingdom, United States and Canada. Perhaps the most significant occurrence, however, was the launch of the first bachelor's degree. The college's confidence to do this emerged from the experience gained from the implementation of the associate degree and its two-plus-two arrangements with the University of the West Indies, coupled with the bold leadership of lecturers who had the lived experience of working and studying in universities in the United States and Canada. This BCC bachelor's degree was not offered in collaboration with or on franchise from a university, although endorsement was sought. It was indeed something new. The second bachelor's degree was easier to implement, but this time, curriculum support was borrowed from Canada.

The Division of Hospitality Studies evolved into the Hospitality Institute, and the new institute ventured into new arrangements for articulation and student exchanges with US institutions. There was also growing influence on institutions in the Caribbean region, funded by international agencies and brokered by the regional Caribbean Tourism Organization. The Nursing department began a new series of international partnerships, accommodating attachments, visiting students from the United States and the wider Caribbean, including Guadeloupe. The Division of Fine Arts had gained new confidence and greater local visibility from its new bachelor's degree status, and students began to show off their new skills in fashion design and graphic arts locally in Portfolio shows, regionally and internationally.

In its strategic plan of 1995, the Barbados Community College signalled its intention to explore a new institutional type – the university college. In 2001, the board of the college agreed on this strategic direction, and later that year, the Ministry of Education endorsed the idea as well. This desired reinvention of form can be seen as a rejection of borrowing (Raby and Valeau 2012), arising from the college's newfound strength and confidence. This aspiration was not limited to the Barbados Community College, which in 2000 was only one of many participants in Bermuda in a regional conference which explored the desirability and feasibility of the university college.

In the period of 2004–2014, associate degrees were developed in new areas of need – sport management and procurement. A new diploma was developed in the growing area of gerontology. Niches for graduates of bachelor's degree programmes were emerging in the allied health disciplines of pharmacy and nursing, and a new emphasis was being placed on professional training for college staff to lead these innovations. The Fine Arts Division was asserting itself as a new centre of excellence in music and the performing arts in spite of the fact that its transition to a university college had not materialized. During the period of 2015–2018, new bachelor's degrees in clinical laboratory science, media and journalism, arts and entertainment, and physical education reflect the institution's reinvention of itself.

Over the years, the college had been validated by Ministry of Education support, by external examinations as well as by the endorsements and articulation arrangements of reputable universities. However, in 2017, it was registered by the Barbados Accreditation Council, with plans and prospects of accreditation – a new approach to quality assurance.

Undoubtedly, the Barbados Community College has been affected by globalization. There is evidence of educational borrowing, including north/south flows of ideas, policies, technology and even curricula from the United States and Canada via staff and student exchanges and facilitation by nongovernmental organizations, development agencies and personal contacts. There is also evidence of the college's participation in south/south flows within the region, aided by the University of the West Indies, University of Guyana and professional regional associations such as the Association of Caribbean Tertiary Institutions, the Association of Caribbean Higher Education Administrators, the Caribbean Tertiary Level Personnel Association, and the Caribbean Area Network for Quality Assurance. There is even evidence of south/north flows, aided by student and staff exchanges and collaboration.

It is true to say that in examining the emergence and development of Caribbean community college counterparts, the leadership of the Barbados Community College has been a reality. However, it took place within the framework of a larger and parallel global movement which was also prevailing throughout the Caribbean. All Caribbean countries have been experiencing global flows of ideas, information, technology and people. Simultaneously, there were emerging regional currents – often aligned, but sometimes counter to global flows. These regional currents provided channels for the exchange of ideas, information, technology and people and offered too opportunities for tapping into regional innovations, successes and failures.

In spite of the shared history, culture and language of the anglophone Caribbean, there are significant differences in local culture, population size, country size, topography and sometimes ethnic composition. These differences create unique local incubators which experience not only global and regional flows, but also local cultural, political and socioeconomic realities. They respond organically and holistically, arriving at solutions, including the emergence of unique local community college counterparts. In these circumstances, educational borrowing would have taken place within Caribbean countries. Policies, systems and programmes would have been transplanted fully, adapted or rejected. In providing this window into Caribbean global counterparts, this book has laid a foundation for much-needed further research in the area.

Over the next fifty years, in the context of an ever-changing global, regional and local environment, the Barbados Community College is poised to create a legacy as an important global player: leading and following, borrowing and lending, as it continues to selectively adopt, adapt, exchange and reinvent itself; thinking globally, networking regionally and acting locally.

Appendices

Appendix 1: List of Principals

Names	Dates
Clyde (Charlie) Best	1969–1976
Arthur Sealy (acting)	1976–1978
Alvin Barnett	1978–1988
Norma Holder	1988–2004
Gladstone Best	2004–2015
Lindsay Waterman (acting)	2015–2016
Samuel Rouse (oversight)	January–February 2016
Ian Austin	2016–2017
Cheryl Weekes (acting)	2017–2019

Appendix 2: List of Deputy Principals

Names	Dates
Norma Holder	1980–1988
Calvin Yard	1989–1993
Nigel Bradshaw	1993–1998
Gladstone Best	October 1998–2015
Angelita Sandiford (acting)	2002–December 2004
Lauretta Hackett (acting)	January 2005–2011
Barbara Babb Cadogan (acting)	April/May 2011–December 2012
Lindsay Waterman (acting)	January 2013–September 2015
Samuel Rouse (acting)	October 2015–November 2016 – renewed monthly
Cheryl Weekes	2017–present

Appendix 3: List of First Staff Members

1. Calvin Yard: Assistant tutor in 1969; tutor in 1972 and senior tutor in 1979*
2. Lucene Bishop: Joined in January 1969; became tutor in 1974 and senior tutor in 1989; retired in January 1994*
3. Merle Arthur
4. Nigel Bradshaw:* Assistant tutor 1969; senior tutor; deputy principal (1993–1998)
5. Hubert Bynoe
6. Marcina Haynes (Williams)*
7. Anne Hewitt: 1969–1981
8. Edmund (Eddie) King*
9. Edgar Manifold:* Joined 1979; tutor in 1974 and senior tutor in 1993
10. Norma Holder: Joined 1969; senior tutor (1978–1983); deputy principal (1984–1988)
11. C. William (Billy) Wickham*
12. Arthur Sealy:* Acted as principal (1976–1978)
13. Grace Cohen
14. S. Ebisemiju
15. Marilyn Light
16. Andrew Bend
17. Edward King
18. Adele Lynch
19. Robert Belgrave

*Eight staff members from Combermere School

Appendix 4: Board of Management Chairs

Name	Dates	Duration of Term
Eric Armstrong	1969–1971	2 years
Dr Keith Hunte (now Sir Keith Hunte)	1971–1977	6 years
Dr Leonard Shorey	1977–1986	9 years
Colin Kirton (also first interim principal, 1968)	1986–1994	8 years
Trevor Hassell (now Sir Trevor Hassell)	1995–2000	5 years
Lolita Applewhaite (first woman to serve as chair)	2000–2003	3 years
Dr Asquith Thompson	2003–2006	3 years
Desmond Critchlow	2006–2008	2 years
Bertram Carter	2008–2011	3 years
Stephen Broome	2011–2018	7 years
Velma Newton	2018–present	

Appendix 5: Registrars, Bursars and Supervisor

Registrar/Bursar

Ambrose Stoute	
Carl Lowe (seconded from the Ministry of Education)	
Eureka Brathwaite	1977–1979

Bursar

Eureka Brathwaite	1979–2000
Norma Hall (for Brathwaite on leave)	1981–1982
Judith Newsam	2000–present

Registrars

Grace Pilgrim	1979–1981
Rosemary Simmons	1981–1982
Grace Thompson	1982–1995
Dianne Medford (assistant registrar)	1989–2000
Sydney Arthur	1995–2015
Roger Worrell	2015 (acting); 2016–present (appointed)

Supervisor

Eric Phillips	Early 1970s–1986

Appendix 6: List of Senior Tutors

Division	Successive Senior Tutors						
Commerce 1969	Henry Moe (1969–1978)	Hubert Bynoe (1979–1993)	Barbara Babb-Cadogan (1993–2011)	Kay Skeete (acting) (2011–2013)	Patricia Gall (acting) (2013–present)		
Community Services 1974–1977	Lomar Alleyne						
Computer Studies 1993	Gladstone Best (1993–1998)	G. McFarrel Howard (1998–2001)	Samuel Rouse (2001–2015)				
Fine Arts 1973 (headed by Tutor)	Joyce Daniel (1975–1990)	Denyse Menard-Greenidge (1990–1998)	Hartley Alleyne (1998–2009)	Allison Thompson (2009–2017) (acting)	Zann Ward (2017–present) (acting)		
General and Continuing Education 1988	Angelita Sandiford (1988–2002)	G.M. Howard (acting) (2002–2007)	Roger Worrell (acting) (2007–2015)	Jean Butcher-Lashley (2015–February 2016)	June Caddle General Education and Physical Education (acting) (2015–present)		
Health Sciences 1974	Alvin Barnett (1974–1978)	Norma Holder (1978–1984)	Vivienne Roberts (1985–1991; on leave 1991–1996)	Vincent Sisnett (1996–1998) (acting) (1998–2003)	Cheryl Weekes (2003–2016)	Keren Worrell (2016–present)

Department							
Hospitality Studies/Hospitality Institute 1980	John Sollaway (acting) (April 1–August 31, 1980)	Hugh Barker (acting) (February 1, 1981–1982)	Bernice Critchlow-Earle (1982–2016)	Deborah Trotman (acting) (2016–present)			
Liberal Arts 1969	Arthur Sealy (1969–1976; 1978–1979)	Calvin Yard (acting) (1976–1978; 1979–1989)	Lucene Bishop (1989–1994)	Neville Badenock (January 1994–2004)	Esther Philips (2004–2011)	Roger Worrell (2012–2015; 2016–2017) Jean Butcher-Lashley (September 2015–February 2016; January 2017–current)	
Science	Alvin Barnett (1969–1978)	Nigel Bradshaw (1978–1994)	Edgar Manifold (1994–1997)	David Hallsworth (1997–2011)	Yvonne Greaves (2012–2015)	Francis Sutherland (acting) (2015–present)	
Technology 1973	Otho St Hill (1974–1980; on leave at Cave Authority, 1979–1981)	Arthur Fingall (acting) (1979–1980; 1985–1992)	Lindsay Waterman (1992–2013)	Peter Peter (acting) (2013–2018)			
Barbados Language Centre	Grace Pilgrim (1981–1994)	Lauretta Hackett (1995–2004)	Terry Ward-Gaskin (acting) (2005–2017)				

Appendix 7: Some Department Heads

Department	Successive Department Heads			
Library	David Trotman (Library Assistant) (1969–1977) Gene Philips	Monica Simmons (Librarian) (1979–2004)	Hetty Stoute-Oni (2004–2016)	Celia Blenman (acting) (2016–present)
Physical Education	Esther Maynard (1980–2004)	June Caddle (Head of Physical Education, 2004; Acting Senior Tutor, General Education, 2015–present)		
Guidance and Counselling	Frederick Inniss (1979–1994)	Vanesa Alleyne (1995–2008)	Cheryl Licorish (acting) (2009–present)	
Curriculum Development	Kay Skeete-Thompson (1998–2011)	Sandra Osborne (2011–2013)	Joseph Inniss (2013–present)	

Appendix 8: Staff Profile 2016

Category	Number	PhD	Master's Degrees
Senior Administrative	7	1	
Senior Academic (Divisional Heads)	10	2	
Administrative Support	117		
Tutorial Full-Time (including Department Heads)	160	7 (4%)	50 (31%)
Tutorial Part-Time	212		
Security	24		
Ancillary	41		
Total	571		

Source: Annual Report 2015–2016

Appendix 9: Establishment Dates of Divisions

Division and Operational Departments	Date of Establishment	First Senior Tutors or Tutors
Commerce	1968 (admitted students January 1969)	Henry Moe
Liberal Arts	1968	Arthur Sealy
Science	1968	Alvin Barnett
Technology	1973	Otho St Hill
Fine Arts	1973 (admitted students January 1974)	Joyce Daniel (tutor until 1984)
Division of Community Services	1974–1977 (discontinued at that time)	Lomar Alleyne
Health Sciences	Established November 1974, commenced 1975 (Nursing added 1986)	Alvin Barnett
Hospitality Studies/ Hospitality Institute	1980 (officially opened February 1997)	Bernice Critchlow-Earle (1982)
Barbados Language Centre	September 1982	Grace Pilgrim
Programme of General Education and First Summer School introduced Short vocational training courses in Ceramics, Batik, Weaving, Printing and Puppetry General and Continuing Education	1979 1980 1988	Anne Hewitt Wendy Donawa Angelita Sandiford
Computer Studies Department Computer Studies Division	1984; Brenda Barrow 1987; Gladstone Best 1993	Gladstone Best
Departments		
Library Services	1970 1979	David Trotman (first library assistant) Monica Simmons (librarian, appointed, reclassified 1984)
Counselling and Placement	January 1979	Frederick Inniss
Physical Education	1980	Esther Maynard

Appendix 10: International Formal and Informal Articulation Arrangements

Date	Institution	Division
July 1975	Penn State University	Technology
January 1977	Florida International University (School of Hospitality and Management)	Hospitality
May 1977	Wilberforce University	
1983	Twinning with St Clair College of Applied Arts and Technology	
1989–1996	University of the West Indies	Certificates and diplomas for matriculation: individual and framework
April 1997	University of North Carolina George Mason University	
April 1998	Johnson and Wales University	Hospitality
March 2001	Monroe College	
November 2005	Mount Allison University	Fine Arts
May 2007	Florida International University School of Hospitality and Management/Florida Culinary Institute	Hospitality
	Shaw University	
	Birmingham College of Food, Tourism and Creative Studies	Hospitality
Informal through Joint Projects		
September 2007	Tompkins Cortland Community College	
January 2008	Florida Institute of Technology	
	Mohawk College	
	South Carolina State	
	Berkeley College, New York	
	George Mason University	
	North Carolina Agricultural and Technical State University School of Nursing	
	Georgia Health Sciences University	
	Bowie State University – Department of Nursing	

Appendix 11: Articulation Arrangements with the University of the West Indies

Date	Programme	Status	Conditions/Criteria
1983	Franchise of Preliminary Sciences (N1) programmes		
1986	Certificate in Business Studies Certificate in Pharmacy Ordinary Technician Diploma in Mechanical and Technical Engineering	Normal matriculation	B average and above Adequate O levels, 65% and above
1987	Certificate in Public Health Inspection	Lower-level matriculation	
1987	Paralegal Certificate	Entry to Law	
1989	Medical Record Technology Certificate	Lower-level matriculation	Minimum GPA 2.5 and faculty entry requirements
	Associate degrees in Arts, Science, Applied Science	Normal matriculation	
1992	Diploma in Land Surveying	Normal matriculation	
1994	Associate degree in Computer Studies	Normal matriculation	
1996	Associate degree in Mass Communication Associate degree in Business Studies Associate degree in Agriculture	Advanced placement 2 + 2	Framework for articulation
1997	Associate degree in Culinary Arts, Tourism and Travel Associate degree in Hospitality Studies		
1998	Joint delivery of bachelor's degree with DHS	2 + 2	
1999	Certificate in Agriculture	Lower-level matriculation	
2002	Associate degree in Pharmacy	Advanced placement	Minimum GPA 2.75
2003	Associate degree in Psychology	Advanced placement	Minimum GPA 2.75
2003	Associate degree in Sociology	Advanced placement	Minimum GPA 2.75

Appendix 12: Dates of Introduction of Programmes

Year	Certificates, Diplomas, Associate Degrees	
1969	External Examinations: Cambridge A levels in Science, Liberal Arts, Commerce London Chamber of Commerce PSC Pitman Examination Institute (intermediate and advanced) Chartered Institute of Secretaries Association of the Institute of Bankers	Divisions of Commerce, Liberal Arts and Science
1975	City and Guilds of London Institute Ordinary Technicians Diploma	Division of Technology (established 1973)
1975	A-level Art Pre-Health Sciences	Division of Fine Arts and Health Sciences (established 1974)
1978	Public Health Inspection, MLT, Pharmacy	Health Sciences
1980	Certificate in Paralegal Studies	Commerce
1985	Erdiston Teachers' Training College/BCC Certificate Technical Teachers (1985) Examination for Art Teachers Course (1984) Barbados Land Surveyors License	Fine Arts Technology
1985	Electronics Course with Polytechnic (started 1985)	Technology
	BCC Certificate in Farm Management	Science
1987	Associate degree launched around A-level majors and Pharmacy and MLT majors Associate degree in Mass Communication Computer Studies Fashion Design Certificate in Business Studies	All divisions
1989	Associate degree in Physical Education	Physical Education Department
1990	Associate degree in Business Studies Associate degree in Rehabilitation Therapy Associate degree in Electronics Post-Basic Cytotechnology	Commerce Health Science

(Continued)

Year	Certificates, Diplomas, Associate Degrees	
1994	Associate degree in Marketing, as evening programme	Commerce
	Associate degree in Agriculture, upgrade of Farm Management Certificate	Science
1995	Associate degree in Performing Arts	Fine Arts
	Certificate in Interior Decorating	Technology
	Certificate in Site Planning	
1996	Bachelor of Fine Arts, with major in Fine Arts and Graphic Design	Fine Arts
1997	Computer-Assisted Transcription Course for Court Reporters	Computer Studies
1997	Bachelor of Education in Industrial Arts and Home Economics	General Education
1997	Associate degree in Hospitality Studies	Hospitality Institute
	Associate degree in Culinary Arts, Tourism and Travel	
1998	Joint degree with the Hospitality Institute and the University of the West Indies	Hospitality Institute
	Associate degree in Performing Arts, with major in Music, Theatre Arts	Fine Arts
	Associate degree in Architectural Studies	Technology
1999	Associate degree in Psychology	
2000	Associate degree in Nursing (Revised)	Health Sciences
	Associate of Science in Social Work	General and Continuing Education
2001	Associate degree in Environmental Science	Science
2003	Diploma in Education by Division of Computer Studies	Computer Studies
	Training for Ambulance Service Personnel	Health Sciences
2003	Associate degree in Foreign Language for Business and Tourism	Language Centre
2004	Associate degree in Office Administration and Management	Commerce
2005	Associate degree in Sport Management	Physical Education
2006	Associate degree in Paralegal Studies	Commerce
	Diploma in Gerontology	Health Sciences
2014	Associate degree in Procurement	Commerce

(*Continued*)

Date	Degree	Division
1996	Bachelor of Fine Arts with majors in Fine Arts and Graphic Design	Division of Fine Arts
1998	Bachelor of Education for Technical Vocational Teachers in Home Economics and Industrial Arts	Division of Computer Studies
2014	Bachelor of Science, Nursing	Division of Health Sciences
2014	Bachelor of Pharmacy	Division of Health Sciences
2016	Bachelor of Clinical Laboratory Science	Division of Health Sciences
2016	Bachelor of Arts in Media and Journalism	Division of General and Continuing Studies
2016	Bachelor of Arts in Arts and Entertainment	Division of Fine Arts
2016	Bachelor of Physical Education	Physical Education Department

Appendix 13: Guild Presidents and Vice-Presidents

1969 – Esther Phillips
1978 – Sanka Price
1979 – D. Browne, R. Moseley
1980 – Dorson Franklyn, Arthur Crawford
1981 – Dorson Franklyn, Arthur Crawford
1982 – Kennedy Dear, L. Douglas
1983 – Peter Dawson, Ian John
1984 – Donville Inniss, Phil Harvey
1985 – Roosevelt King, Anthony Holder
1986 – Richard Bowen, Peter Wickham
1987 – Debbie Simmons, Waveney Gooding
1988 – Ryan Gooding, Melanie Bannister
1989 – Ella Drummond-Hoyos, Karen Whittaker
1990 – Ella Drummond-Hoyos, Karen Whittaker
1992 – Peter Coppin, Troy Sealy
1994 – Alice Walters
1995 – Wayne Stuart
1998 – Gerald Walcott, Jason Martindale
1999 – Ravi Whitehead
2000 – Nadia Phillips, Devon Gonsalves
2001 – Zola Alleyne, Raffael Lovell

2002 – N/A (no active Student Guild)
2009 – Stefan Knights
2010 – Demani Parris
2011 – Marlon Ward-Rogers, Curtis Cave
2012 – Ketisha Joseph
2013 – Krystal Cook
2014 – Jamal Slocombe
2015 – Tenille Graham
2016 – Brian Pereira-Donawa, Kobie Broomes
2017 – Kobie Broomes, Jamal Slocombe

Appendix 14: Scholarship Regulations

1991–1992 – A-level results

A-level students would need to meet the standard of three A's in their majors and an A in the General Paper.

2001 – Based on Associate Degree Results

Barbados Scholarships – Twenty-one years and under, with a GPA of 3.80 or above and a minimum grade of A in Core A, English and Communications I and II and Core B, Caribbean Politics and Society

Barbados Exhibitions – Twenty-one years and under, with a GPA of 3.66 and a minimum grade of B in Core A, English and Communications I and II and Core B, Caribbean Politics and Society

Award for Outstanding Achievement – Thirty years and under, with a GPA of 3.75 and a minimum grade of A in Core A, English and Communications I and II and Core B, Caribbean Politics and Society
(BCC Annual Report, 2000–2001)

New Regulations as of January 31, 2012, for Associate Degree Results

The Barbados Scholarship shall be awarded to students in an associate degree programme (Barbados Community College) who must:

(i) Attain grade A in all courses in their main fields of study;
(ii) Attain grade A in the two core subjects (English and Communication), and Caribbean Politics and Society;

(iii) Attain a GPA of 4.0 or over, no less than 78 credits overall, including not less than 60 credits in their main field of study.

The Barbados Exhibition shall be awarded to students who:

(i) Attain grade A in two-thirds of the courses in their main fields of and at least a B+ in each course in the remaining one-third of the courses in their main field of study;

(ii) Attain grade A in one of the core subjects (English and Communication) and Caribbean Politics and Society and no less than B+ in the other; and

(iii) Attain a GPA of at least 3.81 over no less than 78 credits overall, including not less than 60 credits in their main field of study.

The Award of Excellence shall be granted to students in an associate degree programme (Barbados Community College) who:

(i) Are over 20 years of age, but under 30 years of age on the date on which he/she completes the requirements of the associate degree (Barbados Community College);

(ii) Are not holders of any higher degree or qualification;

(iii) Attain passes at grade A in both core subjects English and Communication and Caribbean Politics and Society; and

(iv) Attain a GPA of not less than 3.75.

General Criteria

(i) Students who repeat a Unit or Course at Caribbean Advanced Proficiency Examinations, CXC associate degree or Barbados Community College associate degree would not be eligible for the award of the Barbados Scholarship/Exhibition;

(ii) Students must complete their programme in two years to qualify for either a Barbados Scholarship or exhibition; and

(iii) Students must not have attained the age of twenty years at the time of the examination.

Candidates must be citizens of Barbados, children of a citizen of Barbados or children of a person who is ordinarily resident in Barbados and has been resident for a period of at least seven years.

List of Awardees

Date	Barbados Scholarship	Exhibition	Award of Excellence	Other
1975–1976	Brenda Shorey			
1982–1983		Anne Marie Hassell		Athletics Michael Slocombe
1985–1986		Wendy Ward Honour Wiltshire		
1986–1987	Colin Collymore Sonya Griffith Hal Hollingsworth Fernando Hood Stephen Jackman (5)	Alecia Banfield (1)		Highest achievement in A levels to date
1987–1988	Suzannah Wilson	Leslie Maxwell Sandra Reece Ingrid Reid Martin Sobers Adam Spencer Vanessa Tudor Andrew Yearwood (7)		
1988–1989	Juliet Skinner	Andrew Forde Kim Goring Toni Marshall Suresh Chatrani (4)		141 Associate degrees; 6 credits
1990–1991	Francene Cadogan Michael Alleyne Lisa Belle Ruth Durant Philip Gaskin Andre Mc Carthy Abdul-Rehman Mohamed Michelle Walcott (8)	Franka Alleyne Kristina Armstrong Tyrone Bowen Kay Goring Antonia Humphrey Angela Jennings Terrence Sobers Chaynie Williams (8)		203 associate degrees; 1 distinction and 7 credits

(Continued)

Date	Barbados Scholarship	Exhibition	Award of Excellence	Other
1991–1992	(Requirements changed) Hazel Lorde Wendy Rudder (2)	Alice Hill Bernadetta Callender Vonetta Drakes Sheila Grazette Elizabeth Wilson Kim Coppin Sandra Eastmond Sonia Inniss Kenson O' Donald Ryan Skeete David Thorpe Lisa Walters Gino Yearwood (13)		259 associate degrees, 5 distinctions; 15 credits
1992–1993	Myles Bradshaw	Karol Springer Connie Goodman Paul Rouse (3)		356 associate degrees; 8 distinctions; 18 credits
1993–1994		Judy Ward		
1994–1995	Shirley Alleyne			
1995–1996	Melissa Hoyos	Johnathan Griffith		
1996–1997	Kishorekumar Pardasani	Shernell Belle Annette Clarke Danielle Eastmond Angela Pounder Penelope Small (5)		422 ADs; 8 distinctions; 17 credits
1997–1998	None			A level separated from associate degree

(Continued)

Date	Barbados Scholarship	Exhibition	Award of Excellence	Other
2001	Marita Griffin Keisha Mc Guire	Zachary Bryant Trina Grifith	Barbados Award for Outstanding Achievement Stacia Brathwaite (General Education) Juan Corbin Maylene Dash (Health Sciences) Sean Ifill (Fine Arts)	639 associate degrees, 22 distinctions. Crop Over Fine Arts Exhibition Brooklyn College Scholarship for Music, Lions Club, Kiwanis for Rehabilitation Therapy, Irvine Burgie Literary and Creative Arts Prize, Past Senior Tutor's awards, CGA Top student, Earl Warner Scholarship, Whitten Bank and Trust Co Award, Latin America and Caribbean Scholarship at University of South Florida, National Development Scholarship

(Continued)

Date	Barbados Scholarship	Exhibition	Award of Excellence	Other
2002	Mfon Boyce Dwayne Branch Kirton Busby Patrice Henry Abigail Jones Marilyn Layne Dawn Williams (7)	Christie Castagne Dabian Cozier Donna Lee Estwick Sarah Harris Jamila Haynes Donelel Knight Lendrs Layne Quennel Reece Tameisha Rochester Leah Welch (10)	Jodi Holder (Rehab Therapy) Andrea Mullin (Rehab Therapy) Justin Worrell (Music) (3)	
2003	Dionne Bowie Shari Clarke-Babb Terry Layne Lemar Linton (4) **Upgraded in 2004** Jacqueline Springer Ella Brathwaite Janielle Nurse Agwe Alleyne Tara Durant **Added in 2004** Nadiege Destang (Total of 10)	Andria Agard Keisha Blades Makayla Catwell Jamar Davis Graeme Downes Jeffrey Evanson Patrice Gill I'Akoni Maloney Alison Murphy Rishika Paryani Suediann Singh **Added in 2004** Shamkoe Pile Jamil Jones Natalia Corbin (Total of 14)	Joy E Archer	5 upgraded from Exhibition to Scholarship, 3 new exhibitions, 1 new scholarship 13 graduates with Bachelor of Fine Arts 18 graduates with Bachelor of Education 59 post-associate degree diplomas 779 associate degrees, 15 distinctions and 67 credits

(Continued)

Date	Barbados Scholarship	Exhibition	Award of Excellence	Other
2004	Christina Campbell Tanya Grimes Valencia James Rhea Mapp Alicia Skeete (5)	Melissa Abed Latoya Bynoe Anna Castagne Ashera Corbin Ashley Davis Michella Decaires Samantha Greenidge Summer Gribble Sasha Holder Dionne Ifill Shontelle Millar Rhe-Ann Niles Sasha Phillips Petra Sobers Kadis Toppin Sasha Walkes-Cumberbatch Kalila Worrell (17)	(Outstanding Achievement) Stephanie Alleyne Marsha Boyce (2)	John Wickham Top CGA student, Cuban scholarship
2005	Asha Chase Christine Flemming Andre Haynes Vijaya Mahabir Remi Obamwonyi Dana Ward Tonya Wiles (7)	Thia Bowen Erica Clarke Ramona Downes Lydia Farley Anthony Francis-Worrell Nicole Garnes Shannon Gibbs Kobie Green Antonia Haynes Share-Anne Ince Jonelle Jones (11)		

(*Continued*)

Date	Barbados Scholarship	Exhibition	Award of Excellence	Other
2006	Emma Chapman Keo Forde Machel Forde Janelle Nurse Kole Reece Cherise Ward (6)	Askia Alleyne Fabien Best Shonelle Birch Shukura Callender Sade Carrington Matthew Clarke Latoya Edwards Paula Franklyn Amanda Goddard William Greaves Leandra Griffith Tiffany Grosvenor Joy-anne Headley Shara Howell Rochelle Lashley Raphael Saul Alwyn Springer Matthew St Bernard (18)	Brook Elliott-Gill	John Wickham CGA Prize (2) Cuban scholarship
2007	Frances Arthur Adrienne Green-Brathwaite Andrew Headley Shontelle Mc Guire Safiya Moore Erika Thomas Terricia Wilson (7)	Sade Batson Natasha Beckles Sanita Belgrave Samantha Bovell Mawena Brathwaite Anthony Browne Benjamin Drakes Kimberley Davis Kyle Farnum Melissa Goring Shakera Harewood Brian Mandeville Rondel Ward Kevin Webster Petra Welch (15)		1 football 1 volleyball 2 music PSC Silver CGA

(*Continued*)

Date	Barbados Scholarship	Exhibition	Award of Excellence	Other
2008	Rachild Crookendale-Ward Kesann Walrond-McClean (2)	Carla Bourne Teresa Carrington Brittany Carter David Castagne Ann-Marie Goddard Akowa Griffith Kerren Griffith Shani Rogers Kasmine Sealy MIkeala Springer Melissa St John Glyne-Marc Toppin O'Shea Vaughn Amanda Worme (14)	Nikita Vaughn	John Wickham Music
2009	None	Kristal_Anne Ally-Clarke Carl D'Aguilar Kyle Smith (3)	Stephen Evelyn	
2010	None	Ezron Alleyne Mercedes Antrobus Richeda Boyce Danica Corbin Leandra Griffith Janielee Kelly Ashlyn Scott-Williams Cecile Sealy (8)		
2011	Lisa Carrington Alexandria Harris (2)	Stephen Blackman Rabiah Butcher Brittany Evanson Camille Jones Saran Lashley Salama Patrick Nickel Pemberton Rickeda Taylor (8)	Fabian Bartlett Ahmad Desai Tamisha Shepherd (3)	

(*Continued*)

Date	Barbados Scholarship	Exhibition	Award of Excellence	Other
2012	None	Asha Burrowes Deimarr Callender Katrina Edwards (3)	Shontelle Hollingsworth Benjamin Knaggs	Emerging Leaders in the Americas Programme Scholars (18) John Wickham (4) Gildan Active Wear
2013	None	Reyda Gay Dominique George Taylor Mirkarimi (3)	1	Emerging Leaders in the Americas Programme (17) John Wickham Gildan Active Wear
2014	None	Janeil Odle (blind)		Emerging Leaders in the Americas Programme (14) John Wickham (5) Gildan Activewear Award
2015	None	Tracey Brathwaite Danielle White (2)		Portfolio Prizes, including Norma Holder Butterworth Bursaries Gilda Activewear Award

(Continued)

Date	Barbados Scholarship	Exhibition	Award of Excellence	Other
2016	Cherise Griffith Lorin Warren (2)	Musa Degia Makeda Edmee Khalil Greenidge Jendayi Worrell (4)		Emerging Leaders in the Americas Programme (5) Barbados Association of Office Professionals Award
2017		Cara Cumberbatch Brittany Gibbons (2)	Malique Marsh (GPA of 4), but Antiguan	

Appendix 15: Annual Student Enrolment

Year	Total	Day	Evening	Male	Female
1969	325	55	245		
1969–1970	497				
1970–1971	600				
1971–1972	825	252	573	469	356
1972–1973	973				
1973–1974	1,190				
1974–1975	1,286 (92)*				
1975–1976	1,383 (145)				
1976–1977	1,447 (134)				
1977–1978	1,605 (102)				
1978–1979	1,619 (102)				
1979–1980	1,697 (150)				
1980–1981	1,945 (110)			930	1,125
1981–1982	1,764 (124)	886	854		
1982–1983	1,600 (140)				

(Continued)

Year	Total	Day	Evening	Male	Female
1983–1984	1,648 (144)				
1984–1985	1,806 (133)				
1985–1986	1,750 (172)				
1986–1987	2,001 (141)				
1987–1988	2,003 (126)				
1988–1989	2,249				
1989–1990	2,408 (272)				
1990	2,522 (170)	1,353	2,382		
1991	2,696 (162)				
1992	2,383 (185)				
1993	2,286	1,601	685		
1995	2,546	1,564	982		
1996	2,994	1,710	1,284	934	1,730
1997	3,093				
1998	3,798	2,379	1,419		
1999	3,540	2,231	1,309		
2000	3,844			1,232	2,512
2001	4,045	2,827	1,218		
2002	4,085	2,924	1,161	1,374	2,711
2003	3,829				
2004–2005	4,114			1,454	2,660
2005–2006	3,865			1,326	2,539
2007–2008	4,535			1,483	3,052
2011–2012	3,994			1,364	2,630
2012–2013	3,635			1,207	2,428
2013–2014	3,620			1,180	2,440
2015	4,264			1,438	2,826
2016	3,697			1,289	2,408

*Cross-divisional registration

Note: Day/evening, male/female registration not available for many years.

Appendix 16: Questionnaire for Past Staff

Name
1. In what year did you join the Barbados Community College (BCC)?
2. When did you resign or retire?
3. If you resigned, why did you leave?
4. What positions did you hold?
5. How would you describe your experience, for example, with: (a) Principals, (b) senior tutors, (c) general administration, (d) Board of Management, (e) students, (f) curriculum, (g) physical environment, (h) library, (i) physical education and (j) community ethos?
6. What is your most memorable positive experience?
7. What is your most memorable negative experience?
8. What do you recall as the most significant moment?
9. What was your greatest achievement?
10. What was your greatest challenge?
11. Is there a particular student that stood out for you and why?
12. Is there a member of staff that stood out for you? In what way?
13. Were there opportunities for staff development and did you use them?
14. Were you involved in any outreach activities or service to the local, regional or international community?
15. Do you think that the BCC should continue to offer Bachelor's degrees and offer even postgraduate degrees if it has the resources?
16. To what extent has the BCC answered the educational, cultural, societal and economic needs of Barbados?
17. As an institution, would you describe the BCC as a hybrid (a cross between a secondary school and a university), a transplant (a North American institution) or a homegrown institution, and why?
18. Are you in favour of a merger with Erdiston College and the Samuel Jackman Prescod Polytechnic to form the University College of Barbados?
19. If yes, why? If not, why not?
20. What implications, if any, do you think the establishment of more sixth-form schools has had or will have for the Barbados Community College?
21. How did the BCC provide educational leadership locally, regionally or internationally?
22. Where do you think the BCC should go from here in its development as an institution and in its offerings?

References

AACC (American Association of Community Colleges). 2012. "The Voluntary Framework of Accountability: Developing Measures of Community College Effectiveness and Outcomes". http://www.aacc.nihe.edu/vfa.

Adamson, Cebert. 2015. "Jamaica's Community Colleges: Responding to Today's Challenges and Creating Tomorrow's Opportunities". In *Global Development of Community Colleges, Technical Colleges, and Further Education Programs*, edited by Paul A. Elsner, George R. Boggs and Judith T. Irwin, 87–92. Prescott, AZ: Paul Elsner and Associates.

Adelman, C. 1999. *Answers in the Toolbox: Academic Intensity, Attendance Patterns and Bachelor's Degree Attainment*. Washington, DC: US Department of Education, Office of Educational Improvement Statistic.

Alleyne, Michael. 1995. "The Community College in the Commonwealth Caribbean: Focus on Trinidad and Tobago". *Caribbean Journal of Education* 17 (1): 137–50.

Alsohybe, Nabeel. 2015. "Yemen's Community College System". In *Global Development of Community Colleges, Technical Colleges, and Further Education Programs*, edited by Paul A. Elsner, George R. Boggs and Judith T. Irwin, 243–50. Prescott, AZ: Paul Elsner and Associates.

Altbach, P.G. 2011. "Patterns of Higher Education Development". In *American Higher Education in the Twenty-first Century: Social, Political, and Economic Challenges*, edited by P.G. Altbach, P.J. Gumport and R.O. Berdahl, 15–36. Baltimore: Johns Hopkins University Press.

Anzai, Shinobu, and Chie Matsuzawa Paik. 2012. "Factors Influencing Japanese Women to Choose Two-Year Colleges in Japan". *Community College Journal of Research and Practice* 36 (8): 614–25.

Aypay, Ahmet. 2015. "The Vocational and Technical Schools of Higher Education in Turkey". In *Global Development of Community Colleges, Technical Colleges, and Further Education Programs*, edited by Paul A. Elsner, George R. Boggs and Judith T. Irwin, 191–202. Prescott, AZ: Paul Elsner and Associates.

Bagley, Sylvia S., and Val D. Rust. 2009. "Community-Based Folk High Schools in Norway, Sweden and Denmark". In *Community College Models: Globalization and Higher Education Reform*, edited by Rosalind Latiner Raby and Edward J. Valeau, 279–98. Berlin: Springer.

Baker, George A. III, ed.; Judy Dudziak and Peggy Tyler, tech. eds. 1994. *A Handbook on the Community College in America: Its History, Mission, and Management*. Westport, CT: Greenwood.

Baldacchino, Godfrey. 2000. "Higher Education in Small Island Territories: Some Frank Considerations for Stakeholders". In *New Approaches in Higher Education: The University College Proceedings from an International Conference at Bermuda College*, 20–30. Hamilton: Bermuda College Press.

Barbados Community College. 1969–2016. Principal's Annual Reports to the Board of Management.

Barbados. 1968. *House of Assembly Debates Official Report: January–December 1968*. Bridgetown: Government of Barbados.

Barnaart, Antoine. 2015. "Australia's Vocational Educational and Training Sector". In *Global Development of Community Colleges, Technical Colleges, and Further Education Programs*, edited by Paul A. Elsner, George R. Boggs and Judith T. Irwin, 323–32. Prescott, AZ: Paul Elsner and Associates.

Barnett, A.F.E. 1985. "Barbados Community College: The Road Ahead". Paper presented at the management seminar for community college staff. 16 December.

Berquist, William, Michael Hammerston and Norma Holder. 2000. Notes from the group discussion following the panel presentation "Confronting the Culture Challenge: Faculty and Staff Development in the University College". In *New Approaches in Higher Education: The University College Proceedings from an International Conference at Bermuda College*, 104. Hamilton: Bermuda College Press.

Best, Clyde. 1987. "Education for Manpower". *New Bajan*, 21st anniversary issue (November): 34–35.

———. 1989. "Barbados Community College: Trendsetter in Education". *New Bajan*, 18–21.

Best, Gladstone. 2013. "Barbados Community College Graduation Report". Typescript.

Bethel, Keva Marie. 2000. "Responding to University College Stakeholders". In *New Approaches in Higher Education: The University College, Proceedings from an International Conference at Bermuda College*, 31–38. Nassau: College of Bahamas Press.

Birnbaum, Robert. 1983. *Maintaining Diversity in Higher Education*. San Francisco: Jossey-Bass Higher Education Series.

Blackman, Annette. 1990. "The Historical Development and Educational Impact of the Barbados Community College". Master's thesis, University of the West Indies, Cave Hill, Barbados.

Bobb-Smith, Yvonne. 2007. "National Report on Higher Education in Grenada". In *Higher Education Caribbean Perspective*, edited by Kenneth O. Hall and Rose Marie Cameron, 257–80. Kingston: Ian Randle.

Boggs, George R., and Judith Irwin. 2015. "Community Colleges in the United States of America". In *Global Development of Community Colleges, Technical Colleges, and Further Education Programs*, edited by Paul A. Elsner, George R. Boggs and Judith T. Irwin, 101–13. Prescott, AZ: Paul Elsner and Associates.

Bragg, Debra D., and Elizabeth A. Barnett, eds. 2006. "Academic Pathways to and from the Community College". In *New Directions for Community Colleges*, 5–19. San Francisco: Jossey-Bass.

Brint, Steven, and Jerome Karabel. 1989. *The Diverted Dream: Community Colleges and the Promise of Educational Opportunity in America, 1900–1985*. New York: Oxford University Press.

Brubacher, John, and Willis Rudy. 1958. *Higher Education in Transition: A History of American Colleges and Universities, 1636–1976*. New York: Harper and Row.

Burgos-Sasscer, Ruth, and David Collins. 1996. "Reform and Quality Assurance in British and American Higher Education". In *Dimensions of the Community College:*

International and Inter/multicultural Perspectives, edited by Rosalind Latiner Raby and Norma Tarrow, 159–75. New York: Garland.
Campbell, G. 1971. *Community Colleges in Canada*. Toronto: Ryerson Press.
CARICOM. 2014. *Strategic Plan for the Caribbean Community 2015–2019*. Turkeyen, Guyana: CARIOM Secretariat.
Cissell, Allen, and Harris Iskandar. 2015. "Community College Development in Indonesia". In *Global Development of Community Colleges, Technical Colleges, and Further Education Programs*, edited by Paul A. Elsner, George R. Boggs and Judith T. Irwin, 151–54. Prescott, AZ: Paul Elsner and Associates.
Cissell, Allen, and Tanom Inkhamnert. 2015. "The Community College System of Thailand". In *Global Development of Community Colleges, Technical Colleges, and Further Education Programs*, edited by Paul A. Elsner, George R. Boggs and Judith T. Irwin, 185–89. Prescott, AZ: Paul Elsner and Associates.
Cohen, Arthur M. 1991. "The Transfer Indicator". Occasional paper. American Council on Education, Education Resources Information Center, Washington, DC.
Cohen, Arthur M., and Florence B. Brawer. 1984. *The American Community College*. San Francisco: Jossey-Bass.
———. 1987. *The Collegiate Function of Community Colleges: Fostering Higher Learning through Curriculum and Student Transfer*. San Francisco: Jossey-Bass.
Cook, Jean. 1996. "Community Self-Help International Development Projects: A Humanistic Perspective". In *Dimensions of the Community College: International and Inter/Multicultural Pespectives*, edited by Rosalind Latiner Raby and Norma Tarrow, 37–52. Garland Studies in Higher Education. New York: Garland.
Cotterell, A.B., and E.W. Haley, eds. 1981. *Tertiary: A Radical Approach to Post-compulsory Education*. Gloucester, UK: Stanley Thornes.
Currie, J. 1996. "Globalisation Practices and the Professoriate in Anglo-Pacific and North American Universities". *Comparative Education Review* 42 (1): 15–29.
David, Hugh, and Geoff Hall, 2015. "From Demand-Led Skills to the Entrepreneurial College in England". In *Global Development of Community Colleges, Technical Colleges, and Further Education Programs*, edited by Paul A. Elsner, George R. Boggs and Judith T. Irwin, 271–88. Prescott, AZ: Paul Elsner and Associates.
Day, Robert W., and Barry L. Mellinger. 1973. *Accreditation of Two-Year Colleges in the South*. Atlanta: Commission on Colleges Southern Association of Colleges and Schools.
De Bresser, Sandra, and David Roldan Martinez. 2015. "Spain's Vocational Education System". In *Global Development of Community Colleges, Technical Colleges, and Further Education Programs*, edited by Paul A. Elsner, George R. Boggs and Judith T. Irwin, 313–22. Prescott, AZ: Paul Elsner and Associates.
Dennison, John. 1992. "The University-College Idea: A Critical Analysis". *Canadian Journal of Higher Education* 12, no. 1: 109–24.
———. 2000. "Characteristics of the University College of British Columbia". In *New Approaches in Higher Education: The University College. Proceedings from an International Conference at Bermuda College*, 106–15. Hamilton: Bermuda College Press.
Dennison, John, and Paul Gallagher. 1986. *Canada's Community College: A Critical Analysis*. Vancouver: University of British Columbia Press.

Dougherty, Kevin J. 1994. *The Contradictory College: The Conflicting Origins, Impacts and Futures of the Community College*. Albany: State University of New York Press.

Douglass, J.A. 2000. *The California Idea and American Higher Education: 1850 to the 1960 Master Plan*. Palo Alto, CA: Stanford University Press.

Doyle, Jim. 2015. "Further Education in New Zealand". In *Global Development of Community Colleges, Technical Colleges, and Further Education Programs*, edited by Paul A. Elsner, George R. Boggs and Judith T. Irwin, 339–54. Prescott, AZ: Paul Elsner and Associates.

Drummond, Mark, and Philip Hartley. 2015. "Higher Colleges of Technology in the United Arab Emirates: An Update". In *Global Development of Community Colleges, Technical Colleges, and Further Education Programs*, edited by Paul A. Elsner, George R. Boggs and Judith T. Irwin. 213–16. Prescott, AZ: Paul Elsner and Associates.

Eaton, Judith S. 1994. "The Fortunes of the Transfer Function: Community Colleges 1900-1990". In *A Handbook on Community College in America: Its History, Mission, and Management*, edited by George A. Baker III; technical editors Judy Dudziak and Peggy Tyler, 28–40. Westport, CT: Greenwood.

Elsner, Paul A., George R. Boggs and Judith T. Irwin, eds. 2008. *Global Development of Community Colleges, Technical Colleges, and Further Education Programs*. Washington, DC: Community College Press.

———. 2015. *Global Development of Community Colleges, Technical Colleges, and Further Education Programs*. Rev. ed. Prescott, AZ: Paul Elsner and Associates.

Elsner, Paul, and Roberto Navarro Sanchez. 2015. "Colombia's CERES Programme". In *Global Development of Community Colleges, Technical Colleges, and Further Education Programs*, edited by Paul A. Elsner, George R. Boggs and Judith T. Irwin, 81–82. Prescott, AZ: Paul Elsner and Associates.

Eskow, Steven. 1974. "Resolution on the Development of World Community College: A College of Colleges Devoted to the Exchange of Information and Assistance on Community-Based, Short Cycle Education". Resolution from World Community College Conference. November, Vancouver, Canada.

———. 1998. "World Community College: Has Its Time Come?" *Community College Times*, November 31.

Ferguson, James. 1999. *The Story of the Caribbean People*. Kingston: Ian Randle.

Fielding, William, and Jeannie Gibbons. 2007. "National Report on Higher Education in the Commonwealth of the Bahamas". In *Higher Education Caribbean Perspective*, edited by Kenneth O. Hall and Rose Marie Cameron, 174–205. Kingston: Ian Randle.

Finegold, D., L. McFarland, and W. Richardson. 1992. Introduction. *Oxford Studies in Comparative Education* 2 (2): 7–24.

Fisher, Glen, and Marianne Scott. 2015. "Public Further Education and Training Colleges in South Africa". In *Global Development of Community Colleges, Technical Colleges, and Further Education Programs*, edited by Paul A. Elsner, George R. Boggs and Judith T. Irwin, 19–35. Prescott, AZ: Paul Elsner and Associates.

Flint, J. 1978. "Darwin Community College: An Experiment in Australian Education". Typescript. University of California, Los Angeles.

Floyd, Deborah L., Michael L. Skolnik and Kenneth P. Walker. 2005. *The Community College Baccalaureate: Emerging Trends and Policy Issues*. Sterling, VA: Stylus.
Free, Coen. 2015. "Creating a Learning Village in the Netherlands". In *Global Development of Community Colleges, Technical Colleges, and Further Education Programs*, edited by Paul A. Elsner, George R. Boggs and Judith T. Irwin, 299–308. Prescott, AZ: Paul Elsner and Associates.
Gagliano, F.V. 1992. "Globalisation of the University". *NCA Quarterly* 67 (2): 325–34.
Gallagher, Paul. 2000. "New Approaches in Higher Education: The University College in the Nature of Knowledge and the University College". In *New Approaches in Higher Education: The University College Proceedings from An International Conference at Bermuda College*, 2–5. Hamilton: Bermuda College Press.
Gershwin, Mary. 2015. "Brazil's Growing Education System". In *Global Development of Community Colleges, Technical Colleges, and Further Education Programs*, edited by Paul A. Elsner, George R. Boggs and Judith T. Irwin, 45–49. Prescott, AZ: Paul Elsner and Associates.
Gershwin, Mary Crabbe, Philip Cary, Marcelo Von Chrismar, Cristobal Silva and Shelley L. Wood. 2015. "The Chilean Experience in Technical and Further Education: Public Policies and Private Providers". In *Global Development of Community Colleges, Technical Colleges, and Further Education Programs*, edited by Paul A. Elsner, George R. Boggs and Judith T. Irwin, 69–80. Prescott, AZ: Paul Elsner and Associates.
Gittens, Cleopatra. 2007. "A Report on Higher Education in St Kitts and Nevis". In *Higher Education Caribbean Perspective*, edited by Kenneth O. Hall and Rose Marie Cameron, 355–83. Kingston: Ian Randle.
Grant-Woodham, Jeanette, and Camille Morris. 2009. "Community College Embracing Change: The Anglophone Perspective". In *Community College Models: Globalization and Higher Education Reform*, edited by Rosalind Latiner Raby and Edward J. Valeau, 299–320. Berlin: Springer.
Greenberg, J.A. 1991. "Exporting the Community College: Worldwide Variations". *New Directions for Community Colleges* 75:69–77.
Grubb, N. 1991. "The Decline of Community College Transfer Rates: Evidence from National Longitudinal Surveys". *Journal of Higher Education* 62 (2): 194–222.
Grubb, N., and R. Sweet. 2005. *Alternatives to Universities Reconsidered. Educational Policy Analysis, 2004*. Paris: OECD.
Hagedorn, Linda Serra, and Wafa Thabet Mezghani. 2013. "Bringing Community Colleges to Tunisia". In *The Community College in a Global Context: New Directions for Community Colleges*, no. 161, edited by Tod Treeat and Linda Serra Hagedorn, 100–113. San Francisco: Jossey-Bass.
Halder, John. 2015. "Three Styles of Community College Development: India, the Dominican Republic and Georgia". In *Global Development of Community Colleges, Technical Colleges, and Further Education Programs*, edited by Paul A. Elsner, George R. Boggs and Judith T. Irwin, 355–63. Prescott, AZ: Paul Elsner and Associates.
Halpin, D., and B. Troyna. 1995. "The Politics of Education Policy Borrowing". *Comparative Education* 31 (3): 303–10.

Hanisch, T.E. 1978. "Norway's Regional Colleges". Typescript. University of California.
Harre, J. 1978. "The New Zealand Community College". Typescript. University of California.
Harris, Mathilda Esformes. 1996. "Culture, Technology, Development: Partners with a Price Tag". In *Dimensions of the Community College: International and Inter/Multicultural Pespectives*, edited by Rosalind Latiner Raby and Norma Tarrow, 211–38. New York: Garland.
Holder, Norma J.I. 2000. "Confronting the Culture Challenge: Faculty and Staff Development in the University College" In *New Approaches in Higher Education: The University College Proceedings from an International Conference at Bermuda College*, 99–103. Hamilton: Bermuda College Press.
Howe, Glenford. 2003. *Contending with Change: Reviewing Tertiary Education in the English-Speaking Caribbean*. Caracas, Venezuela: IESALC/UNESCO.
Howe, H. 1988. *The Forgotten Half*. New York: William T. Grant Foundation.
Humphrys, J.G., and A.M. Koller Jr, eds. 1994. "Community Colleges for International Development Inc.: The Vision and the History. 1976–1994". Brevard, FL: Community College for International Development.
Huxley, Thomas. 1888. "On the Reception of the Origin of Species". In *The Life and Letters of Charles Darwin, Including an Autobiographical Chapter* (1888) vol. 2, edited by F. Darwin, 204. London: John Murray.
Ilon, L. 1997. "Response". *Comparative Education Review* 41 (3): 351–57.
Jones, Glen, ed. 1997. *Higher Education in Canada: Different Systems, Different Perspectives*. New York: Garland.
Kerr, Clark. 1963. *The Uses of the University*. Cambridge, MA: Harvard University Press.
———. 1994. *Troubled Times for American Higher Education: The 1990s and Beyond*. Albany, NY: SUNY Press.
King, Maxwell C., and Seymour H. Fersh. 1992. *Integrating the International/Intercultural Dimensions in the Community College*. Cocoa, FL: Association of Community College Trustees and Community College for International Development.
Kintzer, F. 1979. "World Adaptations to the Community College Concept". In *Advancing International Education. New Directions for Community Colleges*, vol. 26, edited by Maxwell King and Robert Breuder, 65–79. San Francisco: Jossey-Bass.
———, ed. 1982. *New Directions for Community Colleges: Improving Articulation and Transfer Relationships*. San Francisco: Jossey-Bass.
———. 1993. "Higher Education Beyond the United States: A Glimpse of Short-Cycle Higher Education in Other Countries". *Community/Junior Community College Quarterly* 16 (1): 1–8.
———. 1995. "International Developments in Higher Education: New Perspectives on Non-universities". *Community College Journal of Research and Practice* 19 (3): 235–46.
———. 1998. "Community Colleges Go International: Short-Cycle Education around the World". *Leadership Abstracts, Worldwide Web Edition* 11 (6): 1–4.
Kintzer, F. and James L. Wattenberger. 1985. *The Articulation/Transfer Phenomenon: Patterns and Directions*. Horizons Issues Monograph Series. Washington, DC:

American Association of Colleges and Universities (ERIC Document Reproduction Service No. ED 257 539).

Kintzer, Frederick C., and Donald W. Bryant. 1998. "Global Perceptions of the Community College". *Community College Review* 26 (3): 1–35.

Knapp, L.G., J.E. Kelly-Reid, S.A. Ginder and E.S. Miller. 2008. *Enrolment in Postsecondary Institutions, Fall 2006; Graduation Rates, 2003 and 2003 Cohort; and Financial Statistics, Fiscal Year 2009 (NCES 2008-173)*. Washington, DC: US Department of Education, Institute of Education Sciences, National Center for Education Statistics.

Laya, Marrisol Silva. 2009. "Technological Universities: A Relevant Educational Model for Mexico?" In *Community College Models: Globalization and Higher Education Reform*, edited by Rosalind Latiner Raby and Edward J. Valeau, 219–34. Berlin: Springer.

Leslie, P.M. 1980. *Canadian Universities 1980 and Beyond: Enrolment, Structural Change and Finance*. Ottawa, ON: Association of Universities and Colleges of Canada.

Levin, John S. 2001. *Globalizing the Community College: Strategies for Change in the Twenty-First Century*. New York: Palgrave.

Li, S. 2010. "Chile's First Community College Remakes Technical Education's Image". *Chronicle of Higher Education*. 7 November.

Lin-Liu, J. 2001. "China Plans to Build Network of Community Colleges". *Chronicle of Higher Education*. 14 November.

Lingenfelter, P. 1992. *Undergraduate Education Transfer and Articulation*. Springfield: Illinois State Board of Higher Education.

Lombardi, J. 1979. *The Decline of Transfer Education*. Topical Paper No. 70. Los Angeles: ERIC Clearinghouse for Junior Colleges.

Lorenzo, Albert L. 2005. "The University Center: A Collaborative Approach to Baccalaureate Degrees". In *The Community College Baccalaureate: Emerging Trends and Policy Issues*, edited by Deborah L. Floyd, Michael L. Skolnik and Kenneth P. Walker, 73–94. Sterling, VA: Stylus.

Madden, Lori. 2010. "The Community College Experiment in Latin America". *Community College Journal* 69 (2): 10–15.

McGin, N. 1997. "Counter Response". *Comparative Education Review* 41 (3): 357–59.

McMahon, Frank. 2015. "Further Education in Ireland". In *Global Development of Community Colleges, Technical Colleges, and Further Education Programs*, edited by Paul A. Elsner, George R. Boggs and Judith T. Irwin, 289–98. Prescott, AZ: Paul Elsner and Associates.

Morris, Camille. 2012. *Community College Model in Anglophone Caribbean: Relevance and Future*. Paper presented at the Comparative and International Education Society National Conference, San Juan, Puerto Rico, 22–27 April.

Mosa, A.A. 1996. "Why Globalisation?" Paper presented at the Comparative and International Education Conference. Sydney, Australia.

Neave, Guy. 1991. "Into the Charmed Circle, or the Expansion of the Nonuniversity Sector of Higher Education in Western Europe". *Journal of European Education* 23:45–61.

Oliver, Diane, Sandra Engel and Analy Scorsone. 2015. "Community College Development in Vietnam: A Global and Local Dialect". In *Global Development of Community Colleges,*

Technical Colleges, and Further Education Programs, edited by Paul A. Elsner, George R. Boggs and Judith T. Irwin, 229–42. Prescott, AZ: Paul Elsner and Associates.

Pederson, R.P. 2000. "The Early Public Junior College: 1900–1940". PhD dissertation, Columbia University.

Perriot, Leopold L. 2000. "Belize's Experiment with a University College: An Exercise in Quality Assurance". In *New Approaches in Higher Education: The University College Proceedings from an International Conference at Bermuda College*, 63–69. Hamilton: Bermuda College Press.

Peters, Bevis. 1993. *The Emergence of Community, State and National Colleges in the OECS Member Countries: An Institutional Analysis*. Bridgetown, Barbados: Institute of Social and Economic Research, University of the West Indies.

———. 2001. "Tertiary Education Development in Small States: Constraints and Future Prospect". *Caribbean Quarterly* 47 (2–3): 44–57.

Phillippe, K.A., and L. Gonzalez Sullivan. 2005. *National Profile of Community Colleges: Trends and Statistics*, 4th ed. Washington, DC: Community College Press.

Phillips, David, and Kimberley Ochs. 2003.? "Processes of Policy Borrowing in Education: some explanatory and analytical devices". *Comparative Education* 39 (4): 451–61.

Postiglione, Gerard A., and Yiwei Chen. 2015. "Recent Developments in Higher Vocational and Professional Education (HPVE) in China – An Update". In *Global Development of Community Colleges, Technical Colleges, and Further Education Programs*, edited by Paul A. Elsner, George R. Boggs and Judith T. Irwin, 137–50. Prescott, AZ: Paul Elsner and Associates.

Postiglione, Gerard A., and Steven Sai Kit Kwok. 2015. "The Emergence of the Community College Associate Degree in Hong Kong". In *Global Development of Community Colleges, Technical Colleges, and Further Education Programs*, edited by Paul A. Elsner, George R. Boggs and Judith T. Irwin, 137–50. Prescott, AZ: Paul Elsner and Associates.

Postiglione, Gerard A, Liangjuan Wang and Don Watkins. 2015. "Vocational and Continuing Higher Education in China". In *Global Development of Community Colleges, Technical Colleges, and Further Education Programs*, edited by Paul A. Elsner, George R. Boggs and Judith T. Irwin, 121–32. Prescott, AZ: Paul Elsner and Associates.

Raby, Rosalind Latiner. 1996. "Introduction to Part II". In *Dimensions of Community College: International, Intercultural, and Multicultural Perspectives*, edited by Rosalind Latiner Raby and Norma Tarrow, 9–36. New York: Garland.

———. 2000. "Globalisation of the Community College Model: Paradox of the Local and the Global". In *Globalization and Education: Integration and Contestation across Cultures*, edited by Nelly P. Stromquist and Karen Monkman, 149–73. New York: Rowman and Littlefield.

———. 2001. *Community College Model Characteristics*. Washington, DC: US Department of Education Educational Resources Information Centre.

Raby, Rosalind Latiner, Janice Nahra Friedel and Edward Valeau. 2016. "A Discussion on Community Colleges and Global Counterparts Completion Policies". *Journal of Research and Practice* 4 (11): 961–64.

Raby, Rosalind Latiner, and Norma Tarrow, eds. 1996. *Dimensions of Community College: International, Intercultural, and Multicultural Perspectives*. New York: Garland.

Raby, Rosalind Latiner, and Edward J. Valeau, eds. 2009. *Community College Models: Globalizaton and Higher Education Reform*. Berlin: Springer.

———. 2012. "Educational Borrowing and the Emergence of Community College Global Counterparts" (Manuscript #M1701). In *Community Colleges Worldwide: Investigating the Global Phenomenon*, edited by Alexander W. Wiseman, Audree Chase-Mayoral, Thomas Janis and Anuradha Sachdev, 19–26. International Perspectives on Education and Society Series, vol. 17. Bingley, UK: Emerald Publishing.

———. 2013. "Community College Global Counterparts: Historical Contexts". *Research in Comparative and International Education* 8 (2): 110–18.

———. 2014. *Access and Social Capital: A Profile of Community College and Global Counterparts*. DOI:10.5195/ehe.2014.126.

———. 2018. *Handbook of Comparative Studies on Community Colleges and Global Counterparts*. Dordrecht, Netherlands: Springer.

Ratcliff, James L. 1994. "Seven Streams in the Historical Development of the Modern American Community College". In *A Handbook on Community College in America: Its History, Mission, and Management*, edited by George A. Baker III; technical editors Judy Dudziak and Peggy Tyler, 3–16. Westport, CT: Greenwood.

Roberts, Vivienne. 1999. "Programme Articulation. The Making of a Regional Tertiary Education System". *Journal of Education and Development in the Caribbean* 3 (2): 145–69.

———. 2000a. "Access to Tertiary Education in Selected Caribbean Countries: Enabling and Limiting Factors". PhD dissertation. University of the West Indies, Cave Hill, Barbados.

———. 2000b. "Strengthening the Caribbean Tertiary Education System through University of the West Indies and College Linkages". *International Studies in Educational Administration Journal of the Commonwealth Council for Educational Administration and Management* 28 (2): 2–21.

———. 2000c. "University of the West Indies and Tertiary Education Linkages in International Studies". *Educational Administration Journal of the Commonwealth Council for Educational Administration and Management* 28 (2): 40–56.

———. 2001. "The Associate Degree in the Caribbean: Its Viability as a Post-secondary Qualification". *Caribbean Quarterly* 47 (2–3): 20–43.

———. 2003a. *Accreditation and Evaluation Systems in the English-Speaking Caribbean: Current Trends and Prospects*. Caracas, Venezuela: IESALC/UNESCO.

———. 2003b. "Overcoming Barriers to Access and Success in Tertiary Education in the Commonwealth Caribbean". *International Studies in Educational Administration Journal of the Commonwealth Council for Educational Administration and Management* 31 (3): 2–21.

———. 2003c. "Programmes in Tertiary Education in the English-Speaking Caribbean: Responding to the Emerging Niche Markets". Report submitted to Patrick Rowe for University College of Barbados.

———. 2003d. *The Shaping of Tertiary Education in the Caribbean: Forces, Forms and Functions*. London: Commonwealth Secretariat.

———. 2006a. *National Report on Higher Education in Antigua and Barbuda*. Caracas, Venezuela: IESALC/UNESCO.

———. 2006b. *National Report on Higher Education in St Vincent and the Grenadines.* Caracas, Venezuela: IESALC/UNESCO.

———. 2006c. "Tertiary Education in the Commonwealth Caribbean". In *Commonwealth Ministers Reference Book,* 184–86. London: Henley Media Group and the Commonwealth Secretariat.

Roberts, Vivienne, and Nigel Brissett. 2003. *Pathways to Tertiary Education in the English-Speaking Caribbean.* Bridgetown, Barbados: University of the West Indies Tertiary Level Institutions Unit.

Rosen, Alan. 1979. "An Examination of Barbados Community College 1969–1978". PhD dissertation, Florida Atlantic University.

Rosenbaum, J. 1999. *Unrealistic Plans and Misdirected Efforts: Are Community Colleges Getting the Right Message to Students?* New York: Columbia University, Teachers College Resource Center.

Rosenfeld, Stuart, Cynthia Liston, and Hanne Shapiro. 2015. "Further Education in Denmark". In *Global Development of Community Colleges, Technical Colleges, and Further Education Programs,* edited by Paul A. Elsner, George R. Boggs and Judith T. Irwin, 251–62. Prescott, AZ: Paul Elsner and Associates.

Sandiford, Lloyd Erskine. 1969. "Address at the Opening Ceremony of the Barbados Community College". 5 January.

———. 2011. *Fighting for the Just Society: An Autobiographical Note.* Bridgetown, Barbados: Sandiford Centre for Public Affairs.

Sawadogo, Geremie. 2015. "Community Colleges and Further Education in French West Africa". In *Global Development of Community Colleges, Technical Colleges, and Further Education Programs,* edited by Paul A. Elsner, George R. Boggs and Judith T. Irwin, 3–11. Prescott, AZ: Paul Elsner and Associates.

Schugurensky, Daniel, and Kathy Higgins. 1996. "From Aid to Trade: New Trends in International Education in Canada". In *Dimensions of the Community College: International and Inter/Multicultural Perspectives,* edited by Rosalind Latiner Raby and Norma Tarrow, 53–78. New York: Garland.

Sisnett, Vincent O. 1982. "Concept, Philosophy and Role of Community Colleges". *Staff Association Journal* 2 (1): 3–18.

Skolnik, Michael. 2015. "Community Colleges and Further Education in Canada". In *Global Development of Community Colleges, Technical Colleges, and Further Education Programs,* edited by Paul A. Elsner, George R. Boggs and Judith T. Irwin, 55–63. Prescott, AZ: Paul Elsner and Associates.

Song, Yingquan, and Gerard Postiglione. 2011. "The Expensive Dream: Financing Higher Vocational Colleges in China". In *Increasing Effectiveness of the Community College Financial Model: A Global Perspective for the Global Economy,* edited by Stewart Sutin, Dan Derrico, Rosalind Latiner Raby and Edward Valeau, 251–63. New York: Palgrave Macmillan.

Smith, Natanga. 2017. "From Brittons Hill to Berklee". *Sunday Sun.* 5 November, 9–11.

Smyth, D.M. 1970. "Some Aspects of the Development of Ontario Colleges of Applied Arts and Technology". Master's thesis, University of Toronto.

Steiner-Khamsi, G., and H.O. Quist. 2000. "The Politics of Educational Borrowing: Re-opening the Case of Achimota of British Ghana". *Comparative Education Review* 44 (3): 272–99.

Stewart, F. 1996. "Globalisation and Education". *International Journal of Educational Development* 16 (4): 327–33.

Strydom, A.H., and L.O.K. Lategan, eds. 1998. *Introducing Community Colleges to South Africa.* Bloemfontein, South Africa: University of the Free State Publications.

Taylor, J.S., J. Brites Ferreira, M. de Lourdes Machado and R. Santiago, eds. 2008. *Non-University Higher Education in Europe.* Berlin: Springer.

Thayer-Scott, Jacquelyn. 2000. "The Nature of Knowledge and the University College". In *New Approaches in Higher Education: The University College Proceedings from an International Conference at Bermuda College,* 7–18. Hamilton: Bermuda College Press.

Tsunoda, Joyce, and Yasuko Iida. 2015. "Institutions in Transition: Japan's Community Colleges". In *Global Development of Community Colleges, Technical Colleges, and Further Education Programs,* edited by Paul A. Elsner, George R. Boggs and Judith T. Irwin, 155–66. Prescott, AZ: Paul Elsner and Associates.

Tull, Louis. 1977. "Address on the Occasion of the Official Opening of the Barbados Community College Campus". 1 November.

UN Office for South South Cooperation. 2010. General Assembly Resolution 60/212.

Ural, Ipek. 1998. "International Community College Models: A South African Perspective". In *Introducing Community Colleges in South Africa,* edited by A.H. Strydom and L.O.K. Lategan, 106–19. Bloemfontein, South Africa: University of the Free State Publications.

Walker, Kenneth P. 2005. "History, Rationale, and Community College Baccalaureate Association". In *The Community College Baccalaureate: Emerging Trends and Policy Issues,* edited by Deborah L. Floyd, Michael L. Skolnik and Kenneth P. Walker, 9–24. Sterling, VA: Stylus.

Wang, Wei-ni, and Fatma Nervie Seggie. 2013. "Different Missions of Community College Systems in Two Different Countries: Community Education in Taiwan versus Vocational Education in Turkey". *Community College Journal of Research and Practice* 37 (10): 18–36.

Wiseman, Alexander W., Audree Chase-Mayoral, Thomas Janis, and Anuradha Sachdev. 2012. "Community Colleges: Where Are They (Not?)". In *Community Colleges Worldwide: Investigating the Global Phenomenon,* edited by Alexander W. Wiseman, Audree Chase-Mayoral, Thomas Janis and Anuradha Sachdev, 3–19. Bingley, UK: Emerald Publishing.

Yamano, T., and John N. Hawkins. 1996. "Assessing the Relevance of American Community College Models in Japan". In *Dimensions of the Community College: International and Inter/Multicultural Perspectives,* edited by Rosalind Latiner Raby and Norma Tarrow 259–73. New York: Garland.

Zukav, Gary. 1979. *The Dancing Wu Li Masters: An Overview of the New Physics.* New York: Harper-Collins.

Zwerling, L.S. 1976. *Second Best: The Crisis of the Community College.* New York: McGraw-Hill.

Index

Page numbers in italics refer to figures and tables.

accessibility, 9, 61, 72, 161, 234, 244
accreditation, 27–28, 56, 65, 72, 82–83, 157, 179, 195, 196–98, 208, 219, 226, 235, 242, 251. *See also* Barbados Accreditation Council (BAC)
Accreditation Service for International Schools, Colleges and Universities, 69
Adams, Grantley, 93
Adamson, Cebert, 4
Adamson, Frederick, 105
Advocate News, 94, 116, 129
affordability, 9, 23, 27, 28, 53, 61, 72, 161, 189, 234, 244
Africa, 4, 18, 41–42, 48, 49. *See also* South Africa
African National Congress, 41
agriculture. *See* Department of Agriculture
Alberta, 32
alcoholism and addiction course, 167
A-Level Geometrical and Mechanical Drawings, 168
A-level studies/programmes, 50, 66–67, 69, 70, 71, 75, 77–78, 81–82, 95, 105, 106, 109, 113, 116, 118, 119, 139, 140, 143, 151, 155, 156, 165, 167–68, 209, 235, 239, 244, 248
Alleng, Danielle, 222
Alleyne, Alicia, 222
Alleyne, Hartley, *126*, 184, 205, *213*, 256
Alleyne, Lomar, 112, 256, 259
Alleyne, Michael, 4
Alleyne, Rosemary, 107
Alleyne, Rudolph, 221
Allied Health Sciences, 250
Allman, Clemens, 134
All Saints Primary School, 160

Alsohybe, Nabeel, 4
American Association of Community Colleges, 19, 24
Anguilla Community College, 55, 76, 84, 246
Antigua State College, 58, 59, 62–63, 82
Applewaite, Lolita, *97*, 185, 190
Aranda, David Valladares, 4
Archibald, Ken, 147, 193–94; computer familiarization course, 147
Argentina, 145, 250
Aris Qua de Treille, 223
Arizona State University, 43, 220
Arizona Tribal Community College, 43
Armstrong, Eric, *96*, 100, *255*
Arthur, Owen, 160
Arthur, Sydney, *211*, 246, *255*
articulation arrangements, 173–75, 206–7; international, *260*; University of the West Indies, *261*
Arts in the 21st Century, 222
associate degrees, 142–44, 157, *262–64*; new/revised programmes, 165–66, 199–201, 218; scholarships, 223; separation from A levels, 181, 234; sport management and procurement, 251
Associated Examination Board, 101, 113
Association of Assistant Teachers of Secondary Schools, 91, 94–95
Association of Caribbean Higher Education Administrators, 246, 252
Association of Caribbean Tertiary Institutions, 48, 49, 51, 82, 190, 239, 246, 250, 252
Association of International Accountants, 113

Atherley, Rose, 136
Atkinson, Ewan, 224–25
Austin, Ian, 10, *211*, 217, 218, 219, *253*
Australia, 4, 12, 16, 34, 218, 224; binary systems, 12; CCID, 17; further-education institutions, 14; technical and further-education (TAFE) colleges, 17, 20, 37, 38, 45; technical vocational sector in, 45
awardees, list of, *267–75*
awards: community, 186–87; list of awardees, *267–75*; Muscavado Awards, 162; staff, 204–5. *See also* scholarships
Aypay, Ahmet, 4

Babb, Alwyn, 221
Babb-Cadogan, Barbara, *215, 256*
bachelor of fine arts (BFA), 168, 176, 204, 222
bachelor of pharmacy degree, 200
bachelor's degrees/programmes, 218, 234–36, 250; first, 66, 74, 168–70, 178, 190, 229, 250; second, 170–71, 250
Badenock, Neville, 116, 172, 186, *215, 257*
Bahamas Baptist Community College, 78–79, 81
Bahamas General Certificate of Secondary Education (BGCSE), 78
Bahamas Hotel Training Centre, 67
Bailey, Kiara, 221–22
Bank of America, 105
Barbados Accreditation Council (BAC), 195, 196–97, 219, 235
Barbados Advocate, 7, 116
Barbados Arts Festival, 105
Barbados Association of Professional Engineers, 104
Barbados Association of Science Exhibition, 108
Barbados Bar Association, 157
Barbados Community College (BCC), 2, 5; articulation arrangements, 173–75; board of management, 129, 133, 143, 144, 150, 171, 172–73, 180, 181, 187, 188, 189, 198, 209, 219, 225, 226, 236, 237, 242, *255*; bursar/bursary, 130, 131–32; centres of excellence, 242–43; community service/awards, 186–87; controversial beginnings, 90–91; credibility, 114–15; curriculum reform, 238; establishment of, 1, 91; evaluation, 116–18, 149–50; evolutionary journey, 244–45; expansion phase (1973–1976), 103–6; first bachelor's degree, 168–70; homegrown adaptation, 89; hospitality studies, 133–34; impact of, 150–52; international collaboration, 145–46; library, 132–33, 160–61; local collaboration, 144; management and leadership, 237–38; national leadership, 157–58; opening ceremony, 90; organizational reform, 239–40; physical establishment of, 100–103; published work on, 5; regional collaboration, 145; registrar, 130–31; second bachelor's degree, 170–71; semesterization, 186, 250; teachers' union concerns, 94–95; 20/20 vision, 89; twinning attachments, 146–49. *See also* associate degrees; infrastructure development; staff; strategic plans; students
Barbados Community College (BCC) Act, 92–94, 177–78
Barbados Exhibitions, 151, 202, *202*, 230–31, 234, 265, 266, *267–75*. *See also* exhibitions
Barbados Government Information Service, 129, 197
Barbados Hilton Gallery, 110
Barbados Industrial Development Corporation, 109, 140, 169
Barbados Labour Party, 91, 114, 206, 247
Barbados Land Surveyors' Board, 104
Barbados Land Surveyors' Licence, 104
Barbados Light and Power Company, 105

Barbados Manufacturers Association Exhibition, 203, 220
Barbados Scholarships, 109, 115, 119, 151, 157, 175, 181, 190, 202, *202*, 230–31, 234, 265–66, *267–75*
Barbados Society of Architects, 104
Barbados Society of Land Surveyors, 104
Barbados Teaching Service, 110
Barbados Telephone Company, 105
Barbados Workers Union, 138
Barclays Bank International, 105
Barefoot Project, 222
Barker, Hugh, 133–34
Barnaart, Antoine, 4
Barnett, Alvin, 10, 101, 107, 108, 110, 114, 127–52, 155, 156, 168, 173, 193, 209, *210*, *253, 256, 257, 259*
Barrow, Brenda, 193
Barrow, Errol, 143
Basseterre High School in St Kitts, 65
Baylor University, 23
BCC Staff Association College Update 1994, 131
Belgrave, Robert, 101, 106, 114, 254
Bell, Hinkitch, 110–11
Bellamy, Pauline, 169
Bend, Andrew, 101, 254
Berklee College of Music in Boston, 175, 203, 224
Bermuda College, 64, 183
Bermuda University College, 183
Bernard, Nicola, 223
Best, Clyde, 2, 10, 94, 99–119, 122, 127, 146, 149–50, 155–56, 159, 168, 193, 209, *210, 253*
Best, Debbie, 225
Best, Gladstone, 10, 136, 137, *148*, 164, 172, 178, 184, 186, 193–209, *210*, 212, 217, 228, 246, *253, 256, 259*
Bethel, Keva, 183
Bethell, Baltron, 78
Bethell, Hilary, 111
Bethell, Keva, 78

Bethlehem Moravian College, Jamaica, 79
BIM Literary Magazine, 204
Birnbaum, Robert, 23
Bishop, Lucene, 101, 106–7, 114, *214, 254, 257*
Blackman, Annette, 5
Blackman, Gloria, 106
Blackman, Rene, 222
Blue Latitudes: Stories from Caribbean Women at Home and Abroad, 204–5
board of management, BCC, 129, 133, 143, 144, 150, 171, 172–73, 180, 181, 187, 188, 189, 198, 209, 219, 225, 226, 236, 237, 242, 255
Boggs, George R., 4, 23, 37
Bologna process, 13, 18
Bourne, Laticia, 221
Boxill, Hamilton, 108
Bradshaw, Nigel, 101, 114, 116, 132, 138, 194, 212, *253, 254, 257*
Branch, Cleopatra, 137
Brathwaite, Eureka, 130, 131–32, 147, *211, 255*
Brathwaite, L. B., 149
Brathwaite, Ryan, 221
Brathwaite, Stefan, 243
Brathwaite, Workeley, 134, 148
Brazil, 4, 36; higher-income families, 42; high school enrolment, 42; school completion rate, 42; US–Brazil Connect, 42
Brazilian Leadership Connect Program, 42
Breckhow, Jean, 134
Brice, Randolph, 171
Brint, Steven, 23
Britain, 1, 4, 37, 110, 114, 127, 169, 175; Education Acts, 43; educational system, 1; higher education enrolment, 43–44; Open University system, 44
British Columbia (BC), 32, 207
British external examinations, 1

Broome, Stephen, *98, 255*
Broomes, Kobie, *265*
Brown, J. Stanley, 22
Browne, Dianne, 175
Brown's Town Community College, Jamaica, 75
Brubacher, John, 34
Bryant, Clarence Fitzroy, 64
Burnett, Charles, 113
bursar/bursary, 8, 100, 102, 130, 131–32, 240, 255
Business Initiatives Direction in Paris, 187
Butcher-Lashley, Jean, *232, 256, 257*
Bynoe, Hubert, *101, 105, 147, 214, 254, 256*
Bynoe, Jacob, 78

Cable and Wireless, 161, 163, 206
Caddle, June, *201, 232, 256, 258*
California Master Plan for Higher Education, 2
Camera Club, 113
Canada, 2, 4; higher education in, 31; universities, 31
Canadian community college, 4, 17, 31–33
Canadian International Development Agency (CIDA), 2, 146, 148
career and technical education (CTE), 25
Careers Day, 223
Caribbean Advanced Proficiency Examinations, 76, 235
Caribbean Advertising Federation Awards, 204
Caribbean Agricultural Research and Development Institute, 67
Caribbean Community (CARICOM), 48, 225, 229, 246
Caribbean community college, 4–5, 35, 48–88; adaptation of upper levels of sixth-form schools, 74–75, *80*; creation of new entities, 76–78, *80*; establishment date, 56–57; expansion of specialist tertiary institutions, 78–80, *80*; features, 51–53; location, 48–51; models, 53–80, *80*; origins, 56; pre-existing specialist institutions amalgamation, 56–58, 56–74, *80*; similar sections of multiple institutions amalgamation, 75, *80*; tertiary institutions, 54
Caribbean Development Bank, 172, 186, 246
Caribbean Food and Nutrition Institute, 111, 139, 145
Caribbean Secondary School Certificate, 50, 76
Caribbean Tourism Organization, 251
Caribbean University Sports Association Games, 203
Carnegie Mellon University, 163
Carnegie Technology Education, 163
Carrington, Taisha, 223
Carroll, J. M., 23
Carter, Bertram, *98, 255*
Carter-Tuach, Margot, 146
Carus, Titus Lucretius, 100
Cary, Philip, 4
Cato, Arnot, 161, 206
CBC *Morning Barbados* programme, 223
CCID Intensive English Practicum in China, 19
centres of excellence, 242–43
Cercle Français, 113
certificate courses, 166–68, 262–64
Certified General Accountant programme, 202
"Challenge and Promise: Developing 21st Century Education in Barbados," 187
Charles, Eddie, 165
Charlestown Secondary School in Nevis, 65
Chartered Management Centre, UK, 77
Chile, 4, 12, 42–43; technical education, 42–43
China, 4, 36, 38
Cissell, Allen, 4

Index | 295

Clarence Fitzroy Bryant College, St Kitts and Nevis, 64–65
Clarke, Amaris, 222
Clarke, Elizabeth, 106
Clarke, Jai, 222
Clarke, John A., 102
Clement Howell High School in Provenciales, 78
Cohen, Grace, 101, 106, 107, 254
College Industry Services Unit, 163–64
College of Agriculture, Science and Education, Jamaica, 65–66
College of Science, Technology and Applied Arts of Trinidad and Tobago, 67–68
College of the Bahamas, 66–67, 79
Colleges of Applied Arts and Technology (CAAT), 32
College Vibes, 164
Colombia, 4, 12, 38, 43, 135, 249
commerce. *See* Division of Commerce, BCC
Commercial Institute of Santiago, Chile, 42
Common Entrance examinations, 115
communication technology, 2
Communifesta, 162, 190
community college: emergence of, 1–2, 3; future opportunities, 229–30; global development, 4; public perception, 1; scholarship, 2. *See also* Barbados Community College (BCC); US community colleges
community college models, 13–14, 20
Community College of the District of Houston, Texas, 42
Community Colleges for International Development (CCID), 17, 39
community development, 244
community engagement, 9, 156, 160, 234, 244
community relationships, 102
community service/awards, 186–87

Community Services Programme, 111–12
Competency-Based Training Fund, 219
computer studies. *See* Department of Computer Studies
Consortium of Institutions for Tertiary Education, 79
"Contemporary Black Artists" (Charles), 165
Cooke, Howard, 75
Corbin, Khristen, 225
Costello, Jack, 141, *148*
Council of Community Colleges of Jamaica, 4, 78, 79, 80
Counselling Department, BCC, 132, 164
Coward, Antonia, 170
Cox, Michelle, 225, 243
Cozier, Nicholas, 223
Craigg, Lionel, 93, 116
creativity, 68, 83, 132, 156, 187, 223, 230, 237, 240, 248
Critchlow, Desmond, 97, 255
Critchlow-Earle, Bernice, 71, 134, 147, 160, *213*, *257*, 259
Critical Writing, 218
Crovisier, Michelle, 134
C.R. Walker Technical College, 66
Cuba, 202–3, 224
Cuban scholarships, 202–3
Curating in the Caribbean, 205
Current Trends in Health Information Management and Technology, 218
Curriculum Development Desk, 179–80, 226–27
curriculum reform, 238

DaCosta and Musson Ltd, 105
Daniel, Andre, 222, 243
Daniel, Joyce, 109, 140, 142, 168–69, *213*, 256, 259
Darmuzey, Philippe, *159*
David, Hugh, 4
Dawn Princess cruise ships, 165
Dawson, Carl, 76

Day, Robert W., 22–23
Dearing, Don, 44
Debating Society, 113
de Bresser, Sandra, 4
Delaware County Community College, 220
Delfina Foundation in London, 225
Democratic Labour Party, 90, 91, 206, 247
Denmark, 4, 17, 37, 43; demand of skilled labour, 43; Southern Community Colleges alliance, 43; Vocational Education Act, 43
Dennison, John, 183
department heads, 258
Department of Agriculture, 223
Department of Chemistry, 223
Department of Computer Studies, 147, 164
Department of Nursing, 163
deputy principal, 8, 102, 115, 128, 130, 155, 170, 194–95, 217, 228, 253
Desbiens, Brian, 134, 148
diplomas, 262–64
Division of Commerce, BCC, 103, 105, 114, 118, 129, 135, 139–40, 147, 156, 165, 166, 199, 207, 220
Division of Community Services, BCC, 111–12
Division of Fine Arts, BCC, 109–10, 141, 157, 160, 168, 170, 199, 203–4, 222, 224, 225, 241, 242, 246, 251; certificate in interior decorating, 167; Erdiston Teachers' Training College and, 169; Lecture Series, 165; Portfolios, 162, 169, 204; Village of Hope, 163
Division of General and Continuing Education, 226–27
Division of Health Sciences, 110–11, 130, 133, 136, 137, 139, 144, 145, 147, 150, 155, 156, 159, 162, 167, 171–72, 175, 176, 179, 199, 200, 207, 208, 217, 224, 247, 248; alcoholism and addiction course, 167

Division of Hospitality Studies, BCC, 133–34, 139, 159–60, 251–52
Division of Liberal Arts, BCC, 105–6, 129, 137, 139, 144, 152, 162, 204–5, 249; mission statement, 165
Division of Technology, BCC, 103–5, 108, 109, 110, 122, 123, 127, 129, 137, 139, 141, 147, 149, 175, 193, 248
divisions, establishment dates of, 259
Dominican Republic, 4
Dominica State College, 69
Dominica State College Act of 2002, 69
Donawa, Wendy, 136
Doucette, Don, 4
Doyle, Jim, 4
Drakes, Rhea, 243
Drummond, Mark, 4
Dupigny, Clifton, 69
Duquesne University, 137
Dwyer, Thomas Edward (Ted), 74

Eastern countries, 38–41
Eastmond, Rawle, 227–28
Ebisemiju, S., 101, 254
Edna Manley College, 169
educational borrowing, 2–3, 15–16
"Education for Living" exposition, 162
Elcock, Gomell, 232
Elcock, Hortense, 148
Eleuthera, 79
Elsner, Paul A., 4, 23, 37
Emerging Leaders in the Americas Programme (ELAP), 203
"Empower Youth International," 223
Encuentro, 180
Engel, Sandra, 4
England. *See* Britain
English as a Foreign Language (EFL), 135, 167, 199, 221
English-speaking Caribbean, 5, 48–88
Erceg, Arlene, 111
Erdiston Teachers' College, 140, 169, 183, 190, 195, 206, 228
Erdiston Teachers Training College, 127

Estwick, Heather, *154*
Europe, 43–45
European Economic Community, 134
European Polytechnic and Institute of Technology, 14
evaluation, BBC, 116–18, 149–50
Evans, Tom, 149
Eversley, Davidson, 222
Excelsior Community College, Jamaica, 54, 55, 74, 150, 245, 250
Exhibition of Contemporary Art in Geneva, Switzerland, 205
exhibitions, 110, 140, 142, 149, 162, 204, 222, 231, 241. *See also* Barbados Exhibitions

fashion design, 129, 136, 140–41, 157, 162, 169, 201, 204, 251
Ferguson, Nancy, 106
Fernández, Leonel, 45–46
fine arts. *See* Division of Fine Arts, BCC
Fingall, Arthur, *214*, *257*
first bachelor's degree, BCC, 66, 74, 168–70, 178, 190, 229, 250
First European Community College Network, 17
Fisher, Glen, 4
Fitts, David, 111
Flanagan, Lou-Anne, 134
flexibility, 9, 28, 37, 43, 53, 73, 83, 151, 178, 179, 186, 189, 226, 234, 235, 244
Food Service Supervisors course, 111
Foreign Language Programme, 135, 139
Founder's Day celebration, 180
France, 16, 17, 20, 38, 135, 249
Francis, Alister, 59
Franklyn, Claudette, *154*
Franklyn, Gaston, 147, 178
Frederico-Santa Maria Technical University, Chile, 42–43
Free, Coen, 4
French West Africa, 4, 37, 41
Fulbright Scholarship, 222
future opportunities, 229–30

Gardner, Brook, 148
Gaskin, Sherrol, *232*
Gates, Richard, 134
GED 106.1 FM, 164
General Certificate of Education (GCE) O level, 104
General Education Programme, 108, 129, 136, 179
Geography Society, 113
Georgia, 4
Germany, 1–2, 14, 17, 20, 22, 38, 224, 225
Gershwin, Mary, 4
Gibbons, Michael, 243
Gibbs, Nathan, 204
Gibbs, Peter, 149
Gill, David, 165
Gittens, Beverley, *154*
Gittens, Nicholas, 175
Gittens, Roger, 204, 225, 243
Gittens, Stanton, 106
Glasgow, Earl, 116
global counterparts, 14; globalization, 14–15; literature on, 34–36; localization, 18–19; north/south flows, 16–18; pool of, 11, 36–38; reinvention of form, 20–21; south/north and south/south flows, 18; transfer of policies, 19–20
globalization, 3, 14–15, 251–52
Goddard, John, 185
Goddard, Joseph, 185
Golden Grove Technical College, 62
governance, 236–37
Grant-Medford, Dianne, 171
Grant-Woodham, Jeanette, 4
Great Depression, 23
Greaves, Samantha ("Sammy G"), 221
Greaves, Wismore, 113
Greenidge, Geoffrey, 130
Grenada National College, 73, 172, 245, 250
Griffith, Richard, *154*
guild presidents and vice-presidents, *264–65*

Hackett, Daphne, 136
Hackett, Lauretta, 135, 194, 197, 199, 208, 212, 228, 253, 257
Haiti, 4, 225
Halder, John, 4
Hall, Geoff, 4
Hall, Mark, 176
Hallsworth, David, 215, 257
Harding, Shama, 225
Harding, Stephen, 165
Harewood, M., 102, 133
Harewood, Susan, 218
"The Harlem Renaissance" (Harding), 165
Harper, William Rainey, 22
Harris, Versa, 222
Harrison College, 90, 108, 127, 131
Hartley, Philip, 4
Harvard University, 136, 171, 197
Hassell, Trevor, 97, 131, 255
Hatcher, Russell, 168
Hawke's Bay Community College, in Taradale, New Zealand, 19
Haynes, Marcina, 101, 114, 254
Healthy Lifestyle Exposition, 197
Hewitt, Anne, 101, 106, 107, 114, 132, 135, 136, 185, 254, 259
Hewitt, Guy, 198, 219
Hibbard, Dave, 148
Higher Colleges of Technology in the United Arab Emirates, 36
Highland Community College in Washington State, 42
Hinds, Adrian, 224
Hinds, Burton, 93
Hinds, Danny, 136
Hispanic Society students, 106
"HIV in the Workplace," 221
H.J. Robinson High School in Grand Turk, 78
H. Lavity Stoutt Community College, British Virgin Islands, 76–77
Hockey, William, 148

Holder, Norma, 10, 78, 101, 114, 130, 131, 132, 147, 148, *148*, 155–90, 193, 194, 208, 209, *210*, 222, 242, 246, 253, 254, 256
"Holder Heads Success Story," 187
Hong Kong, 4, 40
Hood, Heather, 102, 180
Horne, John, 72
Horton, James, 4
Hospitality Institute, 159–60, 246; internship, 165; World Quality Award, 187
Hotel PomMarine, 160
Hotel School, Barbados, 133–34
Howe, Glenford, 4–5
Howell, McFarland, *213*
Human Potential Programme, 111
Hunte, Keith, 96, 122, 123, 131, 255
Hunte, Quinton, 175
Hurricane Hugo, 76

Ifill, Kerry-Ann, 228
Imperial College of Tropical Agriculture, 67
Improvement of Justice Project, 141
India, 4, 18, 37, 38, 39
Indonesia, 4, 16, 38, 39
industrial relations practice, 195
industry services unit, 163–64
information and communication technology, 238–39
infrastructure development, BCC, 159–61, 198–99, 241–42
Inkhamnert, Tanom, 4
Inniss, Donville, 228
Inniss, Esther, 113
Inniss, Frederick, 114, 132, 138, *216*, *258*, *259*
Inniss, Joseph, 107, 113, 162
Inniss, Peggy, 140
innovation, 9, 12, 36, 44, 68, 91, 115, 118, 141, 152, 171, 187, 189, 195, 223, 228, 230, 234, 244, 248, 251, 252

Inter-American Development Bank, 186, 219
Inter-American Development Fund, 123
interdisciplinary seminar, 162
International Hospitality/Culinary Exchange Programme at Walt Disney World in Orlando, 165
International Labour Organization, 67
internship, 165
Inter-School Christian Fellowship, 113
Introduction to Dance, 218
Ireland, 4, 16, 17, 37, 43, 44
Irwin, Judith T., 4, 23, 37
Iskandar, Harris, 4

Jackman, Rosie, 111
Jaimes, Arturo Nava, 4
Jamaica, 4, 27, 37, 48, 49, 54–55, 65–66
Jamaica Biennial Art Exhibition, 222
Jamaica Province of the Moravian Church, 79
Jamaica School of Agriculture, 65
Japan, 4, 12, 16, 17, 18, 20, 35, 37, 38, 40, 135, 142
Jazz Choir, BCC, 222
Jelani, Kweku, 222
Jemmott, Hamilton, 170
Jessamy, O., 102
Johnson, Anthony, 111, 147
John Wickham Scholarship, 202
Joint Board of Teacher Education, Jamaica, 80
Junior Calypso Monarch Show in Trinidad and Tobago, 221

Kamali, Tayeb, 4
Kangan Technical and Further Education Report, 45
Karabel, Jerome, 23
Kellman, Winston, 224
Kellogg Foundation, 166
Kerr, Clark, 20
King, Clair, 130
King, Edmund (Eddie), 254
King, Edward, 101, 254
King, Juel, 102
King, M., 114
King, Stefen, 175
King, Stephen, 163
Kirby, Tom, 111
Kirton, Aurea, 102
Kirton, Colin, 91, 96, 100, 131, 142, 255
Klotz, Alan, 165
Knox Community College, Jamaica, 74–75
Kovaleik, A., 103

Lakehead College of Arts, Science and Technology in Ontario, 31
Landrum, Bertha, 4
Language Centre, BCC, 105, 129, 131, 134–35, 136, 139, 144, 145, 151, 156, 167, 172, 176, 177, 180, 199, 201, 203, 204, 217, 220, 221, 240, 243, 249
Layne, Aaron, 243
Layne, Kirk, 222
Layne, William, 113
leadership, 237–38, 245–47
Learning Village, Netherlands, 44–45
Lecture Series, 165
Leeward Islands Teacher Training College, 62
Lethbridge Junior College in Alberta, 31
Lewis, Andrew, 114
Lewis, Arthur, 70
Lewis, Olive, 75
L.H. Consulting, 185
liberal arts. *See* Division of Liberal Arts, BCC
Liberal Arts Division. *See* Division of Liberal Arts, BCC
library, BCC, 132–33, 160–61
LIME Academic Enhancement Centre, 221
Literary Society, 113
localization, 18–19

Lodge School, 116
Loi, Sabrina, 4
London Chamber of Commerce (LCC), 101, 113
Louden, Delroy, 76
Lovell, James, 204
Lowe, Carl, 130, 255
Luqui, Bernice, 141, *148*
Lynch, Adele, 101, 106, 114, 254
Lynch, Louis, 93

Macbeth (Shakespeare), 107
management, 237–38. *See also* leadership
Manifold, Edgar, 101, *213*, 254, *257*
Marie, Kerrie, 175
"The Market for Contemporary Photography" (Klotz), 165
Marks, Veronica, 72
Marryshow, Theophilus A., 73
Marshall, Trevor, 5, 135–36, 160, 162, 205
Martinez, David Roldan, 4
Marville, Marcia, 176
mass communications, 129, 137, 162, 164, 173, 174, 175, 176, 198, 222, 227, 228
Matthew, Merrill, 69
Maughan, Raymond, 113
Maxwell, Keith, 130, 180
Mayers, Betty, 163
Maynard, Esther, 132, 186
McCarthy, Thomas, 134
McGill University, 31
McMahon, Frank, 4
Medical Laboratory Technology (MLT), 111
Mellinger, Barry L., 22–23
Melville, H. K., 163
Menard-Greenidge, Denyse, 168, 169, *213*, *256*
The Merchant of Venice (Shakespeare), 107
Mercy Hospital, Pittsburgh, 137
Mexico, 4, 12
Miller, Billie, 135

Miller, D'Sean, 221–22
Miller, Gilda, 140
Milner, Sarah, 135
Misick, Charles Wesley, 78
Mobile Application Design and Development Programme of BCC, 200
Moe, Henry, 105, *256, 259*
Moneague Teachers' College, Jamaica, 79–80
Montego Bay Community College, Jamaica, 75
Montserrat Community College, 70
Montserrat Technical College, 70
Moore, Richard B., 142
Morris, Camille, 4
Morris, Robert, 185
Morris, Wesley, 224
Muhajiri, Mohammed, 114
Murray, Glyne, 164
Muscavado Awards, 162
music students, 203

Nassau Technical College, 66
Nation, 7
National Independence Festival for Creative Arts (NIFCA), 110, 204, 205, 222
National Institute of Higher Education, Research, Science and Technology, 68
national leadership, 157–58
Nations' Cup Culinary Competition, 222
Navajo Community College, 24
Netherlands, 4, 16, 17, 20, 37, 43; Learning Village, 44–45; university-based higher education system, 44
New Bajan, 155
New England Association of Schools and Colleges, 64
New England Culinary Institute, 77
Newsam, Judith, *232*, 255
Newton, Velma, 225, 255

New Zealand, 4, 12, 16, 19, 20, 34, 37;
  bachelor's degree programmes, 218;
  polytechnic system, 45
Nichols, Sheri, 222
The Night Before, 105–6
nonuniversities, 11, 13, 20
north/south flows, 2, 11, 16–18, 33, 38,
  45–46, 119, 152, 251
north/south unidirectional flows, 3
Norway, 12, 17, 18, 20, 34
Nova Scotia Community College, 32

O'Brian, Tom, 148
O'Brien, Gilda, 136
Occupational Therapy Assistants, 111
Oceania, 45, 46
Odle, Janeil, 220, 228, *274*
OECS/HRD/Tertiary-Level Programme
  EDF VII Project, 70
Oliver, Diane, 4
O' Neal, Michael, 77
Ontario, 31–32
open access, 12, 14, 21, 188, 248–49
Open Polytechnic of New Zealand, 45
opportunities, 244; BCC students,
  227–29; future, 229–30
Oraco Consulting, 183–85
Organisation for Economic
  Co-operation and Development
  (OECD), 17
Organisation of the Eastern Caribbean
  States (OECS), 35
organizational reform, 239–40
Organization of American States (OAS),
  114, 134, 135, 137, 141, 203
Owen, Glen, 75

Padmore, Simone, 222
Pan American Health Organization
  (PAHO), 110, 111
Parsons, Eileene, 77
partnerships, 6, 17, 27, 29, 32, 35, 36, 37,
  39, 44, 54, 77, 79, 82, 104, 128, 152, 163,
  174, 183, 185, 190, 196, 206–7, 208, 220,
  228, 241, 242, 243, 247, 251
Passley Gardens Teachers College, 66
Payne, Paul, 147
Penn State University, US, 2
Peters, Bevis, 4, 185
Peters, Donald, 69
Philips, Esther, 107, 205
Philips, Ronald (Gene), 180, *258*
Phillips, Eric, 130
Phillips, Ralph, 148
photovoltaic project, 219–20
physical education, BCC, 128, 132, 140,
  141, 150, 156, 165, 166, 167, 174, 175, 176,
  186, 201, 217, 218, 220, 221, 228, 241,
  242–43, 246, 251
Pierce, Danielle, 223
Pile, Dorian, 106
Pile, Simbah, 222
Pilgrim, Charlie, 106
Pilgrim, Grace, 130–31, 135
Pincott, Mildred, 114
Pine Basin Initiative, 186
Pinelands Creative Workshop, 225
Pitt, James, 73
planning and policies, 176–86;
  Curriculum Development Desk,
  179–80; idea of the University College
  of Barbados, 181–86; joint degree with
  the UWI, 180; lessons learned, 234–36;
  semesterization, 186, 250; separation
  of associate degree from A levels, 181;
  thirtieth anniversary, 180; transfer of
  policies, 19–20. *See also* strategic plans
Plantations Ltd, 105
policies. *See* planning and policies
polytechnics/polytechnical institutes,
  14, 20, 39, 43–44, 45, 104, 144. *See also*
  Samuel Jackman Prescod Polytechnic
  (SJPP)
Ponitz, David, 4
Portfolio Fashion Show, 176
Portfolios, 162, 169, 204

Portfolio Theatre, 218
Portmore Community College, Jamaica, 77–78
Postiglione, Gerard, 4
"Postmodernism in the Caribbean" (Gill), 165
Postsecondary International Network, 17
Powell, A. Wesley, 74
Powlett, Peter, 170
Pre-Health Sciences Programme, 110, 111
Prescod, Aerin, 223
Price, Joyce, 140
Prince Edward Island, 31–32
Prince George Community College in Maryland, 187
principal(s), 2, 7–8, 10, 217, 253; Cambridge examinations, 107; evaluation by, 117–18; interim, 100; ministerial approval for position of, 123; office, 100. *See also* deputy principal; *specific* principal
Project HOPE, 111, 248
Project of Institutional Cooperation, 141
prototype of community college, 2
Proverbs, Lesia, 171, 200
Provost, Theodore, 76
Public Health Inspector's Programme, 111
public protests, 202

Qatar, 4, 15, 19, 38
Queen Elizabeth Hospital, Bridgetown, 137

Raby, Rosalind Latiner, 2–3, 4
radio station. *See* GED 106.1 FM
Recreational Leadership, 112
Redman, Ricky, 169
registrar, 130–31, 237, 255
registration and accreditation, 196–98. *See also* accreditation
regulations for admission, 249

research, 4–5, 7, 9, 14, 20, 22, 25, 27, 30, 31, 28, 36, 52, 65, 67, 89, 108, 156, 178–79, 183, 207, 225, 226, 234–42
Richards, Winston, 143
Rickinson, Peggy, 171
Robbins, Lord, 43
Roberts, Vivienne, 4, 154, 185, 213, 214, 256
Rose, Sheena, 222
Rosen, Alan, 5
Rosenfeld, Stuart, 4
Ross, Bertram, 65
Rouse, Samuel, 217
Rowe, Patrick, 184
Royal Academy of Dance, London, 225
Rudy, Willis, 34
Runaway Bay Heart Academy for Resort Skills, Jamaica, 159

Sai Kit Kwok, Steven, 4
Samuel Jackman Prescod Polytechnic (SJPP), 104, 129, 141, 144, 149, 164, 170, 183, 190, 195, 197, 201, 206, 219, 228, 230
Sana'a Community College, Yemen, 39
Sanchez, Roberto Navarro, 4
Sandiford, Abigail, 243
Sandiford, Angelita, 136–37, 194, 228
Sandiford, Erskine, 6, 89, 90–91, 93, 94, 100, 103, 107, 142, 143–44, 150, 157–58, 159, 163, 187, 192, 193, 204
Sandiford, Irene, 228
Sandiford-Garner, Irene, 107
Sangster, Alfred, 78
Sarjeant, Pauline, 171
Saskatchewan Institute of Applied Science and Technology, 32
Saunders, C. W., 78
Sawadogo, Geremie, 4
scholarships, 2, 7, 67, 140, 176, 202–3, 244, 250; A-level programme, 140; associate degree graduates, 223; Cuban universities, 202–3; national, 175, 177, 189, 231, 250; OAS, 137; overseas institutions, 175; policy review, 137;

regulations, 265–66; revision of requirements, 202; US sports, 202. *See also* Barbados Scholarships
School of Nursing, 64, 65, 69, 72, 139, 140, 144, 245
Schultz, Frank, 143
Sci-Tech Expo, 203
Scorsone, Analy, 4
Scotiabank Junior Calypso Monarch, 221
Scott, Lady, 100
Scott, Marianne, 4
Scott, Winston, 100
Sealy, Arthur, 10, 101, 106, 122–23, *124*, 131, 168, 170, *213*, *253*, 254, *257*
Sealy, Lionel, 106
second bachelor's degree, 170–71, 250
self-study, 83, 197, 219, 221
semester system/semesterization, 186, 190, 250
Seneca College in Canada, 145, 170
Shakespeare, W., 106–7
Shapiro, Cynthia, 4
Sheehan, Bob, *148*
Sherlock, Philip, 66
Shorey, Brenda, 109, *267*
Shorey, Leonard, *96*, 127, 131, *255*
Shorey Report, 115
short-cycle institutions, 11, 12, 35; binary institutions, 12; dual institutions, 12
Silva, Cristobal, 4
Simks, Robert, 143
Simmons, Kerrie, 107, 227–28
Simmons, Monica, 133
Sinckler, Chris, 228
Singapore, 4, 12, 17, 37
Sir Arthur Lewis Community College, St Lucia, 58, 63, 70–72, 78, 80, 82, 150, 167, 176, 201, 203, 245, 250
Sisnett, Vincent, 5, *215*, 217, *256*
sixth-form schools, 1, 74–75, 81, 90–95, 115, 118, 156, 188, 235
Skeete, Kay, 171, 179, 198, 207, 208
Skolnik, Michael, 4
Slocombe, Michael, *232*, *267*

Small Business Management Programme, 174–75
Smith, Arabella, 78, 116
Sollaway, John, 133, *257*
South Africa, 4, 17, 18, 35, 37, 41–42; Advanced Technical Education Act of 1967, 41; apartheid regime, 41; Further Education and Training Act, 42; National Institute for Community Education, 42; postsecondary education in, 41; technical vocational education and training (TVET), 41; US community college concept, 42
South America, 12, 42–43, 48
south/north flow, 3, 18, 35, 152, 252
south/south flow, 3, 18, 35, 152, 250, 251–52
Soviet model, 39
Spain, 4, 36, 37, 43, 45
sport management and procurement, 166, 199, 1251
sports and games, 141, 186, 190, 201, 202, 203, 243, 246. *See also* physical education
Springer, Jameson B., 93–94
Springer, Jeanette, 114, 136, 180
Springer, John, 176
Springer, L. J., 102
Springer, Richild, 136
Springer Memorial School, 133, 220, 235
Squires, Matthew, 222
Sri Lanka, 19
staff, 114; association, 137–39, 172–73; continuing education, 114; list of first staff members, 254; professional development, 171–73, 204–5; profile (2016), *258*
Staff Association, 113, 128, 137–39, 172–73, 184, 226
Staff Association Newsletter, 226
Stanford, Hugh, 108
St Clair College of Applied Arts and Technology in Ontario, Canada, 2, 6, 31, 33, 146–49

Stepwise in Qualification Plan, Denmark, 43
St George Secondary School, 104
St Hill, Otho, 103, 147
St John, Bernard, 92
St Lucia Jazz Festival, 222
St Matthias' Girls School, 159
Stoute, Ambrose, *102*, 130, 235
Stoute-Oni, Hetty, 133, *212*, *258*
strategic plans, 7, 67; of 1995, 182, 251; of 1997–2005, 178–79, 198, 225; of 2016–2021, 219, 227
strengths, 225–26
Stuart, Wayne, 163
student-centredness, 241
Student Health Clinic, 163
students, 112–13, 201–4; activities, 201; attrition rate, 112; enrolment, 112, *275–76*; examination results, 113; extracurricular activities, 113; organization of games, 137; performance, 175–76, 202–4; reflection-first students, 113; scholarships and exhibitions, *202*; sports and games, 203
Students' Guild, 162, 201
St Vincent and the Grenadines Community College, 72–73
Suriname Telecommunication Company Venture, 19
Sutherland, Francis, *232*, *257*

Taiwan, 4, 12, 16, 19
T.A. Marryshow Community College, Grenada, 73–74
Tappin, Arturo, 222
Tarrow, Norma, 4
teachers' colleges, 38, 51, 53, 55, 58, 59, 66, 196
technical assistance, 33, 71, 104, 142, 144, 147, 171, 172, 231, 245–46
technical colleges/institutes, 1, 12, 17, 20, 22, 30, 31, 32, 42–44, 46, 49, 50, 53, 56, 62, 64–66, 91

Technical Correspondence Institute, New Zealand, 45
technical teachers certificate programme, 104
Tercentenary School of Nursing (TSN), 110, 140, 144, 241
Thailand, 4, 15, 16, 17, 37, 38
Thayer-Scott, Jacquelyn, 182
Thomas, Hilroy, 69
Thomas, Leighton, 78
Thomas, Trevor, 75
Thompson, Alison, 205, *216*, 225, *243*, *256*
Thompson, Asquith, *97*, *255*
Thompson, Edwin, 163
Thompson, Eva, 116
Thompson, Grace, 131, 147, 163, *212*, *255*
Trades Training Centre, 93
Transatlantic Technical and Training Alliance, 43
transfer of policies: holistic and autonomous, 19–20; purposeful and planned, 19. *See also* planning and policies
triangular cooperation, 18
tribal colleges, US, 24
Trinidad and Tobago, 4, 48, 49, 53, 59, 67–68, 174, 201, 221, 239, 246
Trotman, David, *102*, 133, 180, *258*
Tsunoda, Joyce, 4
Tudor, James Cameron, 92
Tull, Louis, 116
Tunisia, 4, 37
Turkey, 4, 17, 37, 40–41
Turks and Caicos Islands Community College, 78
tutors, list of, *256–57*

United Arab Emirates, 4, 36, 37, 38, 40
United Nations Development Fund for Women, 67
United Nations Development Programme (UNDP), 110, 248
United States (US), 2, 4; GI Bill of Rights, 23; Great Depression, 23; Higher

Education Acts, 24; higher education institutions, 22; Project HOPE, 111, 248. *See also* US community colleges
University College of Barbados, 181–86, 205–6
University College of the Cayman Islands, 49, 68–69, 181
University Council of Jamaica, 54, 196
University of Guyana, 139, 145, 152, 248, 251
University of Massachusetts, Amherst, 174, 228
University of Technology of Jamaica, 49, 55, 63, 65, 66, 67, 69, 71, 72, 73, 75, 78, 220, 228, 239
University of the Virgin Islands, 76, 77, 82, 176
University of the West Indies, 1, 2, 141–42, 181, 194, 196; articulation arrangements, 261; deputy principal, 194; joint degree with, 180; transfer agreements with, 197
University of Wisconsin-Whitewater, 79
US Agency for International Development, 17, 38, 63, 141
US-Brazil Connect, 42
US community colleges, 1, 2, 34–35, 89; challenges for, 29–30; as contradictory institution, 30–31; as a highly valued commodity, 17; history/development, 3, 22–24, 89; mission, 24–28; multiculturalism and internationalization, 34; open access, 14, 248–49; operations, 3, 28; regionally accredited, 24; values, 28
US Information Service, 164

Valeau, Edward J., 2–3, 4
Venezuela, 12, 17, 106, 135, 145, 159, 250
Venezuelan Cultural Centre, 162, 174
Venezuelan Institute of Culture and Cooperation, 180, 201, 204
Victoria College, 31
Vietnam, 4, 20, 37, 38, 39

Vietnam National University, 39
Vietnam War, 39
Village of Hope, 162–63
vocational education system, 11, 17, 23, 30, 36, 41, 43, 44, 45, 46, 65, 70, 92, 134, 244
vocational schools in Turkey, 40–41
Volkshochschulen, 1–2, 14
Volney, Henry, 69
Volunteer Leaders' Academy in Kazan, Russia, 222
Von Chrismar, Marcelo, 4

Walcott, B., 102
Walker, Giselle, 223
Walker, Kristen, 222
Wallpaper, 164–65
Walthrust-Jones, Natalie, 205, 225
Wang, Liangjuan, 4
Ward, Cherise, 222, 223
Waterman, Ivan, 147
Waterman, Lindsay, 217
Watkins, Don, 4
weaknesses, 226–27
Weber, K., 103
Weekes, Cheryl, 207, 213, 217, 224, 228, 232, 243, 253, 256
Weekes, Yvonne, 204
Welch, Patrick, 184–85
Western Ontario Institute of Technology, 32, 146
West Indian Collection of the Sydney Martin Library, 7
Wharton, Goulbourne, 130, 180
Wheatley, Charles, 77
Wheatley, Jennie, 76
Whitehead, Jeff, 135, 139
Whitehorse Vocational Training School, 32
Wickham, C. William, 101, 254
Williams, John, 185
Williams, Ronald, 113, 222
Williams, Roosevelt, 72
Williams Solar Inc., 219

Wiltshire-Forde, Jacqueline, 136
Wiseman, Alexander W, 4
Wood, Shelley L., 4
Woodvine, Andre, 204
Words, 180
World Bank, 2, 17, 18, 39, 133, 142, 159, 160–61, 171, 175, 178, 179
World Federation of Colleges and Polytechnics, 17–18
World Health Organization (WHO), 104, 114
World of Science Survey, 155
World Quality Award, 187
Worldwide Sport Volunteer Leaders Academy, 222

Worrell, Roger, 243
Writers' Club, 106

Y2K (the coming of the year 2000), 193
Yankee, Bernard, 69
Yard, Calvin, 101, 106, 116, 130, 137, 138, 212, 253, 254, 257
Yasuko Iida, 4
Yearwood, Kraig, 222
Yearwood, Nancii, 204
Yemen, 4, 39
Yiwei Chen, 4
Yoshimoto, Keiichi, 4
Yugoslavia, 12, 17
Yukon Vocational and Technical Training Centre, 32

www.ingramcontent.com/pod-product-compliance
Lightning Source LLC
Chambersburg PA
CBHW021819300426
44114CB00009BA/235